Praise for *THE FULL CATASTROPHE*

"This is a story about true ____ that resilience doesn't mean it's easy to get back up when life knocks you to the ground, but rather that resilience means as humans we can try over and over to seek and find the love we deserve. A searingly beautiful testament to all the ways loss yields to love."

-CLAIRE BIDWELL SMITH, author of *Conscious Grieving*

"In *The Full Catastrophe*, Casey Mulligan Walsh offers a raw and complicated story of love and loss that both bolsters and brings you to your knees. In this beautifully written book, Walsh refuses the simple titles of victim or heroine, instead showing us what it truly means to embody the roles of daughter, wife and mother in the face of profound life-shattering loss."

-MEGHAN RIORDAN JARVIS, author of *End of the Hour*

"*The Full Catastrophe*, Casey Mulligan Walsh's profoundly moving examination of grief and resilience, traces the consequences of loss across decades of confusion and need. Walsh knows well that new losses awaken grief from the past, and this book arises from the depths of her grief as an orphaned child and contends with her grief as a mother, a kind of whirlpool that pulls everything into it and threatens to drown her. It doesn't, however. Instead she bears witness to sorrow, and finds peace. This book is a triumph and an inspiration."

-RICHARD HOFFMAN, author of *Half the House* and *Love and Fury*

"Casey Mulligan Walsh is such a compassionate guide into the deepest reaches of grief, into both the devastation and the surprising peace that can be found there. My heart feels forever altered by this profound, and profoundly moving, search for home and connection and meaning in a world rocked by loss. *The Full Catastrophe* is fully engaging, fully human, fully wrenching, fully healing, fully, ferociously alive."

-GAYLE BRANDEIS, author of *The Art of Misdiagnosis*

"In *The Full Catastrophe*, Casey Mulligan Walsh depicts, in unflinching and impeccably clear-eyed prose, how the marriage she entered too fast and too young and the image of family she so desperately believed in fell apart at first slowly, one shouting match at a time, and then all at once, with the sudden death of her oldest son. Through it all, Walsh keeps going, which is what she learned to do while growing up with sick parents, what she did when her father and her mother died, what she did when she found herself living with well-meaning relatives, what she did when she started seventh grade with the prayer that she would someday again wake up in a place that felt like home. Only when Walsh realizes she can both keep going and change direction does she begin to reclaim herself and her life. This heartbreaking but ultimately hopeful and gorgeously redemptive memoir reveals how one brave woman embraces the wrenching but also tender imperfection that defines the human family and, in so doing, makes her life her own."

-JEANNINE OUELLETTE, author of *The Part That Burns,* founder of Writing in the Dark

"On one of the worst days of her life, Casey Mulligan Walsh has an epiphany, an epiphany that led her to write her unflinchingly honest memoir, *The Full Catastrophe*. She takes us back to losing her parents as a young girl and her search for home and family that followed. What Walsh earned through loss, heartbreak, disappointment, and new love brings hope to all of her lucky readers."

-ANN HOOD, author of *Comfort: A Journey Through Grief*

"*The Full Catastrophe* is a candid and spare look at motherhood, grief, and what it means to claim a life of one's own. Written in lovely and calm prose, this book is both heartbreaking and heart-healing. Walsh's journey shows the potential for a life well-lived, even in the midst of great tragedy."

-KELLY SUNDBERG, author of *Goodbye, Sweet Girl*

"Casey Mulligan Walsh writes her heart out while confiding to readers about "the full catastrophe" of life. Her prose is brutally honest, vulnerable—laced with both insight and resolve to not only survive but thrive beyond the chaos. She is living proof that despite a multitude of griefs, survival is possible. *The Full Catastrophe* is one woman's journey of breakdown and breakthrough moments and a heart-wrenching story about saving oneself. Her storytelling prowess will make you cry, laugh, and even learn a few Sondheim lyrics. Definitely a must read for all of us navigating the rigors of everyday life during this era of loss."

-ARMEN BACON, co-author of *Griefland* and *Daring to Breathe*

"The loss of a parent, sibling, or child can't be undone. In *The Full Catastrophe*, Casey Mulligan Walsh pulls at the strings of identity, family, and love in a true story of heartbreak and tenacity. The frayed ends of loved ones lost too soon is the inheritance of too many Americans whose genetic conditions like familial hypercholesterolemia, which affected Walsh's family across generations, have gone undetected. Losing her father and brother to this cardiovascular disorder and her mother to breast cancer, all by the time she was twenty, set Walsh on a search for belonging that shaped her life and family. When her son, Eric, tragically dies at the age of twenty, Walsh resolves to live even more bravely. The Full Catastrophe is a story of resilience that has a lot to teach us about honoring our grief and forgiving fate."

-KATHERINE WILEMON, Founder and CEO of The Family Heart Foundation

"With courage and curiosity, Casey Mulligan Walsh tells the story of surviving heartrending loss and what telling the truth can mean; *The Full Catastrophe* is unputdownable."

-RONIT PLANK, author of *When She Comes Back* and *Home is a Made-Up Place*

"*The Full Catastrophe* is all that—a warm, generous, tragic yet ultimately hopeful story of a woman's struggle for family, for understanding, for healing. Casey's story had me turning pages all night."

-NERISSA NIELDS, singer/songwriter and author of *Plastic Angel* and *How to Be an Adult*

"*The Full Catastrophe* is aptly titled. Anyone who has suffered great loss, who has struggled with a difficult marriage, or has worked to keep their children safe will identify greatly with this work. With complete honesty and self-reflection, Walsh delves into her past where she has withstood injury and abandonment. Writing in clear, lovely language, we get an intimate portrait of a woman in distress, a woman who will not let loss defeat or define her."

-TAVI TAYLOR BLACK, author of *Where Are We Tomorrow?* and *Serabelle*

"Powerful and compelling, *The Full Catastrophe* captures the bravery required to build our own belonging, both within and outside our families. The way we make sense of suffering and never give up hoping for better days. The joys and challenges of parenting. The terrible realization that we cannot keep our kids safe, no matter how hard we try. With vulnerability and honesty, Casey has crafted an engrossing and universal story that will appeal to anyone who has lost one or more of their essential people and wants to know how–and if–it's possible to build a life in the aftermath."

-MARGO FOWKES, author of *Leading Through Loss* and founder of Salt Water

The Full
CATASTROPHE

*all I ever wanted...
everything I feared*

Casey Mulligan
Walsh

No part of this book may be reproduced, distributed, or stored in a retrieval system, or transmitted in any form or by any means, electronic, mechanical, photocopying, recording, or otherwise, without express written permission of the publisher.
Some names have been changed to protect individuals' privacy.

Text copyright © 2025 by Casey Mulligan Walsh
All rights reserved. Printed in the United States of America
Published by Motina Books, LLC, Highlands Ranch, CO
www.MotinaBooks.com

Library of Congress Cataloguing-in-Publication Data
Names: Walsh, Casey Mulligan
Title: The Full Catastrophe/Casey Mulligan Walsh
Description: First Edition. | Highlands Ranch: Motina Books, 2025

Identifiers:

LCCN: 2024944953

ISBN-13: 979-8-88784-042-0 (hardcover)
ISBN-13: 979-8-88784-040-6 (ebook)
ISBN-13: 979-8-88784-041-3 (paperback)

Subjects:
BIOGRAPHY & AUTOBIOGRAPHY / Memoirs
FAMILY & RELATIONSHIPS / Death, Grief, Bereavement
FAMILY & RELATIONSHIPS / Parenting / Motherhood

Cover Design: Peter Selgin
Author Photo: Kaptured by Krishna
"Still" excerpted from a piece originally published in its entirety
in *Split Lip*, June 2022.

For my children

and

For Kevin—
my love, my anchor, my home

AUTHOR'S NOTE

Barbara Kingsolver writes, "Memory is a complicated thing, a relative to truth, but not its twin."

The way we experience and recall our past is as unique to the individual as the color of their eyes. Each time we revisit our memories, we do so through the lens of our current selves and our imaginations. Each time, our memories shift.

Against this backdrop, this is a true story to the best of my recollection, as it happened for me. Some events have been consolidated in order to maintain narrative flow and cohesion. Though there are no composite characters, I've changed the names and/or identifying traits of some individuals out of sensitivity and discretion.

All of us...are seeking a home, and I don't mean where we were born, or where we now live and have things, but where we can do the big things, the right things. Where we belong, where we fit, where we're loved.

-Tennessee Williams to James Grissom, *Follies of God*

Prologue 1

PART I   Seeking Home 7

   ONE   Waking Up in Oz 9

   TWO   This Time for Good 25

   THREE   First Comes Love 39

   FOUR   Then Comes Marriage 49

PART II   Making Home 59

   FIVE   Lost and Found 61

   SIX   When the Games are Over 73

   SEVEN   Getting Sorted 87

   EIGHT   Night Vision 99

   NINE   Parallel Lives 109

PART III   Home Interrupted 119

   TEN   Candids 121

   ELEVEN   Rupture 133

   TWELVE   Waiting 143

   THIRTEEN   On Trial 155

   FOURTEEN   Out of the Frying Pan 167

FIFTEEN Into the Fire 179

SIXTEEN Keep Going 189

SEVENTEEN Oh, the Places You'll Go!.. 203

EIGHTEEN Pacing the Cage 219

PART IV Death of the Dream.......................... 233

NINETEEN Fly One Day............................ 235

TWENTY All Roads Lead Here 251

TWENTY-ONE Brighter in the Dark 265

TWENTY-TWO Indigo Tears 277

PART V Home at Last 293

TWENTY-THREE The Full Catastrophe . 295

Epilogue 307

Acknowledgements................................. 309

Suggested Resources............................... 313

BOOKS 313

WEBSITES 315

PODCASTS.. 317

About the Author 319

Still

"You can come in now," they say, holding open the door between the waiting room and the inner sanctum of the ER, and I stand, smoothing my wispy summer dress and unsticking my bare legs from the vinyl chair where I've waited for a half hour that's seemed like days, still praying, knowing yet not knowing, listening to the whirr of the helicopter blades on the pad on the other side of the window, never realizing it was there for my son, should he make it, but he didn't make it, that's what the doctor said when she came to tell me moments ago, sadness in her eyes, her shoulders stooped like someone had given her a thousand-ton weight to pass on to me, and everything got quiet in my head, as if snow had fallen all around me and nothing, not the hugest boulder dropped from the highest height, could ever make a sound that would reach me in there...

PROLOGUE

I'm listening to Sondheim and wading through a sea of bills when the phone rings.

"Eric Simonson, please."

"Sorry, he's not here."

You have no idea how sorry I am he's not here. But god, it feels so good to hear someone say his name again.

"We're calling about a $60 check he wrote to Price Chopper on October 7th, 1998. It was returned for insufficient funds."

"Seriously? That was nine months ago."

"With fees, he now owes $82. If he doesn't pay right away it goes to our lawyer."

I drop into my worn-out computer chair and stare out the bank of windows into the back yard. The old barn leans to the left, tilting in the direction of the abandoned basketball hoop.

"Hello? How can we get in touch with him?"

Glancing at the sympathy cards and still-unopened boxes of thank-you notes stacked on the side table, I mumble, "He's dead."

"Dead?" I detect a note of skepticism.

"Dead. He died on June 12th."

Eric's death, so quickly old news for the rest of the world, though it's only been six weeks. But the telling makes it real again. Makes him real. They say his name and it brings him back, if only for a moment.

I have to remind myself Eric isn't away at college or basic training, that he won't burst through the door at any moment, calling, "What's for dinner, Mom?" as he grabs his swimsuit and heads right back out to the lake. Some days—like today—I begin to picture this, then force myself to think about something else. It's too hard, too fresh. Not yet.

It felt as if my own life began when Eric was born. If marriage made me a wife and having Eric made me a mother, then bringing him home made the three of us a family, the very dream I'd been chasing since I lost my own family at twelve. Soon we had another son, then a daughter, and—despite difficulties in our marriage—I thought I'd created the life I'd longed for and the belonging that had eluded me for so long. But it didn't last.

"We're sorry for your loss." The voice in the phone jars me back to the present. "Just send us a copy of the death certificate."

"No." It falls out of my mouth before I even have time to think.

"No? Ma'am, we'll need a copy of the death certificate."

My words come out in a rush. "Sorry, I'm not sending you one. It's public record. What're you gonna do, have him arrested?"

Standing in the great room now, the cordless phone to my ear, a sigh escapes me. My attention drifts, and I use my free hand to wrestle the wooden filing cabinet drawers closed. They're falling apart, overflowing with the bills, family court documents, and school records lawyers insisted I produce during our protracted divorce and custody battle. There is, at last, nothing left to prove.

I've been proving myself forever.

Staying with friends when my parents were ill, living with relatives after they both died, then folding myself into my husband's family as though I'd always been there, I became adept at finding ways to fit in. If I alternated between smiling

Prologue

sweetly and proving my worth, I hoped I could strike just the right balance. Maybe I could fool them all into accepting me as the permanent, no-matter-what-happens family member and friend I longed to be.

"We're attempting to collect a debt. Someone has to take care of this, or you'll have to send us the death certificate."

"I understand. I just won't do it."

This refusing to explain, producing no evidence is strangely exhilarating. Freeing. Sympathetic to the caller— she is, after all, only doing her job—I stop short of being rude, sticking instead to statements of fact. Several volleys later, collection lady wholly unsatisfied, I hang up.

Week after week well into the fall, I answer the phone to hear a new caller with the same familiar request: "We're looking for Eric Simonson."

I'm sure the fact that Eric has died is right there on the screen, so I've run out of patience for gentle disclosures of his passing.

"You're going to have a hard time reaching him."

"Would you like us to stop calling?" She skips feigning ignorance and jumps directly to impatience.

I draw in a deep breath, then let it out slowly. "You bet."

"Then send us a death certificate."

"Sorry, nope. Talk to you soon."

I can't pin down the complicated feelings these calls evoke. As annoying as they are, these requests remind me Eric's still my son. I'm still his mother.

Yet finally I've had enough.

I arrive home from work one evening in early fall, toss a piece of salmon on the grill, and run for the phone jangling inside. Balancing the tongs on the empty plate in one hand, I grab it on the seventh ring.

"Eric Simonson, please."

I stopped what I was doing and ran into the house for this?

"Listen, he's dead. He was dead the last time you called, he's still dead, and he's probably gonna be dead the next time you call. Why don't you just save your breath and stop calling?"

Months later, I realize they did. I couldn't have known we'd had our final skirmish until the phone went deafeningly silent.

I'm sad the battle's over; now there's no one calling for him, saying his name.

But Eric's is not the only name I long to hear.

I'd have given anything to hear "Aren't you Bob and Elizabeth's girl?" just once through my teens and into adulthood, when I yearned to know people who had known them. Their absence left a hole I spent decades trying to fill; no matter how fast I shoveled or how rich the soil, the pit remained.

Though I couldn't rewrite my own history, I'd been certain I could protect my kids from this same ache by putting down deep roots in a small village. Yet even this didn't save them from the pain and struggle I'd have given anything to prevent.

Maybe it's genetic, that elusive sense of being entitled to a place in the world. Maybe some—the lucky ones—inherit the secret code and pass it down to their children.

I wondered how that would be, for far too many years, waking up in the world like you already knew you belonged there.

PART I
SEEKING HOME

I'm resolved to being born and so resigned to bravery.

-Dar Williams, "Spring Street"

ONE

Waking Up in Oz

I take the long way home this February Friday, trudging through the piles of dirty snow all along the mile and a half from my junior high to our four-room house on Locust Street.

Since September, when we moved to Dumont—yet another northeastern New Jersey suburb—I've learned some survival skills I didn't need when I rode the bus a few towns away. But that was last spring, when Dad was alive. Now everything is different: my family, my hometown. Me. And now I walk to school.

The most important thing is to stay alert and plan the safest route. Most days, my seventh-grade girlfriends and I head home in a group, dropping members one by one as they break off toward their own houses until, finally, I walk the last leg alone. On Friday afternoons like this one, though, our schedules out of sync, it's just me plodding along start to finish.

Alone is when it starts.

Crossing Madison and heading into my neighborhood, I see a group of boys punching each other in the arms, playing keep away with their hats. I make a quick left onto Erie, right onto Johnson. Disaster averted.

In my fifth school since I started kindergarten in 1959, I know too well the pain of a snowball against my ear or the sting of teasing about any number of transgressions I'm not aware of until I've walked right into them. But if I'm alert I can change course.

A few blocks from home, the calm that comes from having completed another successful journey sets in, and I turn my thoughts to what I know. Our red-shingled shoebox house. My big brother, Tommy, nineteen to my twelve. Almost a grownup. And Mom. Always Mom.

My mother's been sick for weeks—she's had breast cancer since I was nine—so her sister, my Aunt Sis, has come from Oklahoma to care for her. Mom's friend Azalea's here, too, tidying up. It's time, once again, to stay at Azalea's for a few days while Mom recovers.

In the bathroom, I pack things for the weekend and come out to find Azalea waiting in the hall. She gently turns me toward the doorway of the room I share with my mother. Mom is in her bed, the headboard against the far wall, her feet closest to us at the door. Late-afternoon light filters through the curtains, and her once-thick black hair, dappled with gray, spreads across the pillowcase. She lies on her side, asleep. Regaining her strength. By Monday she'll feel much better. I'll be home by midweek. By now, I know the drill.

"Look at your mother, how she's breathing," Azalea whispers in her melodic Southern Ohio drawl, her ample arm soft around my shoulder. She sounds nervous, which makes me a little nervous, too.

"Yeah?"

"The doctor was here today, Casey. She has pneumonia."

Four years ago, we were unpacking boxes again when Mom developed pneumonia the first time. That word—*pneumonia*—scared me. I stood at the door of my parents' bedroom, Mom nestled under the covers, and summoned the nerve to ask her the question that had been keeping me awake at night.

"Mommy, do you have the kind of pneumonia you can die from?" I spoke softly, but I could tell she'd heard me by the way her face crumpled.

"Oh, pumpkin, you go off to school and have fun now. Make some friends, I'll be fine in a few days, I promise. Things will get back to normal."

She was, and they did. At least for a while.

"She's not going to get better, Casey," Azalea says now, a tinge of sadness in her voice. "I'm so sorry."

I search her face, trying to figure out what she's telling me. Mom's been sick since I was in third grade. She never gets better.

Then it hits me.

I miss my dad, but since he died I've felt all twisted up with a mix of secret gratitude that it wasn't my mother who had left me so suddenly and guilt for feeling that way. I couldn't imagine life without her. Now she's dying too?

"Go in and say goodbye." Azalea's voice sounds far away, and before I have time to think, I'm standing beside the bed where Mom sleeps under the white chenille coverlet, her breath rapid and shallow. I rest my hand on her arm.

"Hi Mommy, I'm home," I whisper.

Throughout the worst of her illness—even on days when she was barely conscious, her friends will later tell me—whenever I came through the front door after school, Mom opened her eyes and asked, "Is that Casey?" This is how it feels in this moment, as though she's more aware. As though she knows I'm here.

I want to kiss her goodbye, but she has pneumonia. Isn't that contagious?

Someone should tell me what to do.

I stand there, listening to the relentless ticking of the

wind-up clock on the bedside table, looking at Mom for the last time. I memorize her face: the bump on her nose where she fell off a horse as a child, her almond-shaped eyes set into the purest white skin. Her high cheekbones are more prominent than ever now. The cancer has turned her into a smaller, weaker version of the mother I love, but she's no less beautiful to me than she's always been. I add this to the list of moments I've already vowed to remember forever.

"I have to go now, Mommy," I say, finally. "Goodbye. I love you so much." It feels wrong to leave, but Azalea's waiting at the door. Eventually, I turn away.

She steers me to the tiny living room and sits me on the sofa next to Aunt Sis, who draws me close, patting my back as I focus on the Van Gogh Sunflowers print hanging on the opposite wall. I can tell they expect me to cry, so I do. I want to focus on the rest of the day—where we'll go, what we'll do—anything but look ahead to the rest of the week. The rest of the year. The rest of my life.

Growing up with sick parents has taught me one thing— the only way forward is directly through whatever happens. The only option is to just keep going.

At Azalea's house later that evening, I'm watching TV with her daughter and older son when Azalea calls me into a nearby bedroom.

"Alone," she says. "I need to speak to you alone."

Alone is never good.

She shuts the door behind us, and I sit on the bed. Azalea perches on the edge of a chair and faces me.

"I'm sure you know what I'm going to tell you."

I don't. I honestly don't know.

"Your mother died a little after six."

"Oh." I said goodbye, but no one told me she'd be gone

so soon.

I stare into my lap and rub my thumb across the hem of the denim jumper Mom made last August. Then, all I had to worry about was whether I had enough money for the carnival in the field across the street and if I'd make new friends when seventh grade began in the fall.

"Tommy will get an apartment here, close to his job. You'll live with your aunt, Esther, now."

Dad's sister Esther lives with her husband and sons in a rural upstate New York side-by-side duplex three hours north. I've visited there each summer since I was in fourth grade. Esther played gin rummy with me and bought my favorite snacks. When these stays began, I couldn't believe my good fortune. This was as close to a vacation as I'd ever had, yet for years Mom had been reluctant to let me go along with Dad on his visits home. The combination of a house full of rowdy boys and Esther's less-than-stellar housekeeping worried her.

"I've always liked her." What else is there to say? Azalea hugs me tight.

At the service a few days later, the minister quotes a psalm I memorized in Sunday School a few years ago. "The Lord is my shepherd, I shall not want," he intones. I believe God watches over me and, through tears, I promise Mom I'll see her and Dad again one day in heaven.

I arrived at the funeral home with Aunt Sis, but when the service is over and I've said my last tearful goodbye, I walk beside Esther. I'm on the direct route to a new life in New York.

There will be years stretching out ahead, crying myself to sleep in the dark of my room, grieving for all that is lost, the people I miss and the things I cannot yet name. But during the waking hours, I'll remember the lessons I learned: Be very careful. Stay under the radar. Cry when you're supposed to. Smile when they expect it.

By now, I know the drill.

———

I stand beside the principal in the doorway of my seventh grade homeroom. He introduces me—the new girl again—and I wait for the ripple of laughter I know is coming. In 1967, Casey has not yet made its way onto the list of acceptable girls' names, especially here in small-town upstate New York. These kids—the Kathys and Debbies, the Peters and Richards—do not disappoint.

Scanning the faces staring back at me, I see the twelve- and thirteen-year-old girls as divided into two groups: the wholesome country kids and those who've slipped into maturity—real or feigned—ahead of schedule. Back in fifth grade, the most popular girl in our class announced she'd stop speaking to anyone who spoke to me. That can't happen again, not here, with a chance to make a fresh start. I'll hang out with the cool girls. Maybe I'll stay safer as one of them.

"What happened to your parents? Did they die in a car accident? Do you have any brothers or sisters?" they ask as we scarf down our lunches in the cafeteria.

"It's a long story." I'll use this opener to introduce any discussion of my family relationships for decades to come. I recite the worst of it, a list of disturbing events. "We were a Russian Roulette family," I say, invoking the flip if slightly off-mark phrase I use to tamp down my grief at the unlikely combination of both my parents dying from chronic illness within a year.

I try to ignore the emptiness that lingers in the pit of my stomach. "After they died, my brother got an apartment in New Jersey. I came to live here in Hoosick Falls with my aunt—you know, Mrs. McCarthy—my uncle Mack, and my four cousins. All boys, all older than me. Mack is the undertaker for Dotson's Funeral Home. I don't think he likes me."

The bell rings, so I pile an empty milk carton and silverware onto my tray beside a half-eaten sloppy joe. "Actually, I don't think he likes anyone."

When he's not embalming bodies and arranging funerals, Mack works in Dotson's furniture and appliance store. It appears his primary responsibility is to sit in the display window, bundled up against the cold and damp of a poorly heated building, and monitor the world as seen from Classic Street.

Each evening, he takes his place at the head of the dining room table in his undershirt and boxer shorts with a quart of Schaefer beer and badgers Esther. A kind woman, she comes home after herding nine year olds to prepare the roasted whatever and boiled vegetables that wait in pots on the stove. Sometimes one of the boys is around for dinner. More often, it's just the three of us.

I've only been here a week but I catch on quick. I fill my plate and settle into the swivel rocker to finish my homework and watch *The Monkees*. The living room is a dreary space, paneled in brown wood. The heavy drapes, an orange-and-gold latticed design on a cream background, are drawn tightly across the windows.

Esther and Mack argue constantly, but I can drown out their voices if I turn up the TV. Still, I know what they're saying. It's the same every night.

"Come get some dinner," Esther calls through the doorway from the kitchen.

Mack barely looks up from his beer. "Too tired to eat."

"Fine, suit yourself."

My dour uncle couldn't be more different from my father. The classic charismatic Irishman, Dad loved being a Fuller Brush salesman so much he often said he'd do the job for free. To him, this meant captivating New Jersey housewives as much with his own personality as with the goods he was peddling. My mother had succumbed to these same charms in World War II Baton Rouge. When Bob Mulligan, the dashing Yankee soldier home from the war, put his mind to something, there was little anyone could do to resist. Elizabeth Williams was no exception.

Dad's charm went only so far until his irresponsible nature got the better of him. Friends refused to ride with him in his eye-catching, fire-engine red refurbished Jaguar Mark I sedan. I imagine his attempts to see how fast the car could go—and one particularly unwise decision to make an impromptu U-turn on a major highway at top speed—made their decision easy.

When he was home, Dad often lit up the place. Whenever my friends and I walked past him as he watched *Gunsmoke* in the living room, he'd call out to us—"Hey Mabel! Hey Matilda!"—hilariously dowdy names that never failed to make us laugh. Then he launched into a vibrato rendition of "Casey would waltz with the strawberry blonde, and the band played on." Dad's disregard for the gender mismatch between the song and his dark-haired, freckle-faced daughter only added to the hilarity.

Here in Hoosick Falls, bickering replaces my father's big band parodies as the soundtrack of my days. Esther pushes away the papers piled on the dining room table, clearing a spot to sit and eat. Mack sips his beer, punctuating the silence with one of his frequent refrains.

"Joey's driving around and around again," he groans. His youngest son's sole purpose in life appears to be irritating his father. "Jeeesus, Esther. He flies past the store. The kid drives way too fast."

Esther looks at the ceiling as if seeking divine patience. "Oh, for goodness sake, Mack, don't you have anything new to say?"

On and on they go until Mack curls up on the dining room floor for the night—his back feels better there, he insists—and soon the snoring begins.

I climb the stairs, crawl into bed, and pray one day I'll wake up in a place that feels like home.

———

With Tommy out of reach, I've inherited four more big brothers. The oldest two are away at college, and sometimes I come downstairs on a Saturday morning to find one of them and several of his friends sound asleep, sprawled on the sofa, folded into chairs, spread out on the living room floor. The third, not much younger than Tommy, attends community college and lives at home. Since my summer visits, he's made me feel special, a gullible foil for his sarcastic humor.

But as the youngest and closest in age to me, sixteen-year-old Joey is the one I see most. I become the little sister he never asked for.

It's Friday after school, and Esther is grocery shopping and having dinner out with a neighbor. Joey tells me to climb into his car with several of his friends and a case of beer. They talk about girls and swear as he drives faster and faster over the country roads, the car sometimes spinning in circles or flying over hills.

I'm nervous and excited, and for good reason. Being invited to hang out with the older boys feels like an honor. Maybe a step toward popularity, or at least a step toward blending in. But Dad and Tommy were fast drivers, and I never felt this unsafe with them.

Please God, don't let us crash. Please let me get home in one piece.

"Pass me a beer," Joey calls to his friend. "Give her one, too." He nods in my direction.

They all laugh. "Drink up!" says the guy in the hoodie.

Doing my best to ignore the disgusting smell and my roiling belly, I put the can to my mouth, tip my head back, and drink.

I got used to staying with other families when my parents were sick. If they offer you liver, you eat liver. If they offer you beer, you drink beer. It's how you fit in.

Back home and more than a little tipsy, I tiptoe into the house, rehearsing what I'll say.

"Not feeling great. I have a headache. Going to bed," I call to Esther, who's too busy putting groceries away to pay much attention. I head straight up the stairs to my room.

The next morning, a hangover makes the sadness I always carry feel more like a weight planted firmly on my chest. I walk downstairs and into the kitchen, where Esther sits with her coffee, and burst into tears.

The first time I cried after arriving in Hoosick Falls five long months ago, Esther tried to comfort me, though public displays of affection (or private ones, for that matter) are clearly not her strong suit. Still, I'm a kid whose parents both died. How can she not have sympathy for how alone I feel?

Instead, she takes a sip of coffee and looks out the window, though I see moisture in her eyes when the splash of sun that finds its way through the old oak catches them just so.

I'd give everything I have for one more day with my mother. Back in New Jersey, I often had her all to myself, and I liked it that way. I loved watching her sew, making most of my clothes as well as her own, and begged until she taught me to knit and crochet. She read constantly and read faithfully to me, the stories I clamored for each night until I was old enough, at four, to read them myself.

Mom prepared waldorf salad and homemade french fries, deep fried then shaken in a brown paper bag to blot the excess oil. Spare ribs ready and Dad and Tommy finally home, we sat around the kitchen table and caught up on our day. On our evenings alone, we made fudge, contraband for my father, who had type 2 diabetes. When I dripped a little of the steaming chocolate into a glass of cold water and it formed a soft ball, we poured it onto the Melmac plate to set. Unable to wait, we dug in with spoons and laughed about how this delicious treat was all ours. Served those boys right for leaving us home alone.

When my sassy side emerged, Mom's Southern "hush" carried far more weight than a Northern "shut up" ever could. She needed to say little more; disappointing her was punishment enough. Evenings, when she hugged me in the kitchen and rubbed my back, every inch of my body knew I was loved.

Aching for my mother's warmth, these days I fantasize about all the ways my future family will differ from the one I see here. At the McCarthys', Joe shouts, "Esther! Grabbing five bucks and the keys to the car, see you when I get back," already driving away as the screen door slams behind him. Though he called his mother Mom before I arrived, if I can call her Esther, so can he.

In my someday home, we'll say good morning and good night, kiss goodbye when we leave and hug hello when we return. We'll never eat dinner in front of the TV; my family will sit together for meals and enjoy good conversation. I'll tend to skinned knees with a Band-Aid and a kiss, listen to my daughter's worries as I braid her hair, read to the kids each night and instill a love of books. Discipline, on the rare occasions it's necessary, will be firm and consistent and doled out with love. The kids' friends will gather at our house, with snacks and games and a back yard for hanging out on long summer afternoons.

Biding my time until that day, I become skilled at the sleepover. School nights are for homework, clarinet practice, a babysitting gig. On weekends someone spends the night with me or I stay at a friend's house, where I'm an honorary daughter, just like a sister.

This is how I know Esther loves me: she welcomes my friends and encourages me to feel like her house is mine, too. But to this woman who grew up in a stoic nearly New England farm family, sharing feelings, hugging and, God forbid, kissing are as foreign as my mother's Louisiana home.

When I'm the mother, I'll be sure my kids know all the ways they're number one in my book. They won't have to wish for affection. I'll be just like Mom.

Esther's response to my tears reminds me that day is a long way off.

"Oh, for God's sake, Casey. You'd think you were going

through the change of life or something." She stands, buttons her housecoat, and brings her cup to the sink.

I trudge back up the stairs and shut my door.

———

The weekend half over, all I have to show for it is a scary ride with boys, my first hangover, and a good cry. After lunch, Louise, Dad's oldest sister, arrives for her weekly visit.

Never married, Louise taught sixth grade for decades and still lives on the family farm north of Hoosick Falls, where all the siblings were born. Her passions include her tractor, her Pontiac, and the stock market. She occasionally showed up at our New Jersey house with my favorite treat (raspberries frozen in Mason jars), raved over whatever display of intelligence I could produce ("Where's my Idaho?" I'd demand as a four-year-old when she hid an obscure piece from my United States puzzle), and debated politics with Dad.

Arguing always made me nervous.

When I was eight, Louise came for an Easter visit. I hid around the corner and eavesdropped while she and Dad caught up. "It's been a rough spring," he said. "Elizabeth and I were both in the hospital, and Tommy totaled his Impala. Then Casey crossed the road one morning to get the bus and ran right into a car."

"What the hell did she do that for?" Louise grumbled.

I played in my room, coming out only for meals, until she was gone.

Tonight, like every Saturday night, Louise hauls bags of produce and baskets of laundry down to Esther's and stays for dinner. After arguing with Mack, bemoaning this year's poor "padayda" crop, and reminding Esther of how derelict her boys are (in case she's forgotten since last week), she turns on the CBS News with Walter Cronkite and I brace myself for another burst of her profanity. Shots of race riots around the country are more than Louise can take.

"Look at them destroying property. For Chrissake, what the hell do they think they're doing?" More nasty language follows—words I never heard at home, where I was taught we all have equal value—and soon she's moved into a full-on racist rant.

Making pudding in the kitchen, I drop a pot, and Louise startles. "Jesus Christ, what the hell was that? Can't she keep quiet?"

Immediately, my stomach hurts. I don't seem to be able to do anything right around her. I walk through the cloud of cigarette smoke in the living room, my eyes cast downward, my chin quivering as I try not to cry, then turn the corner and slowly climb the enclosed staircase toward my bedroom. Hearing hushed conversation, I stop and slink back down a couple of steps to listen.

"God, Esther, you're a queen to put up with her."

Other than displaying normal emotions, which makes Louise visibly uncomfortable, I'm not sure exactly what I did this time. I never am. I turn and drag myself up the stairs, equal parts hurt and angry.

Alone in my bed, I open my tattered copy of *The Catcher in the Rye*, then close it, too distracted to read.

Dad died. Mom died. I hardly ever see Tommy, and here I am in this place, with crazy Mack and nasty Louise who fight like it's a sport. Esther cares about me, I can tell, but no one here hugs me or listens to how I really feel like Mom did.

This isn't normal, right? No one else I know has a life like this.

Mack and Louise's bickering makes its way up the stairs and bleeds through my bedroom door.

I'm doing the best I can.

I don't know how to absorb what has happened to me, that life with my parents and Tommy was my "before" and everything from here on in will be my "after." My childhood increasingly seems like a fairy tale, a story that happened to someone else.

Mom loved JFK, and her gentle manner and beauty reminded me of Jackie. To me, they even looked alike. Though I was only nine when he was assassinated, I knew it was the end of something special. On TV, they called it Camelot. Now I think of those years when my parents were alive as our own Camelot, Dad and Mom the dashing hero and beautiful heroine of their own tragic tale.

Sometimes I picture the claw in the stuffed animal machine outside the grocery store back in Cresskill, where we lived when I was little. I imagine it snatching me up from my New Jersey life, my real life, and plunking me down here—*catch, transfer, release*—with only my clothes, my dresser, and Mom's sewing machine.

But mostly it feels as if Louise's '66 Bonneville, which transported me from New Jersey to upstate New York, has dropped me into Oz instead. Blink and you live in a strange place. Nothing is familiar. Forget you had a family.

That's all over now.

TWO

This Time for Good

Since I was small I've been obsessed with photography, intent on capturing what's refused to hold still. Carrying my Brownie camera everywhere, later a snappy Instamatic with flashcubes, I recorded everything I saw through the viewfinder: my parents, Dad's old sports cars, our dog Junior. My friends making silly faces or posing like movie stars. The radishes and tomatoes Mom grew in pots beside the wraparound porch. My pesky big brother. When my camera was out of reach, at the most random times I paused and promised to remember that moment for the rest of my life.

One day, it'll be impossible to keep it all straight: what year that was, which thing happened first, who was in the hospital (or was it both of them?). Where I stayed while they were gone. Dad's silent nighttime heart attacks, only diagnosed by a visit to his doctor after the fact at Mom's insistence. My brother Tommy totaling his car, then bringing photos of the crushed Impala to show Mom as she recovered in the hospital from a radical mastectomy. Me, a third grader, hit by a car as I ran for the bus across a busy road, Mom watching from the window. Mom watching, again, from the doorway where she stood calling to Dad as the jack holding up the old Jaguar he was working under gave way and fell on him, crushing his chest. She ran across the parking lot to the factory next door and got help until the ambulance arrived, saving his life; I lay on the sofa with a dual bout of German measles and mumps, watching reruns of *Father Knows Best* and *The Donna Reed Show*, oblivious to the commotion outside.

Hospital stays to remove a tumor on my mother's tongue, to resolve issues with my father's heart. And the hysterectomy that revealed her cancer, everywhere it seemed, no organ unaffected.

I never thought to question why this was happening or feel sorry for myself. I went to school and came home. When Mom was hospitalized, I often stayed with one of her friends, Azalea or El.

Children under fourteen were not allowed to visit in the hospital. When my father was a patient, I read whichever *Nancy Drew* or *Mary Poppins* or *Five Little Peppers* book I'd taken out of the library that week while my mother went upstairs to his room. But when the tables were turned, Dad had his own rogue solution, sneaking me up the freight elevator and into my mother's room in true Bob Mulligan form. One Father's Day, when both my parents were patients, their doctor granted special permission, had Mom wheeled to Dad's room, and Azalea brought me in to see them.

We drove home in the dark then, rain pelting the windshield of her wood-paneled Ford Country Squire, wipers keeping time while Roy Orbison's "Pretty Woman" played on the radio. Here was another frozen-in-time scene for sure, setting and theme song ready-made.

When Dad was home, it seemed as if he was always about to leave, off to a meeting or to look at used sports cars with Tommy.

"Why can't I ever go with you?" I asked each time.

"Oh, you wouldn't have fun," he answered. "It's no place for a little girl."

Riding my bike in the neighborhood one hot summer afternoon, I heard Dad's car start up and spotted it backing out of the driveway. My heart pounded, and I could barely catch my breath. If I could make it home quickly enough, maybe he'd take me with him this time.

As usual, I was still furiously pedaling as he rounded the corner and disappeared.

When I was eleven, Dad took to announcing, "I'm not going to live forever, and before I die, I'm going to have a color TV!" When he appeared on Easter eve with the sleek new Zenith of his dreams, I was as excited as he was.

"Oh, Bob, the bills…" Mom's voice trailed off as she headed to the kitchen.

In the morning, I found my Easter basket and settled in to watch cartoons, though I'd never have admitted this to my friends. Soon Dad staggered half-awake through the living room, headed from my parents' off-the-kitchen bedroom to the bathroom upstairs.

"How's the picture?" he asked.

"It's super!"

A wave of satisfaction spread across his face as he climbed the open staircase.

Then a thud. Loud gasps. I ran to Mom, who was still asleep, and shook her hard.

"Mommy, wake up! I think Daddy's having a heart attack!"

She sprang out of bed with more energy than she'd had in months. "I knew this was coming. I'll go to him. You dial 0 and get an ambulance!"

She did. I did.

They came. He left.

This time, for good.

Soon Esther tells me I'll be visiting the nuns at the convent around the corner weekly all summer so I can prepare to convert. It's high time I returned to my Irish Catholic roots.

This is fine with me. Praying has always helped me find comfort when things seem really dark. I can't understand how people get through life without believing there's a God who loves us and is with us always, even when we feel alone.

If someone had asked me at five about what I believed—though no one did—hands on hips, teary and feisty all at once, I'd have set them straight:

"First of all, families shouldn't fight. Daddies should do things with their kids—the girls, too, not just the boys. Big brothers should protect their sisters and say things like, 'Pick on my little sister and you're dead meat.' If you're nice, people should be nice back. Little kids should have a say.

"And families should go to church. In my family, it's just me there in that pew. I go every Sunday in my best dress, right out the front door and across the street to the Northern Valley Evangelical Free Church, where Mrs. Olsen teaches us about Jesus and heaven and how we should love everybody."

One Sunday morning, I worked up the nerve to raise my hand.

"Yes, Casey?"

"Even Khrushchev? We should love Khrushchev?"

"Yes, Casey, even Khrushchev. Love is a powerful thing."

Then we sang "This Little Light of Mine, I'm Gonna Let it Shine." I wanted my light to shine, I really did. I just couldn't figure out how I could love someone who might kill us all.

When I'm the mother, I thought, curled up in bed with my

books and cuddling the matted, floppy-eared stuffed puppy I loved best, *things will be different. My kids will take care of each other, and I'll listen to them just like I listen to the grownups. Their lights will shine all right.*

The world was full of danger—snakes that slithered in the tall grass behind our house, fires burning miles away, mean kids in the neighborhood. But more than anything, I was scared someone might rob or, worse yet, hurt us. After a woman was found murdered in her bathtub less than a mile from our house, we began locking our doors.

"Could someone break in?" I asked Mom. My frequent nightmares wouldn't stop.

But one night, I had another dream. I ran into the house after an afternoon playing outside to find Mommy, Daddy, and Tommy held hostage in the living room. A man—a *Bad Guy*—was holed up in the kitchen, planning his next move.

I looked at my parents and my big brother tied up with ropes, gagged with bandannas, writhing in their chairs. I turned to see the Bad Guy sitting at the kitchen table. He could kill them all.

He's a person, just like us. I'll bet he loves his family, too. I took a deep breath and walked in.

"My name is Casey Colleen Mulligan. Please don't hurt my family."

I could hear Mrs. Olsen's voice in my head: *Use the most powerful thing you have.*

"I love you," I said in my strongest, bravest voice. I smiled my biggest Irish smile.

The Bad Guy stared at me. I stared back at him.

I wasn't scared.

His face went soft. "Your family is safe, little girl. Because of you."

The Full Catastrophe

I woke up to a sunny Saturday. My friend Nancy was at the door, wanting to play. The house smelled like Mom's crunchy French toast, dusted with powdered sugar from the old metal shaker. Tommy let me listen to his Elvis 45's over and over so I could learn all the words to "Are You Lonesome Tonight?" and pretend to be a star. Dad sat in his recliner, laughing and teasing me, his favorite little girl.

Today, everything is just the way it should be. I was pretty sure God could see my light shining all the way from Magnolia Street.

From Cresskill to Northvale, on to Dover and Paramus, we settled in then pulled up roots repeatedly as Dad's career with Fuller Brush progressed. Tommy was often out with friends, but I had my own mission. On Sunday mornings, I waited to be picked up by families willing to take me to church—Dover Baptist, Valley Bible Chapel, and beyond—so I could get my weekly dose of Jesus, right along with my weekly dose of surrogate-family love.

That neither my father nor my brother attended church was something I thought little about. Dad was a lapsed Catholic, and I couldn't picture him in church, anyway; on Sundays, he worshiped at the church of the automotive fixer-upper in our garage, Tommy beside him. But Mom had given me her childhood Bible with notes she'd written along the margins, and she'd been the one to take me to Sunday School when I was barely four.

Maybe the friends and snacks first drew me in. Without extended family nearby, these motherly women became my doting aunts. As I learned about Jesus, who loved me exactly as I was and was with me all the time, and as I worked my way to the top of the Bible-verse-memorizing competition, little could keep me away. My family had dismissed the

30

salvation I'd claimed for myself. If I wanted to get to church, it was up to me.

In second grade, best friends with a Catholic fourth-grader, I learned the Hail Mary, said many a rosary—dutifully omitting the Protestant "for thine is the power and the glory" part of the Lord's Prayer—and dreamed of becoming a nun, or at least a good Catholic girl.

Now I'll fit in with my Catholic friends in Hoosick Falls, and it's all the same God, anyway. I study the Baltimore catechism with Sister Theresa Agnes, and when I'm deemed ready, am baptized. First Holy Communion and Confirmation are not far behind. I learn the rules and follow them, donning a mantilla, going to confession (though talking to God through a middleman never makes much sense to me), and attending mass every Sunday, folding my hands in prayer just so. I survey the congregation from the back, focusing on the young married couples who seem so perfect, so in love. As I pray for peace and for God to keep me safe, I slip in a prayer that my one-day husband and I will be just like them.

———

Though converting is one of many ways I've tried to become part of the McCarthy family, I still avoid awkward exchanges. This presents a problem, particularly when I need feminine supplies, have no money of my own, and am too embarrassed to ask Esther to buy them. Month after month, I fold toilet paper until I've made something absorbent enough to do the job, then carefully dispose of the evidence.

Soon I hit the babysitting mother lode and make enough money, one fifty-cent hour at a time, to buy the things I'm afraid to ask for—personal items and, more importantly, clothes. We rarely leave the village to shop, but I have Mom's sewing machine and can walk to a pharmacy that sells patterns and a five-and-ten with bolts of fabric lined up in rows. Materials gathered, I hole up in my bedroom, figure out how to run the machine and follow a pattern, and emerge only when my mission has been accomplished. Season after season, I stitch short shorts and bell bottom pants, paisley dresses, and woolen kilts with multiple inverted pleats, all the plaids meticulously matched, pinned, and steam ironed to perfection.

When school resumes in the fall, the novelty of the orphan girl has worn off, and I've fallen to the bottom of the pecking order. English class is the worst of it, a free-for-all where I'm as easy a target as I've always been. I never mention my grades, yet somehow everyone knows I'm the one who's ruined the curve. By midyear, when our fifth-period English teacher faces the board and writes out notes for us to copy, kids pitch Sweet Tarts at me.

"Hey, Clearasil Kid! Miracle on Gillespie Street! What're you doing after school?" they hiss, and pass me notes I refuse to read.

I don't get it—my skin is clear, and I never thought I was anyone's miracle. Fighting back will only make things worse, and being nice has gotten me nowhere. I've never been able to change any of it—my parents sick and dying, the endless moving, now living here—but I can control one thing: me. I can work hard and get top grades. I can fend for myself when necessary. I can create the life I dream of, I'm sure of it. And I'll get through this, too.

I make a plan.

A few minutes into class the next afternoon, the stealthy assaults begin as they always do. That's when I leave my body. Just stand and walk to the front of the room. The kids see me ignoring them, reading the assignment, writing out the answers. But I'm not there. Casey—*the Clearasil Kid, Miracle on Gillespie Street*—is leaning against the doorjamb, watching it all from the outside.

They can taunt me and toss things, pull my hair, poke me even, but those things are happening to someone else. They can try to hurt me, but I don't have to let them.

Removed from that girl in the chair, I am safe.

———

The summer of Woodstock—1969—finds me, at fourteen, a little too young to partake. While John and Yoko's "Give Peace a Chance" becomes the anthem of flower children dropping acid in San Francisco and students staging anti-war protests at campuses around the country, I visit my brother Tommy, his wife Rachel, and their eighteen-month-old daughter in Virginia Beach. As I gently run the washcloth across the folds in her tiny neck, diaper her, and pull a sundress over her head, my heart is close to bursting. Can I possibly love my own someday children as fiercely as I do this little girl, as I'll soon love her baby sister?

Rachel, alternately my friend and something else entirely, had little say, I imagine, about whether she'd be responsible for a fourteen-year-old girl for a couple of weeks, maybe longer, while Tommy's off at work. I crave conversation about my mother, whom Rachel knew briefly, but as soon as the topic arises she shuts it down or provides a version of events quite different from my own. As if she were there. Though she wasn't.

And Tommy? When we were a family he liked to tease,

"I was here way before they were even thinking about you." Now he introduces me as his little sister to friends and coworkers with obvious pride. Yet even this feels like a drop of love in a massive empty vat, not even close to filling the gaping hole left by the family I miss so much.

The following spring, it occurs to me that though I haven't seen Mom's best friend El in the three years since Mom died, she's still within my reach. Bursting with nostalgia and longing, I write a letter and within weeks am on a bus to Cresskill for a visit.

"Your mother would be so relieved! She worried you'd end up like Big Mama!" El laughs as I step into her kitchen, into her open arms. I've seen the photos of Mom's grandmother—calling her a substantial woman would be an understatement. Though I'm far from model-thin, she needn't have worried.

El's words hold much more than a wry observation on my teenage form. She has my history. Azalea was a good friend to Mom, but El knew her better than anyone. She knows me in a way no one in my life now possibly can. My entire body—muscles relaxed, heart beating calmly in my chest, breath as smooth as the surface of a still pond—knows before my brain does: I've come home.

Mom and El were inseparable since the day Dad knocked on El's door to sell his wares. Enchanted, he introduced her to Mom. Dubbed "The Gold Dust Twins" by their alternately admiring and jealous friends, they were progressive postwar suburban housewives in pedal pushers and blouses tied up at the waist—no house dresses for these gals—leaving burnt orange lipstick stains on their Tareytons and Lucky Strikes.

One fall day just after I turned four, we arrived midmorning at El and Henry's sprawling white stucco house around the corner from our split level, as we often did. Between giving each other perms, El and Mom prepared our lunch of brown bread and their favorite concoction of cottage cheese, pineapple tidbits, mini-marshmallows, and Vogler's mayonnaise. All afternoon, they drank coffee while completing the *New York Times* crossword puzzle, using the Audubon guide to identify the birds that perched outside El's kitchen window, and discussing their favorite authors—Herman Wouk and John Updike and Ayn Rand.

Meanwhile, I plunked away at the piano, dreaming of being discovered, or explored the rest of the house. The basement held ping-pong and shuffleboard tables and random doors leading to mysterious closets filled with toys El's daughter Sandy and nephew Ricky had outgrown. Others opened into a potting nook or a staircase to the "other room," accessible only from this hallway or one of several outdoor decks. Even the laundry room intrigued me, where El watched *Queen for a Day* on a wall-mounted TV as she ironed.

Sometimes I climbed the stairway to the other room, hoping no one would call to me through the intercom that connected to the kitchen. What would I do then? Rush back downstairs, through the hall and up the other stairs, pretending I hadn't been poking around in here? I couldn't think of anything worse than El being mad at me.

Bored, I wandered behind the house, picked some yellow wildflowers, and shoved a handful of acorns and a couple of feathers into my pocket. A winding maze of cement steps, with random clearings leading to bird baths or small gardens, wound down the cliff separating El and Henry's from the boring houses on the streets below. This place was pure magic. And so was El.

Back in the kitchen, Mom and El were chatting, but I had important things to say.

"El!" I interrupted, but she and Mom kept talking. I needed to show her the treasures I'd found. I knew she'd love them as much as I did. I called her name until she turned to me and held up her index finger.

"I'll be with you in just a minute."

When Mom's other friends said "just a minute," that usually meant *stop bugging me*. That usually meant *I'll be with you never*. But when Mom and El were done, El turned to me.

"Okay, so what did you want to tell me, love?" I showed her the flowers, the acorns, the feather. "Fun!" she said, turning each of them over in her hand. I could tell she really liked them and wasn't pretending, like most grownups did.

I loved Mom, and I knew she loved me, but I worshipped El. I never wished I could belong to her. One day, I would *be* her.

Soon it was time to go. Dad would be home at five, and Mom had to get dinner on the table. Our family had nutritious yet predictable meals and regular bedtimes, but when we were invited to El's house for dinner, she made lasagna, my favorite. On holidays, the four of us joined El's fiftyish extended family members who lined the tables set end to end, stretching from the piano all the way to the bookshelf-lined fireplace wall. Then I'd play until I collapsed in exhaustion and wake up as Dad carried me into our house.

At home, we listened to Nat King Cole and the big bands. El was the only adult I knew who stayed up till 1 a.m. to watch Johnny Carson and get the lowdown on which up-and-coming rock-and-rollers she should carefully follow. My love of A.A. Milne and *Droodles* and, much later, Wouk's *Marjorie*

Morningstar—books I'd found on her library shelves—began, along with all of my best childhood memories, at El's. I knew before I was old enough to say it that I wanted to live in a place like this someday.

Reunited with El after years apart, I soak up as much of the magic as I can to take back with me to Hoosick Falls. I make the New Jersey pilgrimage yearly, and each time we talk until the wee hours. El fills in the blanks around the childhood I barely remember as she rounds out my view of her with more mature discussions of religion and politics, and how to be an adult in the world.

I'm sixteen, and El and I sit on her sofa late one night as we've done many times before. Wrapped in the warm blanket of love and belonging I've yearned for since Mom died, I confide.

"I usually have one or two best friends. But I don't understand why I was bullied at school, why adults sometimes say the things they do to me or treat me like I'm invisible." My voice shakes, betraying how hurt I feel about this puzzle I've been trying to solve since I was small.

Since arriving in Hoosick Falls, I've spent more time than I care to admit trying to understand why when certain kids speak, people listen. I'm keenly aware of subtle signals, the undercurrent within a group of kids (or adults, for that matter), and can sense when I'm being mocked or silently judged.

Though other kids when teased might think *What a jerk* and move on, I was left with a single nagging question:

Why don't I fit in anywhere?

El gets quiet and gives me the look that means she's about to say something important.

"When I was younger, I worked so hard to please everyone I nearly broke. One day, the psychiatrist I saw looked into my eyes and asked, 'What is it that you're afraid of? Are you worried your halo is going to slip?' I've never forgotten that. It changed my life."

I wish it were as easy as that for me. It'll take a lot more than one meaningful phrase to get me out of the hole I've dug for myself. No, I'll continue to analyze what I see others do until I figure out the secret code to fitting in. And praying can't hurt, either.

We move to topics of faith and religion. "If you accept life, you have to accept death–there's nothing more," El says.

Oh, but there is, I think, though I keep it to myself.

Having a conflicting opinion is both sad and empowering. My parents died before I had my own beliefs, separate from theirs. Maybe this is what growing up is all about.

THREE

First Comes Love

A few weeks after I begin my senior year of high school, Will Simonson knocks on our front door. We met briefly at the lake in late August when I visited friends who'd rented a camp there. He lives in Cambridge, one village north. He's cute, of medium height and build, with freckles and wavy brown hair and green eyes like mine. And he's older—twenty, already an adult.

We talk for a long time that first evening and in the weeks to come. Will spent a couple of weeks at college right after high school and decided it wasn't for him. Now he installs and repairs furnaces for a heating company in Hoosick Falls.

All fall, after I get off the school bus, I walk down to High Street and sit on the stone wall outside the convent, watching for him to drive by on his way home from work. He cruises past, tossing a sly smile and a wave in my direction. While the other seniors walk the halls with their boyfriends between classes, Will calls most evenings, me tethered to the only phone in the house, talking in code, just behind Mack's perch at the head of the dining room table.

"Can't wait to see you again," Will murmurs, his tone adding far more to the message than those six simple words.

I smile and whisper, "Me too."

"You have a day off school tomorrow but your aunt and uncle are working, right? Maybe I can run by the house and you can fix me some lunch." Still smiling, I can guess what else he has in mind.

"Sounds good," I answer, careful not to give anything

away in case Esther is listening from around the corner. I've perfected the art of talking about everything and nothing at once, deftly working in the things I really want to say so that no one is the wiser.

Before long, Will's calling or stopping by daily, picking me up in his brand-new metallic gold '72 Dodge Demon, complete with hood scoops, a spoiler, and racing stripes. I watch out the front window for him to pull into our street and listen for the purr of the 340 V8 engine rounding the corner, then dash out the door to meet him. I think of how much Dad and Tommy would've loved this car each time I hop into the bucket seat and kiss Will hello.

Resting our tightly clasped hands on the stick shift, a cigarette glowing between Will's fingers, we drive away. Leaving behind the dark, claustrophobic rooms, Esther and Mack's arguing, and my worry over my social standing at school, I ride beside Will toward what feels like a whole new life. I can't think of a single reason I'd want to look back.

Soon I'm spending every weekend out with Will or at his house with the Simonson clan, where I feel welcome from the start. Will's father Stan tells corny jokes and expects dinner on the table at 5:30 sharp when he returns from work. Birdie, Will's mother, happily obliges. When I'm there for dinner, another plate appears at the table with little fanfare. Will's older sister is out of college and living several hours away, but his younger sister is my age and has a boyfriend. On Sundays, the six of us often pack a picnic and drive into Vermont or Massachusetts for the day. That I'm folded seamlessly into the family goes without saying.

On Christmas, the Simonsons' living room is piled high with gifts, and I'm stunned as each time they pass packages to a family member, they pass one to me. Then the girls and

I set the table, arrange the serving dishes, and fill the glasses in a flurry of preparation for the holiday feast.

"Eat up, girlie," Stan directs me. "Bird can't fly on one wing, you know!"

I agree to give it my best shot while Will's sisters and Birdie groan, then we laugh at what I soon learn is one of Stan's favorite sayings, typically directed at them.

After dinner and cleanup—when Will and the other men carry a dish or two into the kitchen and get comfy in the living room while the "ladies" wash and dry and restore order—it's time for dessert and a round of Canasta. At the end of the night, I reluctantly gather my gifts, and Will drives me back to Hoosick Falls.

I haven't felt this content since my parents were alive. It's felt easy with Will from the start, and though I'm a lover of words and he's a fix-it-yourself sort of guy who wouldn't dream of reading a book, it doesn't seem to matter. I'm in love, and I know he loves me, too. Around Will, I never have to act cool or pretend to be anyone other than who I am. After years of staying strong and counting only on myself, it's impossible to resist the pull of a loving relationship and a ready-made family.

His name, it turns out, is Robert William, but he's called Will. Dad was William Robert, though everyone called him Bob. How could this not be a sign?

I suspect Esther watches all of this unfold with trepidation. Through my parents' illnesses and deaths, the many moves, and the weight of loneliness that never leaves me, academics have been my refuge, and I'm at the top of my class. Though she never says much, it's clear Esther's vision of my educational mastery leading naturally to a wildly successful professional career begins to crumble as I spend more and more of my time with Will.

One day, I open a textbook in class and a piece of paper, wrinkled and folded small, floats to the floor. I study the words scratched in messy yet old-fashioned cursive.

"Can you believe Casey is seeing that Will Simonson? I've heard he's strange. His people don't like the idea either." The gossipy chatter continues, painstakingly written in the style of a note passed in class between friends. But besides the fact that none of it's true, something other than the handwriting is a little off-kilter. No one says "his people." No one but Esther.

Shocked she would stoop to something so juvenile, I don't tell anyone about the note. She could have just talked to me, but Esther never shares her feelings. Our daily conversation revolves mostly around her organizing our lives ("Where are you headed?") and my filling her in on the high points ("We won the basketball game by twenty points!"). She makes her displeasure known mostly through silence or facial expression or lack of enthusiasm. I avoid criticism, and she runs from conflict. We're a perfect pair.

It won't be until I have kids of my own and lay awake nights worrying about their futures that I'll finally understand. Esther is desperate to stop me from making a mistake not unlike the one she made in marrying Mack. Only then will I grasp how helpless she feels as she watches me attach myself to Will, whose lack of education and limited world view she's certain will sentence me to a life far smaller than it could have been. She has to try one last thing. For my mom.

Her fears are not unfounded. Will knows all the best places to go parking after dark and has the keys to his parents' camp at Hedges Lake, across the road from Lake Lauderdale, where we first met. There, unbeknownst to them, we spend many a freezing winter night beside a roaring fire in the light of a gas lantern. I'm by turns eager, cautiously willing, adamantly resistant, and altogether unprepared for the things he urges me to do.

I have desires too, and I want to make Will happy. I want us to belong to each other, like in the love songs on the radio. Yet all of this is complicated by my strong sense of right and wrong, based mainly on the religious teaching I've soaked up over the years, rules that dictate what should and should not occur before marriage.

Nothing below the waist; safer that way.

I make up the boundaries as I go along, allowing what I can rationalize away and protesting when Will crosses a line. The line keeps moving, of course, until, before long, it fades away altogether.

———

That summer, my thoughts are consumed with preparing for dorm life. I was named salutatorian of the Class of 1972 earlier in the year and applied to several schools, though going off to a faraway college feels like taking a forced break from my real life with Will while he gets to carry on without me. Yet who am I if not a star student?

I'm accepted at Cornell in Ithaca, New York—an Ivy and the only private school on my list—but when I think of the roadblocks, they feel like boulders coming at me faster than I can fend them off. Where is Ithaca anyway? How would I get there or get home for Christmas? Most hopeless of all, how would I possibly afford it? When I turn eighteen in September, I'll be on my own. Scholarships will cover my tuition, but it'll be up to me to meet any additional expenses, including room and board, with my small monthly Social Security survivor benefit and the insurance money Esther has saved for me since Mom died.

No one tells me I might receive additional support if I ask, based on financial need and strong academic performance.

The State University of New York at Plattsburgh—commonly referred to as Plattsburgh State—which several of my cousins attended and near where two of them still live, is the logical choice. Will can drive straight up the Northway after work on Fridays to visit, and with many local students there, I'll find rides home.

The camp looks completely different in the July sunshine from the dimly lit, clandestine nights of winter. Will's family spends most days swimming near the dock or riding in the boat. Many weekends, Will, his sister, and her boyfriend water ski. They make it look effortless.

Characteristically cautious, I wouldn't typically clamor for a turn. Since September, I've become one of the Simonson family, but now I need to be part of lake life, too. *Maybe it'll be fun once I learn*, I think as I wade into the water, awkwardly forcing my feet into the skis that refuse to cooperate.

Over and over, Will backs the boat into position and tosses the rope to me, reminds me to keep my knees a little bent ("like a shock absorber!" he likes to say), shouts "Ready!" and guns the engine. Over and over, I jerk forward, let go, and watch the rope handle bounce away across the surface of the water.

Late in the afternoon, everything finally clicks. Suddenly "up," I ski around the lake and cruise back to the dock just in time for dinner on the screened porch of the camp on the hill.

Never again do I struggle to get up on skis. Often, I'll prefer to lounge in a chair by the water with a book or visit with friends. Instead, around the lake I'll go, a huge smile masking some serious self-talk:

This is fun! I convince myself. *I'm so lucky to have this boat and this spectacular lake.*

Some days, I actually do enjoy skimming over the water on skis. Some days, I almost believe this sun-kissed, risk-taking girl is who I really am. Maybe Will and his family are uncovering a piece of me I didn't know existed.

Or maybe I'm twisting myself to fit neatly into the space they've made for me.

I have no idea how to tell the difference.

———

My bubbly college roommate meets Will when he arrives for the first of many visits he'll make my freshman year.

"Casey's had such a difficult life. How is she so normal?" she asks him. He shrugs.

I've never heard anyone say it's remarkable I've gotten through my parents' illnesses and deaths intact. For the first time, I feel something I can't name, something like pride in what I've been able to survive.

I won't hear the word "resilience" until well into adulthood. I don't yet know there's a name for putting one foot in front of the other, day after day, whether you want to or not, whether you think the light at the end of the tunnel is help on its way or an oncoming train. I never consider that I could rebel, go off the rails in any one of a hundred ways.

What would that get me, I'd think, *and who will clean up the mess that I leave?*

With one foot in the world of high achievement and intriguing topics—political science and theater, psychology and music theory—the other foot remains firmly planted in Cambridge with Will. I vacillate between enthusiasm for my classes and anticipation of our weekend reunions. Though at the start it's a toss-up which will win, by spring there's little doubt. Will's sister and her boyfriend are engaged, and we've talked about it, too. Waiting until college is over—four years, maybe longer—is out of the question.

I love Will, but we've had our conflicts from nearly the beginning. I worry about everything from his driving after drinking a few beers to the importance of developing new friendships as a couple, outside of his family and childhood pals. Having a spiritual life is a key part of my identity. Will neither supports this nor argues against it but, if I push, reluctantly accompanies me to whichever church I'm attending and sits passively through the service.

Though we come close to breaking up once or twice, each time I'm stopped by the twin specters of need and fear. What if I go through life solo, with no kids of my own, no one to care where I am for Christmas, no one in the world who cares deeply for me? I need Will in my life, or who will I be?

Maybe there will never be anyone else.

Somewhere between that first summer night in my living room and the many nights spent studying alone in my dorm room, I decide Will is not only my life's destination but also my ride there. I place my wellbeing squarely in his hands, because they feel safe to me. They feel like home.

Will doesn't plan a surprise proposal, get down on one

knee, hold the ring box open, and ask "Will you marry me?" I don't bring my hands to my face in overjoyed surprise and utter a shocked "Yes, yes I will!" My focus on beginning our lives together, sooner rather than later, has eliminated any possibility of this happy drama. It's a small tradeoff for knowing I'm on the way to a life and a home of my own with Will. Nothing, not even a romantic surprise, could make me happier.

Instead, when I go home one weekend in February, we pick out a ring, a small solitaire in a four-pronged white-gold setting. Will slides the ring onto my finger there in the car, and we drive home to tell his parents.

"We're engaged!" I announce as we come through the door into the kitchen. Will is grinning like the Cheshire Cat.

"Lovely job!" Birdie says, one of her most-used British phrases. Stan claps Will on the back, then pulls me in for a hug.

We drive to Hoosick Falls, and I stretch out my left hand to display the ring.

"Don't worry, I'm going to finish college."

Esther smiles weakly. "Well, congratulations, then." Her resigned tone tells me she's seen this coming.

What I see are my dreams coming true. The memory of these years at the McCarthys' and of feeling rudderless fade as the rest of my life unfolds beautifully before me.

I never think of marrying, settling in Cambridge, then driving to Albany daily to finish college closer to home. The persistence that served me well through my teens kicks into overdrive now, and there's no stopping my relentless march toward what I see as a singular goal. I know others are disappointed in me—Esther most obvious among them—but then it's not their life, is it? I'm finally going to have a home of my own. No one can stop me.

When I return to Plattsburgh, I arrange a transfer to a two-year agricultural and technical college and wrap up a secretarial degree in no time. I understand I've limited the places my education can take me, yet the vision of stable love and marriage wins out.

"Business," I'll tell people for years to come. "I have a degree in business."

One day, I'll long for so much more.

FOUR

Then Comes Marriage

"It's perfect," Birdie says as I spin slowly in the wedding dress that's clearly "the one," and I see in her eyes an excitement that nearly matches my own. We wrap our arms around ourselves in the late-September chill as we walk to the car, breathing in the crisp fall air and admiring the showy leaves that float to the ground. I'll be finished with college in a few months, and I've focused my attention on planning the perfect event, a fitting start to the happy life I know awaits.

Last semester, I spent long hours in the college library studying the massive comparative religions textbook, working out what exactly it was that I believed. Whenever I was home, typically staying at Will's, we made the rounds for Sunday service and finally settled on a Presbyterian church in town, where our ceremony will take place.

Esther has little interest in participating in wedding planning, but Birdie has stepped up in a big way. Once she helps me select my dress, we compile the guest list and record the music on a reel-to-reel tape for the Friday night American Legion Hall reception, the cost of hiring a band or DJ more than Will and I can afford.

Tommy, married with two young children and living in Atlanta now, won't be there. "Work obligations," he says. I'm disappointed. Is this a passive protest to a marriage he, too, thinks ill conceived? He sometimes visited Hoosick Falls while I was away at college, giving him and Esther plenty of time to chat about my questionable choices. When we talk on the phone, I can sense his disappointment in my decision to cut my education short and marry Will. I blame Esther for Tommy's opinions, though I can see that Will, nervous around new people, does little to win anyone over.

On a Friday night in January 1975, the church glows with the flickering light of dozens of candles. At the end of the ceremony, we walk arm in arm down the aisle to John Denver singing "Follow Me." We beam, and our guests smile, too. Friends from Cambridge and Hoosick Falls and my college years, Will's family, my cousins, even Esther and Mack all look so happy for us, and—for maybe the first time since I was a little girl—everything feels right.

"I love you so much," I tell my new husband as we wait in the back of the church for the receiving line to begin, squeezing his hand a little tighter, my eyes attached to his. "Let's promise we'll never fight." Will agrees.

We have a three-night honeymoon in the Poconos, then settle into our apartment across town from Will's parents. Once I find a job, our happily-ever-after will begin. No advanced degree could ever have made me as content.

I interview for jobs in Albany, an hour south, but settle on a position in the only bank in Cambridge, within walking distance of anywhere in the village. Though the salary is low, it's a professional-seeming post that will fit nicely into our lives, even when our children come along. I can hardly wait.

Not quite a month after our wedding and scheduled to begin work the following Monday, I drive to the motor vehicle department in Hoosick Falls to update the name on my driver's license. I'm cruising into town when Will passes from the other direction in his company truck, flashes the lights, and motions for me to pull into the parking lot of the heating company where he works. He guides me into the office and sits me down.

"I have some bad news." Will lowers himself into the chair beside me.

"Esther got in touch with me this morning. It's Tommy."

"Yeah?" I'm confused and getting anxious and I wish he'd just come out with it.

"Honey, he died last night."

"What?!" Tommy is twenty-seven, his daughters only four and six. None of this makes sense. "How did it happen? How did you find out?"

"Esther called me this morning and asked me to find you. It was a heart attack. He was in a used car lot, helping a coworker find a car, and he just dropped. They tried to save him, but there was nothing they could do."

My stomach sinks, and I feel vaguely nauseated. I can't believe this.

But of course he died. There's no point in bargaining or denial. People die, that's what happens.

I hug Will, clinging to the warmth of this man I love. Resigned to facing what I know comes next, I drive around the corner to the McCarthys', where Esther and I plan our trip to Georgia.

Packing to leave the next morning, I think about who Tommy was to me. When I was little, he took pleasure in tormenting me as brothers do their younger sisters, but once Dad died, he was often fraternal/paternal in a much kinder way. The last December Mom was alive, he woke me in the middle of the night on Christmas eve by playing Jan and Dean on the GE Wildcat portable stereo turntable he'd bought at Grand Way, where he worked. Mom could never have afforded that.

After I moved to Hoosick Falls, Tommy called a couple of times a month and showed up now and then for visits.

He's been, like Dad, elusive, someone I want and need but who is perennially out of reach. Now he, too, will be permanently unavailable. It seems oddly inevitable.

My parents' funerals were low-key events—closed casket, no graveside burial, calling hours followed by a service in the funeral home. In Atlanta, standing between Esther and Tommy's wife Rachel, I struggle to avoid looking in the direction of his body, which bears little resemblance to the big brother I remember. His hair is thinner, his hairline receding, and I've never seen Tommy with a beard. This sharing space with the body that was once my brother is not what I've come to expect in saying goodbye to a loved one.

I'm running out of loved ones.

———

In the fall, we buy a house, kitty-corner from Will's parents. Every time I round the corner and catch sight of the twin patches of hosta that mark the boundaries of our property, I smile. We paint and wallpaper, hang pictures, and imagine each empty bedroom filled with children one day. Will sends me green carnations on St. Patrick's Day and roses on our anniversary. I'm such a lucky girl.

That Will's parents are right across the street—one big happy family—is a gift, and no one is more supportive, more loving. Ever watching out for us, Birdie and Stan bring us groceries ("Buy one, get one free, might as well share!") and host big family meals every Sunday. What more could a daughter-in-law without parents of her own ask for?

The last of my own family has slipped away just as I'm slipping into this new one. I almost believe they're mine.

Thinking of my childhood is like remembering a book I

once read. The characters are familiar, and dear to me in a melancholy sort of way, but they have little to do with my life now. Yet sometimes, standing at my teller's station or lying in bed at night, a fleeting, unsettled feeling passes through my body in waves. *Something is missing,* it whispers. I shiver, tense, and will it to pass.

I've been meaning to schedule a physical since I got home from Tommy's funeral, but the excitement of buying our first home and Will's opening a gas station/ auto repair shop repeatedly pushed it down the priority list. Now, a year later, I make an appointment with a village doctor, leave with an order for blood work, and return for a follow-up.

"All the results are normal but the lipids," he says, his brow tightly knit under a shock of white hair. "Your total cholesterol is over 400, off the charts. Looking at your family history—it's a tough one—this appears to be genetic, and we need to take it seriously."

He tears a sheet from his prescription pad and presses it into my hand. "Fill this, take it daily, and check back with me in three months."

For years to come, each evening I'll drink cholestyramine, a gritty orange powder that morphs into revolting glop when mixed with water, and eat the low-fat version of every food I can find. I'll make sincere but erratic attempts at regular exercise and monitor my cholesterol numbers. Tommy's early death frightened me, but I feel strong and healthy. I'm doing all I can, so there's no need to worry, at least for now.

———

We've been married three years when I can't wait any longer for our first baby. I've agreed we should find stable jobs, buy a house, and fix it up before we start a family, but now it's time. I finally convince Will, who hasn't been as intent on taking this next step as I have, and within a month, I'm pregnant. I throw myself into decorating a gender-neutral room with rainbows and gingham and dream of the day our two will become three.

Nearly two full days after I felt the first contraction, a spinal block is administered, and our baby is delivered with the aid of forceps.

As much as I've hoped for a girl, the moment this little boy bursts onto the scene I'm captivated. We name him Eric Thomas, his middle name chosen to honor my brother and my mother's father. No one could replace Tommy, but having my baby carry his name comforts me.

I hold him in my arms, encouraging him to nurse, and he grips my finger with his tiny hand. I examine his head and run my fingers across the forceps marks on his ruddy skin— the result of my water having broken more than twenty-four hours before delivery. I soon learn the nurses have taken to calling him Eric the Red, which I find incredibly endearing.

"I wonder if you'll ever know how much I love you, little man," I murmur as he settles into a sated sleep.

He opens his eyes and looks up at me—*he knows my voice*—and a chill runs down my spine. I'm overcome with a love so deep, an intensity I've never known was possible.

"You're going to have a wonderful life, and I'll do everything in my power to keep you safe. There's nothing you could do to make me stop loving you. I promise you that. You'll be my baby till the day I die."

In fewer than forty-eight hours—a shorter span than the labor itself—it's time to go home.

"He's pretty enough to be a girl," says the Gray Lady, a

Red Cross volunteer who stands over the bed, swaddling my pride and joy in the blue blanket knit by a friend obviously rooting for a boy. "What are babies for but to love?"

I settle into the wheelchair they've insisted I use for the ride to the front door and take baby Eric in my arms. No one is more ready than I am to break out of the maternity ward and start my career as a mother. I was born for this.

——

El and Henry arrive a couple of days after we come home from the hospital to keep me company this first week as I learn to be a mom.

"You're the perfect combination of your mother and father," El observes, sitting beside me on the sofa as I nurse late one night.

"Honestly?" I look down at Eric and well up, blaming raging hormones for my frequent emotionality. How many people are there in the world who could or would tell me this? Every moment with El feels like a gift, another dose of her signature magic.

During the day, between diapering and feedings and visits, we discuss parenting. I mention friends who shield their kids from struggle or difficult truths.

"All children really need is love and consistency. You raise your children to live in a world where everyone doesn't love them," she says.

I agree. I want my kids to know how to relate to all sorts of people and learn from situations where things don't go their way. Yet dealing with those who don't love (or even like) me is admittedly not my strong suit. Her comment as she leaves me with my first newborn—"You have the most

The Full Catastrophe

common sense of any new mother I've ever known"—keeps me steady until I can actually believe it myself.

When Eric's older, I'll finally appreciate how El's approach to mothering has so clearly influenced my own. I grow to see in myself an amalgam of her pragmatic influence and Mom's Southern warmth. I couldn't hope for anything more reassuring than this.

———

A week later, I proudly push the shiny navy blue Silver Cross pram my British mother-in-law insisted we have along the sidewalk, Eric snuggled beneath another blanket a customer at the bank has knit for him. People driving past us on Main Street pull to the sidewalk and hop out of their cars to ooh and aah over the little one who has finally arrived.

"Such a beautiful baby," gushes one of the sweetest women I know, "and three weeks late, can you believe that?"

I've never felt more like I belonged to a place.

The first weeks with my newborn are challenging— alternating periods of nursing and fruitless attempts to console the screaming, colicky infant throughout the day with a blissful though abbreviated stretch of sleep at night. Eric warm against my shoulder, I pace the floor and sing him unconventional lullabies punctuated with coos and kisses. I run through them all—"Goodnight Sweetheart," "You Are the Sunshine of My Life," "Put Your Head on My Shoulder"—until I reach my favorite, "Build Me Up Buttercup." Upbeat lyrics begging him not to break my heart seem a perfectly silly juxtaposition to soothing my innocent baby, the bit of comic relief I need to stay sane.

Even on the most exhausting days, I wouldn't trade this for anything. I'm hopelessly in love.

PART II
Making Home

I hope you live a life you're proud of.
If you find that you are not, I hope you have the strength to
start all over again.

-F. Scott Fitzgerald, *The Curious Case of Benjamin Button*

FIVE

Lost and Found

Watching Nickelodeon most evenings, two-year-old Eric dances to Toni Basil's "Hey Mickey," The Go-Go's' "Vacation," and his favorite, the theme from *Fame* ("I'm going to live forever!" he belts out along with the talented teens). He ends with a somersault and leaps to his feet with arms spread wide. Whether Eric's shouting, "Goodnight, Dan!" in response to Dan Rather's farewell on the CBS Nightly News, "Go Blooty!" as Black Beauty races through the fields of England, or "Good answer!" at the Family Feud folks, Will and I are never at a loss for entertainment.

Every few weeks, Birdie and Stan—now Gram and Pop to all of us—invite us to dinner at a restaurant near the lake. We settle Eric into a high chair and before long he's waving and smiling. I follow his gaze to the couple at the next table.

"Hi, sweetie!" calls the woman in her talking-to-children voice. She begins a round of peek-a-boo, and Eric is delighted, squealing whenever she pulls her hands away from her eyes. Her husband can't help but smile and doesn't seem to mind he's no longer the center of her attention. It feels as if my charismatic dad has returned to me in our boy.

It's my job to be sure our son is as healthy on the inside as he appears on the surface. When I insist his cholesterol be tested at age two, his pediatrician is unprepared for the results. Eric's levels are nearly double those expected for a child. He has clearly inherited the potentially deadly family gene, and I pray he'll be saved from a sudden heart attack like the one that killed Tommy.

They're all dead now—the family I was born into—but I'm still here. Though it's been hard living without them, somehow I've gotten through. But how could I possibly survive if anything were to happen to a child of my own?

These are the questions that will haunt me, years later, the ones we ask from the safety of the theoretical, not really believing such things could happen. *What if I'm diagnosed with cancer? What if his plane crashes?* Imagining can never capture the reality of traumatic events. We can never prepare. All we can do is hope we'll be the lucky ones.

A lipid specialist finally gives us the name for what we have: familial hypercholesterolemia, known as FH. I learn all I can about this condition, resolved to protect Eric from my family's tragic outcomes. He explains our livers don't work the way they should to rid the body of "bad" cholesterol, regardless of lifestyle modifications. We adjust our approach with the release of each new medication or study and see a pediatric cardiologist. Knowledge and action are a comfort.

Soon my own doctor detects an irregular heartbeat and prescribes a heart-pacing medication. Two weeks later, I notice a vague numbness in my left hand. Within hours, I'm in intensive care at the local hospital.

I chat cheerfully with nurses. But late at night, alone in my bed in the eerie glare of the monitors, I'm overcome with despair. Will brings Eric to visit, and the sight of my lively little guy in his double-breasted navy pea coat, matching cap fastened under his pudgy chin, is more than I can bear. I spent my childhood visiting sick parents as they recuperated—or didn't—in rooms much like this one. Is this the beginning of that life for Eric, losing me by bits, as I did my own mother? Will his memory of a loving, involved parent fade away, as mine did?

A few weeks later, I'm relieved when the cardiologist prescribes another heart-pacing drug, which he predicts will solve the arrhythmia. He advises close monitoring.

"But about your high cholesterol—you need to think of it as a congenital birth defect, much like type 1 diabetes."

This is oddly reassuring. No one I know has heard of this genetic form of high cholesterol, but people have heard of diabetes. People with diabetes can take care of themselves, follow doctors' orders, and live with their condition. Eric and I will do the same.

———

Satisfied we've gotten the cholesterol issue under control, it's the perfect time for a sibling. We're thrilled when Kyle is born ten days before his big brother's third birthday.

Eric welcomes *his* baby with open arms, offering him his blankie and reciting the rhymes he's learned in preparation for his brother's arrival. He sits beside me on the sofa flipping through board books while I nurse Kyle. *Look at our family: two lively boys, a mom and a dad. No one sick. No one dying.* I can hardly believe this is my life now. I can hardly remember how lost I used to feel.

As Eric is regularly swept up by his daddy, his grandparents, even neighbors, off to become a part of the world, Kyle becomes mine. We spend long hours together, rocking and singing, reading and playing, Kyle surprising me again and again with his precocious abilities. As Kyle grows, Eric climbs into the crib with him to make him laugh. Thus begin years of joint birthday parties and matching outfits; "Seriously, Mom, how could you have done that?" Kyle will

The Full Catastrophe

admonish me decades later.

At three, Eric kneels on his grownup-sized double bed, snug in his footie pajamas, for the tucking-in routine. I lie beside him, struggling to keep my eyes open long enough get my busy little boy to sleep. He finagles his way into yet another cover-to-cover reading of *Richard Scarry's Best Mother Goose Ever* with his impervious three-year-old resolve, then takes a few minutes to chat with the man upstairs.

"Hi God, whatcha doin'?" he asks, and I hide a smile. They're obviously on an enviable first-name, just-checkin'-in basis.

Snuggling down beneath the covers with his favorite blanket, Eric wiggles his little body over to the edge of the bed that threatens to swallow him up and waits for me to pull the zoo-animal sheet up under his chin.

"Leaving room for your wife?" I tease, playing my part in our nightly ritual. He giggles, and I notice his left thumb, only recently forfeited as a sleepy-time pleasure, lingering dangerously close to his mouth. If it's going to "accidentally" slip between his already slightly parted lips, he'll be sure to wait until we exchange I love yous, I run my fingers through his silky hair, kiss his freckled face for the hundredth time, and turn away, leaving the door open a crack behind me.

———

On a frigid February day in 1983, when the boys are almost four and one, the phone rings. Esther has died in her sleep at sixty-nine. The family gathers in Hoosick Falls, and Louise arrives, wringing her hands and sighing incessantly.

"God, Casey, you must feel like the world is coming to an end," she says. I understand this is the only way she can express her own distress at the death of her younger sister. Esther is gone, and Louise is lost. She will never be entirely found again.

I feel many things today, though lost is not one of them. At twenty-eight, I have my own family now. Still, I grieve Esther's passing. My life with her wasn't perfect, and she wasn't my mother, but I know how lucky I was to have her take me in. Though she expressed her love nothing like Mom did, like I do, she loved me nonetheless.

A few months later, El's daughter Sandy calls; her mom has cancer. Turns out, watching my mother's long, painful battle through ineffective treatments to address metastatic breast cancer strengthened El's resolve to ignore the lump in her own breast for decades. When she dies the following June, I'm prematurely at the end of the line. Without parents or siblings, without a guardian aunt or the surrogate mother I've had in El, I have no caring relationship left from my life before Will, no direct link to my parents and brother.

El had rejected the idea of any service when she was dying—no flowers, no memorial of any kind. "When it's over, it's over," she always said. "You need to accept that."

But I won't accept it. Who she was to me, what she means to me now, lives on, just as Dad and Mom, Tommy, and Esther are with me still. It will never be over for me.

When Mack lands in the hospital early in October, eighteen months after Esther's death and only four months after El's passing, I visit regularly. Since Esther died, I've tried to be a good...daughter? Ward of his wife? I'm not sure what exactly I am to him. Ironically, when he finally passes, his son's wife and I—neither of us blood relatives to Mack—are the two by his side.

Yet at the funeral home a few days later, Will and I are

seated in the back with the guests. After the service, we stop at the house where I lived for the eight years between Mom's death and my marriage. I feel like a visitor, greeted politely by some of my cousins, avoided by others. I'm hurt and confused to realize all the years I convinced myself I had five brothers, not one, were a lie.

"Let's go," I mouth silently as I catch Will's eye and head for the door carrying Kyle. Will leads Eric by the hand, and we hurry to the car that will take me back to my real home, the one I have made for myself. There is nothing left for me here.

———

Eric arrives home from kindergarten on a spring afternoon red-faced and breathless, props a hand against the doorjamb, and announces, "I need to call the police. Those teenagers are smoking in the path again!" Mr. Melodrama, even at five. I laugh as Kyle, balanced on my hip, struggles to get down and play with his brother who's finally home. They're a perfect pair.

"It's time to take our cholesterol meds," I call to Eric. He takes medication approved for a child his age and learns what not to eat, telling the ladies in the cafeteria, "No gravy for me, I have high coleshrol!" with his impish grin. Now, on a break from climbing the mountain of dirt at the house under construction next door and jumping off with a wild "Yahoo!" he trudges into the kitchen, resigned to choking down another glass of cholestyramine. He gets it done and heads right back out again to play catch with his dad.

That night when I tuck him into bed, Eric confides that a friend wouldn't play with him at recess that day. I gently

66

wipe his tears, kiss his forehead, and tell him how nothing is forever.

"Give it time. Things work out. I promise," I say, trying not to feel like an imposter, considering how often I feel left out myself.

In years to come, I'll wonder whether Eric got his melancholy from me, prone as I was to waves of sadness and a sense of something missing, while Will appeared to plod through life with little thought about any of it. Though later yet, I'll realize this was never so.

Eric is not me, I think as I watch him sleep. *He'll feel loved and accepted. I'll be sure of it.*

Yet as the school year draws to a close, I learn my own sensitive nature doesn't always serve me well in guiding Eric through life. While I comb his hair and adjust the last-day-of-school outfit he's been dying to wear since we bought summer clothes weeks ago, we chat about how much he loves his teacher, whom we've known for years.

"Today's your last day of kindergarten! You do know that Mr. Green won't be your teacher in the fall, right? Maybe you should thank him for such a terrific year, buddy."

Later that evening, the phone rings. It's Ed Green.

"Just thought I'd call to fill you in on how the end of the school day went."

"Hi, Ed. Is everything okay?" I'm hoping my boy's first year of school hasn't ended on a sour note.

"Everything's fine. You know Eric's the only kid I have who walks home. After we got the rest of the class on the buses, Eric just stood there beside me. He couldn't bring himself to leave. We sat under a tree for a while and had a good chat about what a great year we've had and how we'll see each other next year, too. He got a little weepy."

"Ohhhh." I remember again why we'd hoped Eric would have Ed, "the pied piper of kindergarten," as his first teacher.

"I'm going to write 'sensitive' in red letters on his permanent folder. It's something the adults who work with him should be aware of. Not because he's overly sensitive, but because he usually hides it well."

One day I'll understand how true this is.

———

Will's a hard worker who's there to lend a hand to anyone who needs it. I love this about him. While I take care of the house and the boys or cook or read, he spends his free time working on cars and building things in the garage. I appreciate this, too.

Soon after our wedding, I began attending a small Congregational church just outside the village. Our kids are part of this close-knit church community where everyone feels like family, attending Sunday School and singing in the children's choir. Prayer and talking silently with God throughout my day are as natural as breathing. Though Will reluctantly joined me at church when we were dating, now he only comes on special occasions, preferring working on projects at home to sitting in a pew. So like my father.

The friction that's elbowed its way into almost every area of our lives from the start has gradually loomed larger. I put together outfits with care; Will resists regular showers and wears his grimy work uniform with "Will" emblazoned on the chest into the evening, complaining, "Jeez, you want me to wear a tuxedo or something?" if I suggest he change his clothes.

The garage Will opened just after we were married provided a modest though unreliable income that left us with little to no savings. He railed against finding a regular position that would make our lives more stable until he agreed to take a maintenance job at a factory in Hoosick Falls not long before Kyle was born.

And Will has rules. He insists we spend every Sunday with his family. I loved this when we were dating, but once we were married I hoped we'd become a family of our own. Instead, we're often an extension of his parents, and the benefits of making our home across the street from them are increasingly outweighed by the costs.

Will pulls into the driveway after work most afternoons and his father appears, leaving us no private time to hash out issues we left hanging that morning. Will can't grasp my frustration when his mother is upset we haven't consulted her first before enrolling Eric in preschool or when later I learn she's approached his new teacher with "inside information" on his learning challenges, and doubtless things more personal. The more I fight to establish healthy boundaries, the less Will understands or values them.

When I share fantasies of a life somewhere warmer with more opportunities, where we could grow closer on our own, I learn we're never moving to another town, much less another state. In fact, moving outside the village itself is out of the question, since Will's fire department duties can't possibly be fulfilled out of hearing distance of the siren.

We can never own a foreign car. Will's a Chrysler man, preferably Dodge.

I can't cut my hair. Will likes it long.

I've had assumptions, too. One of them is honesty. When money is missing from my purse, it'll be years before I accept that he took it, mostly for beer he didn't want me to know he'd bought.

I've learned never to repeat stories Will's told me. Too many times, I've innocently mentioned a nugget he shared only to learn he concocted the whole thing.

"I hit a cat on the road and had to stop into Club 22 to tell the owner," Will tells me upon arriving home late one evening. I sense true regret and mention this to his friend, who laughs me out of the room.

"Will stopped in to have a few," he says, shaking his head, amazed I could be so gullible. I blush with embarrassment.

———

We've felt sure for years that we're done having babies, for reasons good (two healthy boys) and not so good. Will, as it turns out, seems much happier with his sons than with their mother. He and the boys come through the door laughing after a trip to the lake or an afternoon working on projects in the yard, so unlike our bickering about nearly everything. Though I'm repelled when I notice how he stinks of the beer he drinks in the garage, seeing him with Eric and Kyle, I soften.

I couldn't be prouder of our boys. Alongside emotions that run deep, Eric's had an adventuresome streak from the start. As soon as he could walk, he ran. As soon as he could run, he rode his bike as fast as he could. Repeatedly, he bursts in the back door with a breathless, "Hey Mom, you won't believe what just happened: I flipped over the handlebars. Right over them, really! I can't believe I'm alive!" his freckled face splotched with red, hair dripping with sweat.

At six, he practices juggling a soccer ball on his knee for hours, waiting for the big boys who coach his PeeWee team to walk by our house on their way home from sports practice.

"Hey, PJ! Hey Dougie! Where's Paul? See you at soccer on Saturday!" he calls to them. "I've been practicing my shots!"

"Okay, Mayor!" PJ often shouts back, over his shoulder.

"Why d'ya call me that?" Eric asks one afternoon.

"Cause you know everyone," laughs PJ. "You're the leader of all the cool little kids in town!"

Kyle—who thankfully has not inherited FH—scrambles along behind Eric, wanting to do everything his big brother does: kick a soccer ball, ride a bike, dig in the garden with Gram. Soon we'll see that though Eric is an extrovert, Kyle is equally introspective, enjoying his friends and the lake and the mountain in winter, yet as inclined to fly solo as his brother is to run with the pack. His love of music—piano and clarinet, guitar and bass and anything else he can get his hands on—will eventually be joined by passions for cooking and reading and his own brand of humor.

Will's current enthusiasm around having a baby is unusual for him. "Wouldn't it be nice to have a little girl?" he cajoles as we discuss the idea of growing our family.

I worry about my own heart-related issues and family history of heart disease and cancer. I question whether having a child in my thirties is the best idea. What if I have a heart attack before the kids are grown? What if I find a lump in my breast, like my mother did? But the draw of three children is too much to resist.

When our two kids come home with their families years from now, that'll be fun, but with three, it'll be a party. *It'll be okay,* I think, doing the math in my head. *I'm thirty-two, so if I live till I'm fifty, she* (so sure I am it'll be a girl) *will be eighteen. I will have gotten all three of them through to adulthood.*

The Full Catastrophe

Our first attempt ends in an early miscarriage, but at long last, four-and-a-half years after Kyle, we have Kaitlin—our Katie, born with her thumb in her mouth and an unexpected shock of dark hair.

I've believed since I was old enough to picture my one-day family that if I were to have a close relationship with a child it would have to be a girl. Yet in recent years, I couldn't imagine feeling any more in love with a daughter than I already was with my boys.

Now, staring into the deep blue eyes of this sweet baby girl nestled into my arms, I can hardly take in what's happened. Lying in the hospital bed late at night, I drift off, then jar myself awake with thoughts of finally buying dresses—pink, frilly things. Will I have her ears pierced? Paint her room lavender? Will we shop together? Do our nails? We'll be as close as a mother and daughter can be.

Sleep eludes me for days as I grow accustomed to the foreign, exhilarating idea that I have a girl, one like me, who can complete that mother-daughter circle broken so long ago. When I wake each morning, it takes a few minutes to return to my consciousness, this miracle that's happened.

I have a daughter! I think, new news every time. It's too good to be true.

SIX

When the Games are Over

"Run, Eric! Block him! Good save!" I shout in the direction of a field full of sweaty eight-year-olds, then peek into the stroller to check on Katie, who's just turned one. She looks up at me from under a warm fuzzy hat, the pink blanket I crocheted tucked tightly around her to ward off the nippy fall air.

I glance across the field, where Kyle's kicking around a soccer ball and wrestling on the ground with his U6 teammates. They played earlier this morning, when the grass was wet with dew. Now the sun has dried the field and illuminates what's left of the leaves, a burst of orange and red and yellow surrounding the field as if God created this picture-perfect day just for us.

When the games are over, we trudge through the path darkened by a canopy of maples, emerge into the dappled light of a tree-lined street, then continue around the corner to our house, Eric and Kyle each with a friend. While Katie naps, I put dinner on the stove to simmer, a hearty chicken stew to warm us after a day spent outside. I fix a bagel and a cup of tea and climb the stairs to read and maybe take a nap of my own, while Will stokes the fire in the wood stove and builds a blanket fort with the boys.

When I dream of these days in years to come, it'll most often be of this time I think of as the placid middle years. Our lives are busy now, and I like them that way. We spend long fall days like this one at the soccer field, all shin guards and cleats, apples and rain gear and camp chairs, the heady scent of burning leaves a constant. The country kids gather at our house in the village, and we host sleepovers most weekends. I'm happiest when we have a houseful, our three with their buddies and occasionally their parents, too.

In summer, friends head up to the lake with the boys and Will, sometimes all of us, to spend an afternoon on the boat, tubes or water skis trailing in its wake. Midwinter, I drive on scary, slippery roads to nearby Willard Mountain for skiing, later snowboarding, picking up friends on the way, all for kids who insist it's essential they be there on a day like today.

No matter the season, I often have a camera in my hand or a camcorder propped on one shoulder. It's never far from mind, that one day the kids will be all grown up, and I'll give anything to see these scenes again.

These nights, all three kids asleep in their beds, Will and I sink into the sofa, tired, a little overwhelmed. Content.

But the days aren't all like this. Though I love Will, it's nearly impossible to untangle the web created by my need for family and fear of living a lifetime alone. It's become clear we're two vastly different people. Perhaps that was the draw; I'm worried it may be our downfall.

We argue frequently lately, typically about raising our kids. Though Will's usually up for his own set of preferred activities—mostly involving the lake—when it comes to approving the kids' other social events, more often than not it's an emphatic "no."

"Can Doug and John sleep over?" Eric asks his dad.

"It's not a good night, but go ask your mother," Will says, setting up a lose-lose scenario. Go along with him to keep the peace? But then I worry the kids aren't developing the close friendships I missed in a childhood of frequent moves. Overrule their father, ignoring his opinion altogether?

When the Games are Over

Determined to prevent them from experiencing the isolation I've never forgotten, I often choose the latter, driving them places or supervising overnights, complete with home-cooked meals and movies from the video store.

We'll talk this through so it doesn't happen again, I resolve whenever conflicts occur, and I try to protect the kids from our disagreements.

Yet whenever they struggle with homework, Will is eager to empathize. "Don't worry about it," he soothes, as they balk at trying something difficult or worm their way out of doing their best. "We can't all be a genius like your mother."

The more Will isn't the husband and father I pictured, the more I try to control him. I invite friends for a barbecue, then complain afterward about comments Will made that were obviously exaggerations and half-truths. When he pulls into the driveway, a cigarette dangling from his lips, or when I see stomped-out butts littering the back yard, all I feel is disgust. I knew he smoked when we met, when we married, but I didn't account for how repulsive it would become. And I didn't understand how I'd eventually filter everything Will did through the lens of what kind of example it set for our children.

I nag him to join us at church, and worrying about his salvation feels like the purest form of love to me. If we could just look like (and actually *be* like) the other young families united in their faith, I'm sure everything would fall into place. I surround myself with people who think like I do, alienating Will all the more. When he refuses to join me in counseling with a local pastor, I go alone, hoping that rethinking the way I react to him might improve our situation even without him there.

Our increasing discord does not go unnoticed by Will's

mother, who becomes increasingly unhappy with me. Returning with Kyle from their grandparents' house one afternoon, Eric innocently repeats her criticism.

"Gram asked us what we ate for dinner. When I told her we had soup and salad, she said, 'Is that all? That's not enough!' and gave us more to eat."

I seethe until Will gets home, then meet him at the door.

"Your mother talks to our kids about me. You need to tell her this is not okay. You need to remind her that I'm the mother—not her—and she has to keep her opinions to herself."

It's likely that message will be hopelessly lost in translation.

When we're together, though, Gram keeps up appearances. I continue as if nothing were amiss and hope for the best. We still look forward to our annual Christmas cookie-baking day and weekend shopping expeditions. She's been like a mother to me and loves my kids as if they were her own. These remarks hurt to hear, but I'm still certain she loves me like a daughter. I can't risk believing anything else.

Despite all of this, I remain hopeful we can turn it around for the kids. In truth, it's more like a cover-up, troubling events smoothed with a skim coat of spackle, then papered over with the fabric of children and time. I prefer not to think about a day when the wall itself might come tumbling down.

———

For years, on and off, Will has arrived home from work around 3:30, seeming pleasant enough, then headed out to the garage to "put his tools away." Hours later, he comes back inside surly, what little he has to say difficult to

When the Games are Over

understand. Though I know he drinks beer out there, I've attributed his garbled speech primarily to fatigue.

He's developed a list of my transgressions, and some nights things go downhill fast.

"Where's the checkbook?" he demands.

"It's in my bag. I bought groceries today."

"You don't need to be carrying that around with you all the time. That's our money, not yours."

"*Our* money, exactly."

"I've never denied you anything."

"Seriously? Are you worried I'll empty our account and run off with your money? All $150?"

"Where does it all go, then? I just got paid and there's hardly anything left."

"I paid the bills! The boys needed ski pants! Just because I write the checks doesn't mean I'm the one who spent the money. What do you want me to do?"

Will paces, fuming, while I try to make him see what's so obvious to me: we need to be a team, united in our singular quest to raise wonderful kids in a close-knit family. I use words as weapons, firing them fast, drowning him in language he can't escape. I picture their sharp edges bouncing off his head, his arms shielding his face for protection. It's more than Will can process. He has nowhere to hide.

Finally, one of us goes silent and stomps away. I wipe my tears of frustration and disappointment and return to being a mom.

Other nights, Will walks through the house from the garage and goes straight to our room with barely a word. I sneak up the stairs late at night, hoping to find him asleep. I'm not always so lucky.

"Why were you at church so late on Sunday?" he begins,

The Full Catastrophe

the lead-in to theme one, a tirade repeated nearly verbatim.

I answer, my voice low and steady. "The kids and I were chatting with friends. You're welcome to join us there."

Might be a better plan than drinking in the garage all day.

"Who have you been talking to? I can tell when you've been talking to one of your friends," his voice louder now, moving on to theme two. Themes three, four, and five can't be far behind. "You get an attitude."

Maybe I need more of an attitude. Maybe that's my problem.

"You're having an affair with that minister. Everyone knows it. Who do you think you're fooling?"

"You know I'm not."

Like I haven't heard this a million times before.

"You think people like you," he sneers then, wrapping things up with the taunt he's sure will hurt me most. "You should hear what people say about you in town."

You hate that I have friends.

"What are you doing for sex? I can get what I need elsewhere, you know. I'm done putting up with your shit. It's payback time, and payback's a bitch."

It's been tough to feel like being intimate when there's no affection between us, and worse. And does he really think threatening "payback" will get us there?

Asking him to keep it down, hoping to keep the kids from hearing, only amps things up.

"Ah, Miss Perfect, hiding behind the kids again." His voice louder and more tense, he bangs a fist on his chest. "What about me?"

I'm not even close to perfect, and I'm becoming angry, too.

"What about *you*?! They're the kids. You're supposed to be the father. And why would I want to be around you when you're such a shitty husband? I have real friends who care about me, which is more than I can say for you."

It's getting harder and harder to like who I am when life is like this so much more often than not.

When I can't listen any longer, when Will stomps in and out of our bedroom, up and down the stairs, close to losing it altogether, and it gets harder and harder to not take the bait, I bury my fingers deep into my ears and move them in circles, creating a *whoosh* that muffles the endless recitation of everything that's wrong with me.

Periodically, I pause to check whether the rant is over. Inevitably, Will returns to our room, mutters something I prefer not to hear, and drops to the floor—much like Mack did all those years ago—huddled under a blanket, facing the wall, seething, until he drifts into a fitful sleep.

I arrive home one night after a counseling session on a chilly evening to find the house we leave open—no need for keys in our village—locked up tight, I refuse to leave while my kids are asleep inside with Will. I spend the night on the floor of the enclosed porch and think long and hard as I shiver, pulling my blazer tight around me. I don't want to live this way. But what's the alternative?

I'll make sure Will knows he can never do this to me again.

And I'll carry a key.

———

On this otherwise-quiet Saturday afternoon, Katie napping in her room and the boys playing outside, I'm scooping a dish of ice cream when Will bursts through the back door.

"Get the baby and get out of here. I'm getting my gun," he says, his voice flat and low. "I'll shoot myself." He's shaking with rage.

I catch his eye briefly, searching for a clue to what's actually happening here. Am I seeing someone truly despondent? Or is this a dysregulated man with a desperate need to up the ante, to find any way he can to frighten me so I fall in line? What I see on his face is pure anger, and I can't take a chance.

He's mentioned a gun—as a hunter, he has several—and I need to get my babies out.

Will's late-night rants have become more frequent in recent weeks, and now they happen nearly nightly, sometimes all evening. Once, all night long. Earlier this week, I walked across the street to my mother-in-law's. There in her kitchen, my protective maternal instinct overcoming my need to keep our troubles private, I came clean on what's been happening in our home.

"I don't know how this will end," I told her, "but we may need you soon. If something frightening happens, can I come here with the kids?" Surprisingly understanding, Birdie reassured me she'd be there for us, though I hoped I'd never have to put her support to the test.

I dash up the stairs and gather Katie from the crib. Back in the kitchen, I grab my purse, run outdoors and, feigning calm, direct the boys to follow me across the street to Gram and Pop's. Together, we retreat to the safety of Will's parents', a house with no guns.

For two nights and a day, Will holes up in our house, refusing to speak to anyone. In a fit of rage, he throws everything he considers mine—books, clothing, photos— out onto the front porch, spilling into the shallow yard for everyone to see. Even his father's appeals for diapers and a bottle for the baby fall on deaf ears, so we keep the boys busy and buy what we need.

Finally, at a loss for what to do, I speak with the pastor I've been seeing for counseling. He's advised me in our sessions to let Will "own his own problems," to stop trying to fix things for him. Now he says the only way to end this standoff is to have the village police—some of whom Will grew up with—take him to the mental health wing at Glens Falls Hospital, nearly an hour to the north.

That afternoon, I stand at the window in a friend's house and, as our kids play, watch the police car pass. I catch a glimpse of Will, subdued in the back seat, and soak in the reality of what's happening to us. Will isn't the only one in trouble. The kids are handling things as kids often do in crisis, keeping it all inside. And me? There'll be no masquerading as a happy family now.

It takes the better part of the day to restore the house to some semblance of order, get the kids, and settle them into bed. Tomorrow there'll be more to do, things to fix for days and years to come, but for this one night, there will be peace.

Close to midnight, I'm sleeping soundly for the first time in weeks when the phone rings. I answer, disoriented, and it's ten minutes before I can process any of it—where I am, what has happened, who would be calling me and why—much less the words cascading through the receiver. When at last I'm fully awake, I realize the pastor's been explaining he's been to visit Will.

"He doesn't belong there. He's on a locked ward, but he's calm and rational now. He's afraid, and he's sorry for everything that happened. You need to go over there tomorrow and make sure he gets to the kind of place where he belongs."

Will's breakdown was intense and public. He refused to respond to his parents' pleading, much less mine, and threatened gun violence. Both law enforcement and this pastor himself urged me to have him taken to a place where he would no longer be a danger to himself or to us. Taking this step wasn't easy, with the eyes of the village trained on him. On me. Now, without even one night of rest, I need to examine how wrong I've been?

I'm stunned but dutiful. My kids are out of danger because I protected them, but this is their father—my husband—after all. I meet with the doctors, who agree a move is in order, investigate our insurance, and locate a more suitable facility. I'll need to drive him there.

In a hospital closer to home, Will has a couple of in-patient therapy sessions, meds are prescribed, and he's released, seeming calm and contrite. Our family doctor makes a cryptic comment suggesting antidepressants don't typically work quite so quickly. The words he leaves un-spoken won't land with me until much later: drying out can look a lot like an epiphany.

We sign up for counseling with Mike, the Christian counselor recommended by our pastor, a few towns away. Will, visibly shaken by his stay in a mental health ward, is grateful for a do-over. Week after week we wade into the deep muck of our deeply flawed relationship. Week after week we begin again, as though the previous session never happened. Worse yet is Mike's *Psych 101* counseling method.

"Tell me about yourself, Casey. What was your family like growing up?" He locks eyes with me and waits.

"My parents died ten months apart when I was eleven and twelve, and I was sent to live with cousins in another state. My only sibling, an older brother, died when I was twenty. I don't have any immediate family."

He lays his pen carefully on the notebook in his lap. "That's the saddest story I've ever heard." I'm not sure whether to feel grateful he cares so much or worried about his emotional well-being.

When we get into the thick of things, dissecting our fights, doing the post-mortem on who said what and our respective reactions, Mike appears convinced it's essential he help me understand emotions I can't possibly have figured out for myself.

He leans in. "How does it make you feel when he says those things? You worry someone else is going to leave you, don't you?"

Wait a minute. Will threatened to kill himself with the kids at home, threw my entire life out on the front yard for the world to see, was taken to a mental health unit, had to stop drinking altogether, and I'm the focus here?

"No," I respond in careful tones, hoping to mask my frustration with his utter lack of insight. "My fear is that I'll have to go through *this* again, listening to him hurl insults at me, trying to keep him calm so the kids don't hear. He's my husband, and I want to make this work, but I don't know how much longer I can do this."

We stop counseling soon after.

Will treads carefully for a while, spending more time inside with us and drinking non-alcoholic beer, until his shock fades. Then we gradually go back to the way things were before our lives turned upside down. It's not ideal. It's not what I've prayed for. But it's a bargain I'm willing to make to keep my family intact.

The Full Catastrophe

In the midst of the chaos of Will's emotional meltdown, I step out of my comfort zone like never before. I call his new boss, Ray Presley, who's just arrived from South Carolina to oversee operations at the factory where Will works, and explain what's happened. Ray encourages me to focus on helping Will get well. His maintenance job will be there when he returns.

Weeks later, I learn the Presleys have bought a house in Cambridge. I pay them a visit with freshly baked bread in hand, Katie in the stroller and our dog on the leash. Ray's wife Hope and I hit it off right away and, as it turns out, each of our kids has a counterpart in the Presley clan.

Our lives fall into the same rhythm nearly seamlessly. I job-share at the bank, and when I'm not working, Hope and I spend our days together at home with the babies or make the long trip to the mall with strollers in tow. We arrive back in town just in time for school to let out, when the pack of boys—her three, my two—gets off the bus at Hope's or walks home through the path to our house. Weekends, we have dinners together, barbecues on the deck or holiday parties inside by our wood stove. Sunday mornings we're all at church, though typically without Will.

At work, Ray is Will's biggest supporter, recognizing talents in him others have ignored. Ray does his best to make others see them, too, and rewards Will with raises and promotions. This makes me respect Ray all the more.

But at home, our problems continue. When we're with the Presleys, I hide my frustration well, or so I think. But when no one is watching, I alternate between pretending everything is fine and trying to talk with Will about things

When the Games are Over

he's done or said that have embarrassed me. His short-lived abstinence from drinking is over, and now he's become a "maintenance drinker," retreating to the garage to down enough beer each evening to take the edge off. He's alternately angry with me, then conciliatory, insisting he's trying. It seems to require an awful lot of trying for Will to simply be honest and kind rather than hostile and secretive.

We argue in front of Ray and Hope, and I feel defeated. Isn't one area of my life safe from the damning effects of our discord? Can't we have close friends without their having to be dragged into our drama? Evidently the answer is no.

When nearly two years later, Ray is transferred home to South Carolina, for weeks I fail to hide the tears that flow when I least expect them. I've played at having a big close-knit family, a sister, and now that's coming to an end. I force myself to let go, spending time with other friends while Hope and I plan visits in both directions. By the time we wave goodbye in June, I've made my peace. Goodbye is something I dread but have learned all too well to understand.

SEVEN

Getting Sorted

A timeline is what I picture when I think of my life now, like the ones in history books depicting key events—a death, the discovery of new lands, a significant battle. On my line, there's one imposing black slash, far bolder than the rest, marking the end of the family I was born into. Everything that precedes it seems out of focus, populated with fictional characters. Everything that follows is real.

In another story, I might have grown up with my doting dad, my loving mom, and who might I be then? Imagining parents and a brother in my life—people who look like me, who love me no matter what—is more than I can bear. Best to avoid that altogether, though when I watch sad movies late at night alone on the sofa, Will and the kids in their beds asleep, I find myself sobbing for my parents, for Tommy, for Esther and El, all of them lost to me.

I cry for all the goodbyes, all the grief of the world. I cry for soldiers who die and lovers who part, for pets that pass. I cry for the weight of all I've lost, even as my babies lie sleeping safe and warm in the rooms above me.

By day I'm the responsible adult in more ways than I expected or desired, but during these lonely nighttime waves of grief, I mostly want my mommy. I'm seven again, and I can feel her arms around me, hugging me in the kitchen and rubbing my back, telling me everything will be okay.

Next I'm eleven, in another kitchen, and it's me comforting her now, her body shrunken and weak, ravaged from the cancer that will soon win. I remember our last year together, the twelfth birthday party I organized, doing the limbo with my friends in our basement. I dissolve into tears, only now understanding that while we danced she was surely resting upstairs, fighting the pain, happy that I was happy.

Again I think of how oblivious I was as a self-absorbed preteen to the reality of her life. I grieve having lost her, and I grieve for her losses, too, how hurt she must have been by my occasional selfish outbursts ("Why can't I have friends overnight, Mom? Everyone else can!"), how disappointed in the way her life had gone. How sad it was that it ended so soon.

But lying there, I often return to my late-night conversations with El.

"Whenever I think about all of it, I feel so guilty and angry," I told her, after we'd reconstructed, yet again, the sequence of events I could never quite keep straight: who was sick when, which hospital they'd been admitted to. Where I stayed. How old I was.

"Didn't anyone think I deserved to know Mom was going to die? I was so bratty that year, giving her such a hard time when she had just lost Dad. Tommy wasn't home much, and she was so weak. I would've been so much kinder."

El absolved me with a single line.

"Casey," she said, with a kind yet rueful smile. "You were twelve."

———

The year is 1989, and it's Christmas Eve. We put up our tree in the corner of the living room weeks ago. This spot, directly across from the front door, is the only place we can imagine it could ever belong. Our Scotch pine is short and bushy with long, sharp needles that drop easily, mounding up beneath the tree like nature's holiday gift to us. Its fragrance fills the house and multiplies the coziness exponentially. We've attached strings of large colored lights, hung gaudy reflective tinsel, draped a garland of faux cranberries, and added the modest collection of ornaments we've amassed since our marriage along with those we've bought for each of the kids—one for every year they've been alive—and a few treasured heirlooms from my parents. We let Eric climb the ladder to place the angel on top.

There.

All the gifts have been saved for, selected, purchased, and wrapped. We've dressed in our holiday best and gone to church for the candlelight service, and the kids—three, seven, and ten—are out, like lights themselves, in their new Christmas pajamas.

The neatly wrapped packages and stockings stuffed to overflowing are at Gram and Pop's, stored there like they are every year, safe from the kids' impatient sleuthing. Now that they're sound asleep, Will drives his pickup across the street, fills the bed, and drives carefully back to the mouth of our driveway, where the unloading begins.

Back and forth he goes from his truck, up the steps and onto the porch to our front door, his arms piled high with boxes that nearly topple.

I hold the door open, arms outstretched. Christmas music plays softly in the background.

"I'll take them from here. It's a bucket brigade!" I say. We both laugh and press on, eager to finish up and get into bed ourselves.

I place boxes and bags carefully around the tree and, without a fireplace, we prop the stockings on the floor, leaning against the stacks of gifts. With the living room lights off and the tree lights on, the warm glow only adds to the sense of peace and comfort and joy and all the stuff of which the someday Christmas of my teenage dreams was made.

One day, when this idyllic scene is only a memory, a neighbor will confide how he looked forward to Christmas Eve each year, watching Will's Ford F150-turned-sleigh make its late-night delivery to our house. I'll think of how I looked forward to it, too. I'll remember there were good things, things to miss from these years, just when I've almost forgotten everything but what happened later.

The kids are up early and come to get us up, too, though nearly as excited as they are, I'm already awake. Will and I go down first, while the kids wait dutifully on the stairs for the all-clear. I video them as they run for their stockings, unpack each one item by item, and give me a rundown of what Santa has brought.

After we've all showered and dressed, I call Gram and Pop.

"Merry Christmas! We're ready for you. Come on over!"

"Yeah!" shout the boys, who stand so close I can't move.

"Hurry up!" Katie squeals in agreement.

All of us settled into the same places we claim every year, we unwrap gifts one person at a time all morning long.

"Here, Kyle," calls Gram. "Hand this one over to Pop."

Pop pulls out the pocket knife he always carries. "Got my handy-dandy," he says, and we all groan at another of his signature phrases.

We love his signature phrases.

We take it slow, preferring to savor this day we've waited for—prepared for—all year. Halfway through, someone calls it.

Getting Sorted

"Intermission!"

I set out the breakfast of sausage-egg casserole, toast, fruit, and Gram's homemade coffeecake, then pour coffee and orange juice and hot chocolate, a Christmas morning treat. We sit around the dining room table and savor this, too, while Katie rocks her new baby doll, shushing it like a seasoned mama, and the boys exclaim over the gifts they've already opened.

"I can't believe I got my own skis and boots. No more renting!" Eric, wearing his new ski cap and scarf, is wide-eyed. That the skis are lightly used matters not at all to him.

Kyle is practically bouncing. "Mom, I have so many K'nex now, I can build everything! With these little motors, I can make things move on their own. And I got the new Calvin and Hobbes book, too. I can't wait to see what else there is!"

When we return to the living room to finish opening gifts, I pause and take it all in. Here we are in our warm house with a fire in the wood stove. Gram and Pop wouldn't be anywhere else but with us today, and the kids are overjoyed. Our relationship has remained challenging this year, and it would be easy to focus on the troubles in our marriage, but today Will and I are working together to ensure everything goes as planned. Today is a good day. Today, we're a team.

Everything goes still, and there's nothing but this life I dreamed of. I have a family of my own, a home that's mine, and a place I'll always belong. I can't imagine a single thing that could ever make me give this up.

—

In a mix of optimism and wishful thinking, we add on to

the house the summer before Katie starts school, giving our growing family more room to spread out, and it feels like things might settle down a bit for us. Yet this respite turns out to be short-lived.

Katie was a challenging toddler and tempestuous pre-schooler, alternately loving and passionately oppositional. Having grown up intent on avoiding negative attention, I sometimes felt as though she embarrassed me wherever we went. When I couldn't find her in a department store, there she was in the window rearranging the display. At dance class, while the other little girls spun in their tutus, Katie crawled under the racks of costumes. These may have been the amusing antics of a lively child were it not for the way she stiffened her body, shrieked, and refused to cooperate when I tried to get her to stop.

She wants friends and begs for play dates, though they often end in her sobbing in frustration over something seemingly inconsequential that has not gone her way. I begin to think of "It's My Party and I'll Cry If I Want To" as her own personal theme song.

But just when I'm about to admit defeat, she asks to cuddle up with me to watch a movie or make cookies together. It's tough to keep up.

Sometimes I watch her from across a room, curled up on the sofa or coloring or playing with her dolls. I study her—dark blonde hair half up or in pigtails, sapphire eyes deep in concentration, chunky freckles splashed across her nose and cheeks—and feel a surge of love so strong my breath catches.

"Mommy, can Laura spend the night? Can we have an ice cream party?" Katie asks, and though we've had a tough morning, I agree. I'd do anything to see my little girl happy, making friends.

Getting Sorted

Now she bursts through the door from kindergarten, and I unpack her book bag as I do each afternoon. I remove the half-eaten lunch—carefully packed to align with a heart-healthy diet, as she, too, has inherited FH—then pull out her school-to-home communication notebook. This is the daily event I dread most.

"Katie had a tough day today," her teacher writes. I steel myself for the familiar list of my daughter's grievous transgressions.

"She took thirty minutes to get her coat and boots off and join us on the rug."

"She doesn't pay attention when it's required. While the other children are reading and writing together, she's fiddling with pencils or playing with her hair."

'She was rough with another girl on the playground and became unfriendly when I tried to speak to her about it."

I ask her pediatrician if there could be a medical explanation for Katie's behavior. She's so unlike her brothers.

"Probably not. Some children are just more challenging than others. Try a structured reinforcement system," he suggests. "Be consistent. It takes time to see results."

Positive behavior plans and sticker charts with highly desirable rewards—lunch out or a movie with Mommy, a trip to the lake with Daddy—help, but Katie's still not quite the student her teacher expects her to be, and I know she feels it, too. I want the rest of the world to see the funny, loving little girl we get glimpses of at home. Katie shines when she knows she's done well, but as I lay awake at night, I feel as if I'm the one with the fatal flaw. In a combination of grief and frustration, my thoughts are less than positive.

What does her teacher expect me to do? Lock her in a room for the weekend and send her back fixed? If I could go to that classroom and be her, make her behave as she should, I would.

Maybe I should get rewards for trying hard. A sticker now and then, a thumbs up? A bit of a respite for Mommy when I've made good choices?

I can't help but smile. There's a positive reinforcement system I could get behind.

———

Though Katie's taking much of my emotional bandwidth these days, the boys worry me too. Occasionally they're upset with their dad, but most often they're mad at me. The transition has been gradual, from *Mom as protector* to *Mom as obstacle.* Sometimes I inhabit both roles at once.

One Sunday, cleaning up from a sleepover I orchestrated with the usual opposition from Will, I find the boys in their bedroom with him, hatching a scheme to forget the homework Eric has due tomorrow morning in favor of a trip to the lake. I understand Eric's motivation, but I can't believe Will supports this, ignoring the importance of working hard in school. The close bond I crave with the kids is fading away.

I wake up many mornings already in tears. Desperate self-talk...*I'm a failure as a mother, everything I've tried to build has gone to shit. Why doesn't my own family listen to me? What is it that makes them think they can treat me this way?* Even the nonsense Will has thrown at me for years, things I've previously been able to ignore...*no one likes you...there's something wrong with you...you think you're so much better than everyone else*...consumes me in waves that crest and crash. I'm simply too exhausted now to fight them off.

Spiraling downward, I zero in on other relationships. Though on the surface I'm an extrovert, easily making friends at the bank and at church, I'm plagued by the sense that people outside my small circle of close friends don't respect me the way they do others. I return again and again to the mental Rolodex, flipping furiously through each card to be sure I still have someone who is there for me.

What is it about me that makes me easy to dismiss? Is it my marriage to Will or the cute Irish girl facade that makes people think less of me?

Will I never feel loved in the way that I crave?

———

It seems as though the passion I've poured into fixing our relationship has run dry. Yet neither my failing marriage nor my fear of winding up alone is as all-consuming as my constant worry for the kids.

Within a year, a psychologist confirms my suspicion that Katie has attention deficit hyperactivity disorder. I begin to see that ADHD explains much of what Eric is experiencing, too, how he mostly does what feels good without considering the results, how he craves movement and avoids boredom at all costs. I recall how he used to love to crawl into bed with me, then wait for me to tickle him until he fell to the floor laughing hysterically, of how he craves sensory input and adventure and risk. The more exhilarating, the bigger the thrill, the better, much to my dismay. He's so much like my father. He couldn't be more different from me.

In junior high now, Eric's struggle with focus continues to affect his schoolwork. He'll do anything to get on the soccer field, out to the mountain or up to the lake, devise any scheme to avoid doing homework or the demands of the classroom. We held him back in third grade, bowing to the solution *du jour*—the notion that repeating grades can solve delays in reading and writing—hoping he'll catch up. Now he has the third evaluation of his school career and is finally diagnosed with a learning disability.

In coming years, I'll realize that ADD, the type without hyperactivity, explains much of Kyle's disorganization and low frustration tolerance. I'll move from annoyance to full-on laughter as I clean his room one afternoon while he's at school, pulling crumpled papers and half-eaten apples, orphan socks and the missing net for his fish tank from under the dresser until all I can think of is a magician pulling one rabbit after another from inside a tiny hat. Even later, I'll learn of the highly genetic component to this diagnosis. My three are children of an alcoholic and grandchildren of my father, for whom moderation and focus were beyond comprehension. The only surprise will be that I didn't see it sooner.

One afternoon, as I sit with Katie in the waiting room of the neuropsychologist who monitors her ADHD medication, a poster calls to me from the bulletin board.

DO YOU CONSTANTLY WORRY ABOUT YOUR
PARTNER'S MOODS?
DO YOU CHANGE YOUR BEHAVIOR TO DEAL
WITH THEM?
YOU COULD BE THE VICTIM OF DOMESTIC
VIOLENCE.

Watch for these Red Flags:

Emotional and Psychological Abuse
Substance Abuse
Financial Control
Fear of Volatile Behavior

Getting Sorted

I run over our situation in my mind. I pay the bills and handle the finances, but Will constantly berates me for having the checkbook, insisting I call for permission before ordering vacuum cleaner bags. He drinks too much, but I don't cover for him. Well, not most of the time. He's clearly emotionally abusive, but I don't believe the things he says about me and don't cow to his attempts to intimidate me. That's one of the many reasons we fight so much.

This is all so confusing, and how can I figure it all out while every day I spend all my energy focused on being a good mother? Physical abuse feels much clearer; maybe that would make it easier to draw the line. To know it's time to get out.

As we're called in to see the doctor, a fleeting thought flashes through my mind.

I wish he'd hit me. Just once.

EIGHT

Night Vision

As the kids grow older and the glow of the relationships I thought would save me dims, I spend a lot of time thinking about why I can't make our marriage work. Though I know it takes two committed partners, I still believe I can fix things if I try hard enough. Yet approaching forty, married nearly half my life, I see some of the decisions I've made through a different lens.

My childhood was difficult, but feeling proud of my achievements in school was the one constant. I could have done anything, been anything, but instead I chose what I wanted most: a family. So why am I so unhappy?

My kids see their father as part of a tapestry, woven into his family, a son, a brother, valued by virtue of belonging. They go to the same school he did and know some of his lifelong friends. They live on the street where he grew up. His life makes sense to them. My family, on the other hand, exists only as a story they've heard. I often wonder if they believe I ever had parents and a brother.

Seventeen years into our marriage, I've come to think of myself as a single flower in the middle of a vast meadow, beaten down by the elements. Unprotected.

I think of what I might say, if I had the nerve, to Will's family, for whom I've been almost one of their own, at a time when the "almost" has taken on increasingly greater emphasis.

"I had parents once. I wasn't *like* one of their children. I was their daughter."

Tears well up as I imagine this scene, and I know what's stopping me: I hardly believe it myself.

But things are gradually becoming clearer. In grasping for family I've created a life where my intellect is of little value. Worse yet, intelligence is the very thing Will uses against me whenever he can.

What will it take to turn around and save myself?

—

I've thought about going back to school often over the years, though I set conditions. Afraid to drive on icy roads, I'd have to participate in Empire State College's new distance learning model, or maybe I could take classes through an extension course, closer than the Albany universities an hour away. I'd keep my job, since we couldn't pay our bills without my salary.

And what would I study? Though I'd been a self-taught photographer for years, shooting family portraits and weddings to augment our income, this didn't feel like the right career for me. Maybe accounting, something I could do from home, something that would fit seamlessly into the life we had.

But small shifts in my perspective have been accumulating, and now everything has changed. Having worked at the bank, mostly as a teller, for more than fifteen years, it's become obvious I'll either move on now or stay for the duration; thirty-five or forty years in that same small building in our tiny village feels like a life sentence.

Our finances aren't improving, either, and as the kids grow, my worries about paying for our futures grow along with them.

Gone is my commitment to being sure Will isn't threatened. I need to use my mind, to feel challenged, to remember what it's like to work hard and succeed at something not everyone else can do. There has to be a way to make it happen.

"I've been thinking of going back to school," I tell a social worker friend who's currently a career counselor.

"Oh, you definitely should," she responds with enthusiasm. "You're so underutilized at the bank."

Those six simple words are all I need to hear.

Completing my education becomes my sole focus. I chat up friends who returned to school in their thirties and forties, order catalogs from local colleges, research potential majors. I'd forgotten how much I enjoyed working as an aide to the speech therapist when I was in high school, and in light of my lifelong love of reading and language, I contact The College of Saint Rose in Albany, which offers a major in Communication Disorders. I crunch the numbers and investigate funding streams. Painstakingly fitting my college credits, all nearly twenty years old, into a grid of prerequisites, I plot out how each semester might look and which courses I'll need to take before entering as a full-time junior in the fall.

"I know we need my income, but here's how we could make it work without it," I explain to Will, outlining how a combination of grant money, student loans, merit-based scholarships, and our home equity line of credit could get us there.

"It's a lot of money. Things seem fine the way they are," he argues, never one to take a risk.

"But Will, we struggle to pay our bills. We have credit card debt. What will we do about college for the kids? What about retirement? There's never anything left for a vacation or unplanned expenses. Once I graduate, we'll repay the loans and still have some breathing room."

"You really think you're going to do this? You hate to drive in the snow. Who will be here for the kids? I just don't see it happening."

"I won't be at school every day, and sometimes I'll be home before they are. You're home by 3:30 most afternoons. Eric will be fourteen by the time I start, and your mom's right across the street. There's a good chance I'll be able to find someone to ride with when the weather's bad. I know I can do this. One way or another, things will work out."

Will has no problem highlighting the same fears I've used to limit myself for years in attempting to derail the train that's already gaining steam. But he's misjudged the strength of another of my qualities: determination. Finally, he realizes the train has already left the station. Might as well get on board.

Besides taking a couple of in-person night classes, I prepare for the college equivalency exam in educational psychology. Hidden away in our bedroom with the texts I borrowed from the library piled beside me on the quilt, I come to a discussion of Maslow's hierarchy of human needs. People are motivated to fulfill certain needs, Maslow asserted, and those that are most basic, such as physical survival and safety, must be met before we work to meet higher-level needs, such as belonging, love, self-esteem. When a deficit is more or less satisfied, we are able to move forward. Finally, self-actualization—achieving one's full potential, satisfying needs that arise not from lack but from a desire to grow as a person—can be addressed.

The book open on my lap, I pause to mull this over. I've pushed past my own unfulfilled needs to focus on the personal growth I crave. Maybe immersing myself in an environment that values thought will lead to the belonging and confidence I've sought for so long.

Change is calling to me in a voice so loud it's difficult to sleep. Hard put to imagine what the next few years will bring, I'm sure of one thing: whatever happens, there'll be no going back.

———

Driving out of town at 6:30 a.m. on my way to class the following fall, an hour's ride "over the river and through the woods" ahead of me, I can't stop smiling. It feels as though someone has let me out of prison. No more dirty looks from the other tellers for returning three minutes late from lunch, no more being told where to stand and for how long. I'm pretty sure I'll never have to say, "May I help you?" again.

Now I spend my days in and out of classrooms, studying alone or with a group of other students, most nearly two decades younger than I am. On nice days, I stroll the city neighborhood, such a contrast from the village streets I know so well.

Occasionally I bring one of the kids along with me to class. It amuses me when fellow students are surprised I have a son who's sixteen or remark on how much they all resemble me. I like feeling accepted and respected by younger students, who often ask to study with me. I take pleasure in introducing my kids to my professors and have frequent chats with my advisor and mentor about the challenges of raising children with ADD and ADHD.

The field of communication disorders is broad, and an educational, rather than medical, focus suits me best.

Hospitals make me uncomfortable, the result of a childhood spent imagining the frightening things that might be happening to my parents there. I've watched my kids struggle in school, each in their own way, and have wished someone could help them more effectively. I intend to be that person for my own students.

I have the kids I've always wanted, who are everything to me, and now I have this life, too. The work gets harder by the semester, and the demanding practicum placements add another layer of challenge. Because I've entered as a junior, my schedule is packed with content-area classes, each more fascinating than the last. All at once I'm learning to transcribe speech, break down the anatomy of speech and hearing, analyze and improve spoken and written language. I discover voice and resonance and the emotional and physiological components of stuttering. Every class seems to open doors to new ways of seeing the world, to a new understanding of how the ways we learn and think and speak and write influence who we are, who we become. I've found my calling.

Sometimes I'm teary, grasping for the first time the root of the challenges my own children face, wishing I could help them in ways I don't see happening at their school. Eric struggles with written language. Kyle is disorganized and easily frustrated, though academics come easy. Kate has trouble attending and working through math. The study of language and learning and communication has become intensely personal.

Here, I'm more than "the lady at the bank." People listen to me. Faculty respect me. Quickly, I'm comfortable juggling a course load and field work and family, and the nearly two decades since I've been in college seem like no time at all. I'm at home in academia.

Night Vision

More at home, in fact, than in Cambridge with Will. He seems proud, at first, when I'm successful, acing tests and earning a 4.0. Soon, however, he can't contain his frustration. Often, I return home to find him seething. He has no explanation for his anger, but he holds onto it like it's his best friend.

Will hangs laundry and rakes leaves at midnight, still in his work uniform, the spotlight trained on him to ensure neighbors can see how hard he works. When it gets back to me that one of our friends has lamented to another that I've "abandoned my family to go back to school," it's clear he's spread his sad story far and wide.

I'm gobsmacked, since as it's turned out, I often have more time to spend with the kids than I did when I worked at the bank. Most semesters, I have at least one free day each week when I don't have to be in Albany at all. Often, I arrive home at the same time they do. And oh, how wonderful it is to be off the entire summer between my junior and senior year, to spend all my time with the kids, something I haven't been able to do for this long a stretch since they were born.

Yet when I have evening classes, Will tells his parents he has no idea where I am. I feel them withdrawing from me in ways I don't understand, though I suspect it has to do with the things Will says. I have no way of knowing this for sure, and what can I do about it anyway?

Pop maintains his typical jovial exterior but is the slightest bit removed. Gram is more obvious. On the rare occasions she comes into the house when I'm home, I see her looking around for anything new I might have purchased, from filing cabinets to dishes to the curtains on the windows—more evidence of my abuse of her son.

Over time, she's freer than ever to judge my performance

as a mother and to share these opinions with the kids.

"Gram said, 'I don't know where your mother is all the time. She's only going to be a speech teacher,'" Katie reports.

When I'm inducted into the college honor society and invite Will's parents to the weekend ceremony, they drive there on their own rather than ride with me. On Monday, arriving at class a few minutes early, I take a seat next to a friend.

"I have to tell you about what happened on Saturday," she says. "I saw your mother-in-law standing off by herself, and I thought she'd feel more comfortable if I said hi."

"Aw, thanks. That was so kind of you."

"That was the goal, anyway. I figured your kids would be a safe topic, so I said, 'You have lovely grandchildren.'"

"Nice."

"Not so fast. She looked at me with an odd smile, then said, 'Why, yes I do. I practically raised them myself.'"

I begin to think of them as Birdie and Stan, no longer the caring Gram and Pop I have loved.

One Sunday afternoon, fourteen-year-old Eric comes into the kitchen just as Will and I have finished an argument. He watches his father storm out the back door onto the deck, retreat to the garage spewing profanities, and flip me the bird through the window.

"I'm so sorry this is how things are for you." I tell Eric, who's perched himself on the Formica countertop of the peninsula. I shake my head and lay a hand on his knee. He's wearing his usual oversized rugby shirt and baggy jeans slung low to reveal his plaid boxer shorts. I launch into one of the chats I jokingly call my "fifteen-minute infomercials on how to be a healthy adult."

"I can handle this, Eric, but it breaks my heart that this is your example of being a father."

"You do know Dad drinks a twelve-pack a night out there, right?"

No, I actually don't. I know Will drinks daily, but I haven't understood how much. What else have I missed?

The sparks of hope that have kept me going for so long now illuminate other realities: the family I've felt so much a part of is increasingly shutting me out. Worse yet, the family I fought so hard to build is crumbling, one brick falling away, followed by the next, all of my attempts to cement them back together fruitless. There's nothing to do but keep moving forward.

NINE

Parallel Lives

I've known Mary for years, as a customer at the bank and preschool teacher to many of Eric's friends. But it's a single phone call to arrange a play date on a snowed-in February day in 1994 that begins our lasting bond. I'm in my first year at Saint Rose, and Kate (having recently aged out of "Katie") and Mary's younger daughter, Corinne, are second-grade classmates. Our friendship is forged over wet boots and snow pants, tea in vintage china with cloth napkins and treats from the bakery around the corner from our respective houses, situated on parallel streets.

That first day in my kitchen we chat about our kids, five in all—my son, her daughter, my son, her daughter, my daughter. I ask about her job as a second-grade teacher; she asks how my first year back in college is going. Eventually, inevitably, our conversation turns to the struggles in our marriages, about how quickly sunny relationship skies can turn stormy at home, and we have that defining moment C. S. Lewis so aptly described: "Friendship is born at that moment when one person says to another, 'What! You too? I thought I was the only one.'"

Oh, I know you, I think.

Soon we're having coffee together most Saturday mornings and catching up by phone in between. The perfect mix of Connecticut gentility, earth mother, and tell-it-like-it-is commiseration—no mincing words for her—Mary is the tall, gracefully slender blonde to my short, brunette, comfortably padded version of my gentle Southern mother.

The Full Catastrophe

Though I haven't been accustomed to dropping the f-bomb, I'm getting there, thanks to an onslaught of events for which profanity was invented and Mary's no-holds-barred proclamations.

"Ugh." My sigh is deep, the subtext bottomless. "Have we ordered the wood chipper yet?"—our frequent facetious reference to disposing of a body like they did in *Fargo*.

"Yeah, I'll get right on that, but you'll have to share." She rolls her eyes and tops off our mugs.

"Seriously," I agree, laughing. "What would I do without you?"

We walk almost daily, sorting out our lives as we tick off the miles, set on making our marriages work. Our little girls, best friends, best enemies, and everything in between, may have begun it all, but Eric and Kyle, too, each takes his own turn bonding with Corinne and her older sister, Lorna.

It seems as if our whole lives happen as we chat at Mary's dining room table or mine, the older kids at first riding up on their bikes, later seventeen-year-old Eric driving in, too fast, to tell me where he's off to next, his radio blasting a thumping beat. I thought our Friday night routine would last forever: dinner first, then the little girls creating treasures with beads as we watched a *film* (never a *movie*)—from *The Shawshank Redemption* to *First Wives Club* and everything in between.

At the end of the night, I walk around the corner under the streetlights, choosing that route over the too-dark backyard path that leads straight to my door. I look up at the canopy of stars as I make my way. *Will I be walking these same streets, looking at the same sky, in ten years?* Something tells me the answer is no.

Parallel Lives

—

It seems that nearly everything of significance begins like this. One moment, it's the ho-hum events of everyday life. The next, not an earth-shattering change, just another little thing to take in stride. A new thing, to add to the last thing, followed by the next thing, and so it goes. It's not until later—sometimes much later—that we look back and see that that call, that conversation was the one thing that changed everything.

The boys are thirteen and sixteen now. I'm learning how much I enjoy this age and love bantering with these not-quite-adults. They're more vocal than ever about how they think things should be, which rules should be loosened and what they should now be allowed to do, but we talk things through. I'm happy that, for the most part, we've remained close.

One fall Saturday, I'm upset about something Eric hasn't done—working on homework that's due or helping with something around the house. Funny how later I'll have no memory of the specifics. What I will recall with razor-sharp clarity is what follows. Standing in the living room, I deliver the news.

"I warned you yesterday, Eric, that when you ignore what you've been told to do, there are consequences. You knew going to the football game today would be off the table if you did that…so, I'm sorry, but you'll have to stay home."

I don't expect him to like this, but I'm blindsided when he marches out to the garage and reappears minutes later.

"Dad says I can go. I'm going."

He turns to leave. I can't believe this is happening. I have to try to make him understand.

The Full Catastrophe

"I don't get how you can do this, Eric. We had a deal, you ignored it, and now you run to your dad?

What about all those years I stood up for you with him? All those times I made sure you had friends over or drove you places when he didn't want to bother? All the times I listened to how you felt and why things were important to you when he just stomped out to the garage? All these things run through my mind, though I leave them unsaid.

I can't keep myself from crying, though I wish I could. Eric just looks away. I know he only sees the melodramatic mother who stands between him and freedom. In an instant, he's out the door, down the street.

It feels as though there's been a death today, and in some ways for me there has. I've taken all the love intended for family—for my parents, my brother, all dead for more than half my life—and plunked it soundly down on Eric. And now this.

———

College friends visit on weekends to study or work on projects. Will comes into the house briefly, rarely making eye contact, then leaves as quickly as he arrived.

"Who's that?" he barks when friends call, pacing in and out of the kitchen. "Who are you talking to? Do you know how long you've been on the phone? You're talking about me, aren't you?" he badgers till I hang up, worried the caller has heard Will's rant.

We came together out of need—mostly my own. Now, as Will watches me pulling myself together, he crumbles. It's been this way with us for years: if I'm up, he's down. I've suspected my returning to school would be more than we could weather together. Yet now that I've torn off the blinders that have kept me from seeing my own needs, there's no going back.

It's been freeing, breaking out of my role as the bank teller married to the guy who ran the garage, and I'm not ready to be honest with my college friends about my precarious situation at home. I'm weary of being cast in the "poor Casey with a difficult marriage" role I've grown accustomed to at church, where few secrets stay secret for long. Will uses this to his advantage, knowing when he gets too loud, I'll end the call.

In town, however, it's another story. Little by little, I've let go of my dedication to keeping up appearances. Without parents to rebel against, I've come late to the individuating game. After covering for Will since I was seventeen, rephrasing the ridiculous things he said or making excuses for his antisocial behavior, I finally see my identity needs to be independent of his.

I'm tired of being a person I never intended to be, angry all the time, not the fun-loving mom I envisioned back when the kids were babies. Would they be better off with two happy-but-separate parents than with us together and hostile? I know the answer, of course, yet I can't see how I can make that happen on my own.

Even after the nun who provides free counseling on campus advises I make plans to leave the marriage, my thoughts still revolve around how my new career might help me right this sinking ship. Incredulous, she points out how I've learned to smile, to say everything is fine, even when that ship is taking on water faster than I can bail it out.

"You need an eighteen-month plan," she declares. "Find an apartment, figure out how you'll make the move, get your degree, and follow through. And those in-laws of yours? Let me say it this way: I'd give them a ride to the hospital if they were bleeding, but otherwise? You owe them nothing."

I'm not yet ready to go that far, remembering how they welcomed me into the family all those years ago, imagining the upheaval that would cause for all of us. I file her advice away under "things I'll think about later" and continue my own eighteen-month plan to fix my marriage.

But the next time Will starts following me from room to room, firing the same volley of tired threats he's used for years, I look at him with a calm that surprises even me.

"I know you don't believe this, but I mean it. I'm not going to do this forever." Hearing those words come out of my mouth, I begin to believe they might actually be true.

Soon, Mary and I realize neither of our marriages will survive, though we take turns supporting each other in staving off the inevitable for as long as we can. Once Rome begins its furious burn, we become a two-woman bucket brigade, alternately dousing the fire and nursing the wounds of the other. I'm grateful not to have to fight this blaze alone.

———

On a summer-like Saturday in early September of my senior year, Mary whisks me away for an appointment at the nail salon, a rare treat. When we return, many of my favorite people are gathered on our deck to celebrate my 40th birthday, including Hope Presley, who has flown in from South Carolina. I'm blown away that they've taken time from their busy lives to celebrate with me.

Though at this point my relationship with Will swings from cautiously civil to outright hostile, friends tell me he enlisted their help in planning this surprise party. His thoughtfulness is touching, yet it's awkward when he pulls me in for a kiss in front of everyone, as if having an audience is the point. It's also difficult to feel genuine affection, in spite of this grand gesture, when Will does little to hide his disdain and derides me when no one is watching. When he presents me with the pièce de résistance—a round-trip ticket to South Carolina so I can visit Hope and his younger sister, who lives in Myrtle Beach—I'm grateful. Perhaps some time apart will do us good.

In January, once the kids have gone back to school, I board the plane filled with anticipation. In the southern warmth, I observe the natural affection between Hope and Ray and admire their ability to negotiate minor conflicts and work together to raise their sons. I talk with Will's sister into the night about her new relationship. Free from the daily pressure of holding everything together at home, I see things more clearly now.

I call home each evening, and each cloyingly solicitous conversation is an approximation of the one before it.

"How are you doing, sweetheart?" Will asks, *sweetheart* a jarring juxtaposition to the names he typically calls me.

"I'm fine." I fill him in on the events of that day and my plans for the next. After talk of the kids' schedules, updates on school and sports practices and music lessons, we arrive at the point in the conversation I've come to dread.

"I love you," he whispers. It's the kind of quiet moment of intimacy we haven't had in person in years. I can't play along.

Absence may have made Will's heart grow fonder, but it's done the opposite for mine. I've had an immersive experience in living authentically, seeing how people can be unafraid to be themselves, and I'm ready. When I get home,

The Full Catastrophe

I will be civil, kind even, and I won't intentionally make waves, but I'm done acting.

No more "lovemaking" without a drop of love involved. Pretending is no longer an option.

PART III
HOME INTERRUPTED

If you're going through hell, keep going.

-Winston Churchill

TEN

Candids

In August, I see an ad in the newspaper seeking a speech-language pathologist for Tamarac, a centralized school district much like Cambridge forty minutes southwest, and I know my job has found me. Within days, I take the position and purchase the first decent car I've had in years. I can hardly wait to start the next chapter.

As I settle in at work, Eric throws himself into soccer season. A junior now, he arrives home from away games still humming the songs that rocked the bus ride, "Eye of the Tiger" and "We Are the Champions." No time for losers, indeed.

Week after week, Eric and his buddies work together to dominate the teams they play. He makes the regional newspaper's All-Star Team and is mentioned in print coverage of the games. But the award he receives from his coaches at the annual banquet—"The player who lives, eats, and breathes soccer"—is the honor he treasures most.

Throughout his life, Eric has been passionate about many things—water-skiing and snowboarding and even tennis. But soccer was his first and longest-lasting love, holding his devotion for the better part of fifteen years. It's the whole package for my gregarious son: constant motion, time spent with his best friends, and the thrill of excelling at the sport he loves so much. The intensity with which Eric plays, celebrates victories, and works to eliminate defeat makes it clear that soccer touches a place in him little else does. I stand on the sidelines, nearly as happy watching him on the field as he is playing. I couldn't be prouder or love him more.

Wearing a heavy coat and wrapped in a blanket one cold Saturday evening in late October, I sit in the stands and watch a semi-final game at a school thirty miles from home. My hands are wrapped around a hot cup of coffee, which I've bought as much for the warmth as the energy.

"Push wide! Watch that runner!" Eric continually barks to the players upfield of him, on high alert from the starting whistle. He's the sweeper, the player tasked with the job of "sweeping up" any attackers and providing the last line of defense against the goal. It's the perfect position for a guy like him.

The freckles stand out on Eric's ruddy cheeks as he lifts his jersey to wipe the sweat from his brow. From the muscles that bulge in his strong legs to the powerful arms that propel the ball back into play to the intensity on his face throughout, there's no mistaking how at home he is on the field. He uses everything he has to keep the ball away from his goalie. When he's called to execute a sideline throw-in, I hear his trademark grunt even from this distance, and I smile. That's my boy.

Maple Hill, today's adversary, is a long-time nemesis of the Cambridge boys' team. No matter how skilled they become, our boys haven't been able to get "over the Hill" for many years. Now, midway through the second half with no score on the board, the ref calls a penalty on Maple Hill, and Eric runs up to take the kick.

It all happens so fast I nearly miss it. But when the other spectators stand, shouting, I stand too.

Eric takes several steps back, then runs and kicks the ball, sending it airborne. It soars sixty yards, just above his teammates and their opponents, who watch with mouths agape as it drops with ballet-like form gracefully into the net.

There's a moment of silence, then a cheer goes up all

Candids

around me. "I can't believe that shot!" "Did you see that? No way!" Now it's our game to lose.

When it's over, there it is on the board: Cambridge 1, Maple Hill 0.

Our players, in the glow of victory—incredulous, really—run down the field with arms raised, shouting and hugging and dumping ice over each other, over the coach. Eric stands arm in arm with Kevin and Luke, Evan and John and Paul. His boys. Later, Eric will say it was the most perfect moment of his life.

I climb down from the stands and throw my arms around Eric's sweaty neck as he walks toward the bus. He hugs me back, briefly, though it's clear I'm just a quick stop on the way to the victory celebration that will be the team's ride home.

Years from now, I'll feel as though this was the last I saw of him, the Eric I'd known. Photos from this time show a wide grin, closely cropped hair, and bulked-up body with thick neck and broad shoulders, so different from the boy of even a year earlier.

I take dozens of pictures this fall, action shots and team photos and others I snap at home, but one in particular will forever capture this time for me. I corral the kids for the annual Christmas card photo and take a roll of thirty-six, hoping for at least one good frame, one without a shove between brothers just before the shutter releases, or a pout on the face of the little sister, or those pasted-on smiles everyone hates. Especially me. No, what I'm after is a perfectly natural-looking scene, brotherly-sisterly love abounding. A candid shot—which I carefully orchestrated, from the clothing to the mums and pumpkins on the steps to the placement of the sibs.

The Full Catastrophe

Cooperation is not high on their to-do list, but I get that keeper in spite of them: Eric on the left, leaning slightly forward, elbows on thighs, hands clasped, grin wide. Kate, her arm looped around his neck with a matching smile. And Kyle in all his middle-school bleached-blond glory (at least it's not his Smurf-blue phase, eyebrows and all), sitting just a bit to the right, the smallest of separations between him and the others.

Despite my continued efforts to create the perfect family, or at least the aura of one, the knowledge that our marriage will not endure weighs me down like stones in my pockets. My need for a family, which brought Will and me together in the first place, has kept us together way too long. I've worked as hard making things look good on the surface of our lives as I did in those Christmas photos of the kids, the subjects caught just in time, before they revealed their annoyance with me or with each other, away from the camera's probing eye.

As with most marriages that end badly, we've had good times along the way. The roses on Valentine's Day, the handmade cards Will helped the kids make for me, the gifts he helped them choose and wrap. Quiet words of love and support. The dreams we once shared. But these all seem so distant now. I grasp for them but they slip through my fingers, float to the ground, and scatter to the wind.

Beneath it all, there's bubbled a stream of discontent that flowed in both directions, and now it's become big water, turbulent and unsettled. Ours was a mismatch of major proportions. We have little in common, it turns out, beyond the desire to settle in and make a family. Though I've accepted that I forfeited the hope of ever having a fulfilling relationship, I've remained determined to keep this family together, on my own, if need be.

Determination, I see now, is not always a positive quality. It can spur you to great things. It can also make you blind, unable to see when enough is simply enough. Yet I'm unwilling to be the one to blame for blowing apart the family I've spent my adult life fighting to hold together. No, I reason when I can bring myself to think about it, I'll work a while and we'll get our feet on the ground. When we're in a more stable position financially, when Eric is set with college, then maybe Will and I can find a way to part on civil terms.

But deep down, I know there will be no peaceful parting, that this volatility can only end in a violent explosion. I wonder, sometimes, what the activating event will be, and if there will be any warning before the big bang destroys it all.

———

Meanwhile, outside of sports and an active social life, Eric's transition from upbeat teen to prospective college student has not been smooth. He's never been a natural at the demands of the classroom; sitting still for long stretches of time is not in the particular cocktail of genes he inherited. But now his friends, smart and, for the most part, focused, are on a clear trajectory toward the university of their choosing, including, for some of them, the world of collegiate sports. Eric's dream.

My attempts to keep track of where Eric is and who he's with have become futile. Soccer over, snowboarding season is in full swing. Many afternoons and all weekend, every weekend, the boys are off to the mountain with friends. Given the combination of the car he saved for and a father who lets him do as he pleases, the best I can do is try to keep the lines of communication open. Yet Eric seems untethered, or maybe it's that he hasn't changed at all. He's stuck in life as it is and resistant to any discussion of future plans. It's tough to put my finger on it, whatever's not quite right, but I'm worried.

The kids are each having their own growing pains, but Eric's seem to carry greater weight, more ominous consequences. There's less time left, time for him to figure out life, time to get it together. Everything feels urgent. Every event is fraught with meaning, laden with full-blown teenage angst. Most of it's directed at me.

But in January 1997, only days after the new year, comes an event I'll always think of as the beginning of the end. Of our marriage and of our family as we've known it.

It's Sunday evening, the last night of holiday break. Kyle and Kate are already in their rooms, asleep or close to it. But Eric's on the move again.

"I'm outta here, Mom. Be back later."

"Not so fast," I say. "Christmas break's over in the morning, Eric. You haven't done a thing for school. Honey, you really need to stay put and do some homework. Just give it half an hour and go out a little later, okay?"

"No!" He's shouting again, agitated, twirling the keys on the end of the heavy chain attached to his belt. I see him inflate like a balloon full of volatile gasses on the verge of explosion. "Fuck that, I'm leaving. Dad says it's fine with him so you can't stop me."

He's out the door, his car peeling out of the driveway.

Turning back to the computer, I try with little success to focus on the work on the screen. Time drags. I've become gradually less shocked by Eric's anger, but I'll never get used to it. I'll never reach the point with my son that I've come to with my husband, the steely you-can't-hurt-me place. So I cry. I reassure myself this is not uncommon. Boys Eric's age go through this phase, rebelling against their parents as they define themselves.

And Eric knows his father looks for ways to gain his favor by allowing anything I won't. There's nothing new about Eric's willingness to join in this tug of war, one I've been equally guilty of playing. I run through scenes over the years that have been building to this, times when Will has overruled in less obvious ways, like the football game that October Saturday a couple of years ago when he first gave Eric carte blanche to do as he pleased.

Hours later, I hear Eric's blasting stereo and see his car pull into the driveway. He bursts through the door and, before I can either threaten or cajole, storms through the house and shoots up the stairs.

Over the past year or so, I've learned to give Eric his space and stay in mine when he's upset. But something's off tonight. So I follow him, prepared to make another ineffectual attempt at setting boundaries, employing the tough love armchair psychologists advise will save a kid like him. I stop halfway up the stairs, where the wall gives way to an open banister.

"I can't stand it here anymore, Dad. I have to get away from *her*."

Her? Is he talking about *me?* Eric's been erratic lately, sometimes annoyed with me and frustrated when I offer any guidance or limits, but I haven't understood he's been this upset.

Will won't go along with this.

"Don't worry, I won't tell her where you go. You'd just better be on my side."

There are sides?

I freeze, then sink into the stair, this betrayal like a knife landing deep in my belly. In one crystalline moment, I see: I've been biding my time, praying we'll avoid conflict at the end. But there's a full-out battle ahead.

After losing my own parents so young, having a fractured family has been out of the question. It's seemed selfish to leave Will, choosing to seek a fulfilling relationship with someone more suited to me, over giving my kids a two-parent home. No, I'd do it right for them, all of it: stay with their father, show them how much I love them. See to their social and physical development. Help them with homework, enroll them in sports. Take them to church, teach them kindness and empathy and respect. How could that kind of selfless love be wrong?

I've given up the hope of a happy relationship in payment for the life I want my kids to have. But they've never had that life, not really.

Now I have no one to blame but myself.

When I recover from the initial impact and begin to process what I'm hearing, it's a one-two punch. Will's telling Eric it's okay to leave.

It's okay? And he won't tell me where Eric goes?

The very thing I've dreaded and fought against is happening. Everything I've sacrificed to keep is already gone. It's time to find a lawyer and make things right.

I throw on my coat and run to Mary's, the only safe place I know.

———

Candids

Awaking from a stupor in the twin bed made up with lovely Martha Stewart sheets and a handmade quilt, I'm instantly uneasy. I lie face up and take stock of my surroundings. The pale cream walls, cutwork curtains, and antique bedside table confuse me at first. This feels like home, yet not, which is in a strange way congruent with the vague, pervasive sense I have of things in general being Not. Quite. Right.

As the realization hits that I'm at Mary's house, the rest of it comes thundering down in one dull, nauseating heap. In a state that feels strangely similar to being hung over, memories form, dissipate, then form again, fuzzy. I recall bursting through her back door late last night, numb, sobbing, angry.

"It's finally happened," I said, staring off as if I'd landed in the wrong film, certainly not the happy one I've been scripting since I was small. "And I have no safety net. If I'm on the street without money to feed the kids, there's no one to save me now. And you're no help,"—dark laughter here, a nod to Mary's own shaky mid-divorce status—"you don't have any money either."

Mary hugged me tight. "Oh, sweetie, stay here tonight. I'll take care of you."

"Remember when that nun at the college suggested I develop an eighteen-month plan?" I reminded Mary. "She sounded pretty out there then. Now I can't imagine how I'll make it through tomorrow."

Life as I've known it has collapsed. Yet here I am the next morning, trudging through the back yard and across the street to my house just as the sun peeks over the roofline.

I go through the motions. Will is just heading out to work and Eric has already left for school. I'm grateful for this. He'll cool down soon enough, but less than twelve hours after last night's events, this is clearly not the time to sort things out. Kyle drags himself out of bed and out the door, and I help Kate through the morning routine. We leave together, Kate walking around the corner with friends, me driving in the other direction to work.

It takes a work week of days and an equal number of sleepless nights to absorb the full extent of what's happened. By Saturday morning, here's what I know: Will has checked out of the marriage, but he's just as definite about not leaving *his* house. I've hired a lawyer, and Will has, too; I'll be shocked when I later learn Will first met with him more than a year ago. There's no question divorce is in the works.

But the worst of it is Eric. He's gone. I haven't seen him since I watched him take the stairs on Sunday night. On Tuesday morning, I left the house early to try to catch him as he drove into the school parking lot. No luck. He spotted me, parked his car, and ran into the building like a fugitive running from the cops. If I thought my heart was breaking when I heard Eric tell Will he had to get away from me, it's completely shattered now.

I've become a good detective in the six short days since my life exploded. It doesn't take much to figure out Eric's been sleeping at his grandparents' (though when I call, Will's mother insists she has no idea where he is). I've seen his car hidden in the driveway on the other side of their garage late in the evening, then cruising past our house on his way to school in the morning. It's obvious he's been stopping at home each afternoon while I'm at work to pick up clothes and drop things off; he hasn't made much effort to hide the ever-changing piles on his unmade bed. Finally, I left him a note.

Candids

"I understand how hard this has been for you, Eric. I know you've felt torn between your dad and me, and that hasn't been fair," I wrote, hoping he'd read with an open mind. "You're angry. I get it. But I'd be grateful if you'd come by so we can talk. I love you so much. I know you know that."

Now, as I sip my coffee and sink into the release of the weekend, I see Eric take the stairs again—this time from the driveway onto the deck—round the back of the house, pass the great room windows, then walk quietly through the French doors.

I reach up for a hug, and he tentatively hugs me back. The smell of cigarettes is strong. At any other time I'd push him on this, but it's the least important thing today. Eric pulls a chair away from the table and sits, coat and boots still on, arms folded across his chest. "You wanted to talk. I'm here."

Judging by his body language, I can see he isn't going to do much talking unless I get things started.

"Oh, honey. You're dealing with a lot right now. I get that. First of all, school can't be easy these days. Your friends are all talking about getting into college—you're almost eighteen and have another year of high school left. You see them ready to leave home and be independent, or at least it feels that way. You're stuck here, and having rules seems ridiculous. 'Bullshit,' I know."

I pause, waiting for him to speak, watching for a gesture, a facial expression—something to let me know where he is with all of this—but he's not giving anything away. I feel stuck, too.

"Dad will say yes to anything if it means he can use you to hurt me," I say softly.

I don't want to put Eric in the middle of our conflict, but

The Full Catastrophe

that's exactly where he's been since Will told him he'd hide him from me. I have to address this.

"You've seen that happen again and again. I'm so sorry this is how it's been for you. I wish I could change that."

Fiddling with the chain to his wallet, Eric's quiet, but he's listening.

"I was your age once. I know how tempting it can be, having everything go your way. It seems like there's no downside, right? But trust me, there is. It's not okay to treat someone who loves you like that—not caring how much they're hurt as long as you get what you want—and it's not who you are."

If I didn't know my son as well as I do, I might've missed the subtle softening I read on his face, in the way his body relaxes into the chair.

I lean forward. "This has been coming for a long time, Eric, and it looks like we have a rough road ahead of us. Please come back. We'll figure this out together."

Eric's calmer than I've seen him in months. He thinks a while, then nods.

"Okay, Mom, I'll come home. I'm sorry about the way it all happened. I was just so pissed. About everything."

I try not to let Eric see my relief, how frightened I've been I might lose him. With all my children home again, I can finally breathe. My marriage is ending, but we can still be a family, the kids and me. I'm sure of it.

ELEVEN

Rupture

Life, impossibly, continues. January passes and gives way to February in a snowy, frigid blur. Each day I rise at 4:30 and wade through therapy plans that should've been made the week before, when I was scrambling to get through that week's sessions. I drive to work, my head foggy with lack of sleep, often sobbing the whole way. Then I wipe my eyes, drag myself into the building, and operate as though everything were the same, when the world has, in fact, been turned upside down and shaken, hard, till the coins fell out of its pockets and rolled away, just out of reach.

Back in the car at the end of the day, my mind wanders again, transitioning from work to home, from problems I can solve to dilemmas with no solution. I often arrive to find the boys just leaving, bent on squeezing the last bit of action out of snowboarding season, and Kate off with Will.

This first year as a public-school speech-language pathologist hasn't been easy. Tossed into classes with no real idea of what's expected or dealing with challenging students in the therapy room and no go-to strategies developed with experience, I put on my best "I can do this" face and figure it out.

I have my suspicions about which of my coworkers might develop into full-fledged friends. Ira is intriguing— spending time in his class is often like watching the best kind of children's movie, with that layered humor that reaches the kids on one level and the adults in a whole other, subtle way. From our conversations in the hallway or between activities

The Full Catastrophe

in class, I've gathered we share much of the same philosophy about what's important for children.

So I have hope in this department, fueled by those who, like Ira, invite me into their classrooms to become part of the team or ask my advice about a student with delays, but it's too early to tell. It's far easier knowing whom to avoid, faculty who make a nasty comment whenever I arrive to pick up a student as scheduled ("Seriously? We're just starting math now," or, with a pointed glance at the clock, "Weren't you supposed to be here three minutes ago?"). Others barely speak to "that new 'speech teacher,'" a label considered dismissive of the wide range of expertise speech-language pathologists possess.

A phone hangs on the wall in my shared office, but there's not a shred of privacy there. Because of this, and because of the countless phone calls required to keep my head above the pending divorce waters, I'm starting to feel as if some of the most monumental moments of my current life take place in the janitor's closet.

One morning, I end a call with my lawyer, hang up the phone, slide the wheeled buckets holding wet mops in dirty water to the side, then slink out of the closet and down the hall to the corner room I share with another therapist and a special education teacher. Winding my way around the room dividers, random toys, and mismatched bookshelves, I fold myself into the child-sized chair at the kidney-shaped table hidden in the back corner. My relatively empty plan book and a full schedule stare me in the face.

What made me think I could do this?

From behind me, I hear a rhythmic jingle and, immediately following, a voice.

"Hey! How's it going back here?"

It's Suzanne, a first-grade teacher. We work together in

her classroom several days a week, and I've admired her style, both in and out of class. A little larger than life, she commands the room, the sort of outside-the-box teacher who can make students feel special at the same time they have the tiniest fear of letting her down. It's a winning combination.

I brighten as she enters. Suzanne towers over me. My eyes land on her ankle bracelet ringed with bells then sweep upward over her long flowing skirt, batiked tank, chunky earth-toned necklace of natural stone, and dangly celestial earrings.

I'd have heard her coming sooner had I not been so distracted. Damn that lawyer, anyway. I'm paying him money I don't have, to do…what? I filed for divorce, but I've quickly learned the wheels of the legal system inch along with sluggish indifference, regardless of how urgent our situation feels to me. I've been up till close to dawn, scanning and printing every document I could find to support my case. I'd file the bloody documents myself if I had the credentials.

How naive I was at the start of this mess, thinking that since everyone who knew us could attest to how I've been a loving parent, the stable one, there would be relatively smooth sailing.

"I'm a little overwhelmed, but I'm okay. Just trying to catch up here," I say, smiling weakly.

"You're doing a great job with our kids, and you might as well forget about being caught up. It's not going to happen." She pauses for a moment, tucking her unruly blond curls behind one ear, then meets my eyes. "I'm not sure how I'm going to make it through the school year."

"*You're* not?" I've never seen Suzanne as anything but competent and authoritative, qualities I may feel but definitely don't project. "I know you have some challenging kids this year, but I see you doing such amazing things in your class."

"Yeah, that's not really it. It's my marriage…it's never been great, and I just can't keep up the charade any longer." Learning of her tumultuous personal life, I suddenly understand why she's seemed a bit distant.

"So how are you making out, honestly?" she tries again.

"You sure you want to know? My life sucks at the moment. I'm in the middle of a divorce and my husband refuses to leave the house. My ten-year-old daughter does whatever he says and ignores me. The boys are fourteen and seventeen, and they're both upset and slipping in school. I have no idea how I'm going to pay the mortgage this month. Oh, and my back is killing me. Any questions?"

"Whoa. Maybe you win. I had no idea." She flashes a sympathetic smile, then glances at the clock. "Gotta pick up the kids from music. I think we need to continue this conversation."

With that, she's off, leaving me to stare at the blank page on the table in front of me. Maybe this job will get easier with time.

And maybe, I think with my own small smile, *I've just found a friend.*

——

Will still refuses to leave and commandeers the bedroom. I'm on the pullout sofa in the living room and happy to be away from him.

Most evenings, just after dinner, Eric's in his room off the kitchen, on the phone with one of his friends, and Kyle and Kate are watching TV with me in the living room when Will staggers in from the garage. One night he rounds the corner, looking gaunt and jittery, stomps up the stairs, and slams the bedroom door.

"What an ass," Eric says. Kate is glued to the TV. Kyle, as usual, seethes in silence.

As the weather warms, Will often whisks Kate away right after school, bringing her back close to 11 p.m. When she's home, she argues about doing homework and goes to bed when she feels like it, alternately following rules or disregarding them altogether, which Will supports through his silence.

Kate's preferred Will's company since she was small. Why wouldn't she, when I set the boundaries, and he makes her laugh when she misbehaves? He offers trips to the lake and a get-out-of-homework free pass. Kate and I have had good times together, shopping and cooking, taking long bike rides, reading and going to dance class and play dates. But I care about more serious things, too. Though Will gives lip service to the importance of being responsible, he's mostly left it to me to be the enforcer. The bad cop.

It's no surprise my daughter and her father have become a duo, Kate the center of Will's universe.

Will has said little to either of the boys in weeks, as if he's abandoned any concept of himself as their father. Their disdain for him grows as they watch what's happening with Kate, and it's only a matter of weeks before they stop speaking to him altogether.

The many years of accepting our dysfunction as status quo ground to a screeching halt the minute I heard Eric and Will plotting in our bedroom. Though every day brings another crisis, anxiety is my constant companion, and my heart hurts for our kids, I feel an overarching sense of being on the right track, maybe for the first time in my life.

Suzanne and I have quickly become close, chatting during the school day and on instant messenger at night, and she regularly gives me mixtapes of music by her favorite artist, Bruce Cockburn. His lyrics evoke a subtle transformation in the way I see the world. Songs like "Dialogue with the Devil" and "Pacing the Cage" describe the exact pain and helplessness I feel and the spiritual connection I seek. Listening as I drive to and from work or when I'm alone in the house, I'm broken open in a way that allows me to grieve the demise of the family I wanted so desperately.

Bruce also reminds me that love is stronger than all the pain, that this darkness won't last. When soothing melodies give way to the lively percussion and upbeat rhythms of "The Gift" and "I'm Gonna Fly Someday" and even instrumentals like "Sunwheel Dance," joy bubbles up and I know I'll be okay. I allow myself the genuine smile, rare these days, I feel spreading across my face. A tiny ray of hope has worked its way through the cracks, a message from the inside.

——

I've never had a moment of back pain in my life until last September, when a nagging pull in my sacrum grew gradually more persistent, eventually accompanied by shooting pain from hip to ankle. As a new faculty member, I've refused to take sick days, but on a Friday in May, when I'm unable to endure the forty-minute drive to work, pressing on through the pain is no longer an option. I call a friend, who takes me to the doctor.

Back at home with medication and instructions to rest, I discover the only way to find relief is to lie face down on the floor. Around me I arrange the few things I need to survive hour to hour: heavy-duty painkillers and muscle relaxants, water, a cordless phone, and an alarm to alert me when it's time for my next dose.

So quickly my busy life has been reduced to this, my world shrunk to what I can see from the living room floor. Days pass with me there, in and out of sleep, the kids bringing me food and helping me when it's time for a trip to the bathroom or a dose of meds. The alarm goes off one afternoon, and Eric counts out the pills and hands them to me with a glass of water. I look up, grateful.

"More drugs." I plead with a weak smile. "Drugs are good."

He grins. "Whoa, wait till I tell my friends my mom said that."

For a while, there appears to be a moratorium on hostilities. Kate is in the sweet-little-girl mode I'm grateful to still see on occasion, but even with Will, there's a shift. In my diminished state, he becomes unusually attentive, speaking to me for the first time in months. He tries to be kind, looking at me with his sympathetic face. It makes me angry, and though I'm not doing myself any favors, I can't play along.

"Can I get you anything?" he asks one afternoon with a forced smile.

"Nope, don't put yourself out," I snap back. It occurs to me this isn't exactly consistent with my spiritual quest to connect peacefully with others, but I can't seem to help myself. "You wouldn't have thrown me a rope if I were

The Full Catastrophe

drowning a week ago. Don't bother now."

With the look on his face hovering between deflated and incensed, he stomps out.

After a couple of long days on the floor, I awake in the middle of the night and realize I've slept through the alarm and have missed my meds. Still half asleep, I'm in the bathroom before I'm fully aware of what's happening. I hear myself shriek, and suddenly the whole house is awake.

I crawl back to the living room and it continues, pain exploding in my lower back and the sensation that someone is plucking a nerve in my left hip over and over, shooting blinding pain to my ankle. But there's something new, muscles tightly cramped all up and down my leg and a wailing I can't suppress. I struggle to catch my breath before a new wave begins, which reminds me of the hours I spent laboring with each of my babies. Finally, mercifully, the meds take over and the pain and cramping subside.

Eric insists I go to the hospital. I protest—weakly—then lie on the back seat as he drives me up the hill. It seems like only a few years ago that five-year-old Eric came careening in the back door and, failing to negotiate the turn to dash up the stairs and put on his swimsuit, struck his forehead on the woodwork and split the skin wide open. When I arrived at the hospital, leaving my Friday-night post at the bank, there he was, hair dripping with blood, stitches just at the hairline, smiling broadly.

Now he helps me into the ER and waits with me as they read the X-rays. The doctor orders an MRI for tomorrow and schedules a visit with the neurosurgeon directly afterward. A disk in my lumbar spine has ruptured. Surgery is the only answer.

The ten days it takes to get cardiac clearance before the

procedure give me time to get everything in order and gives Will, back to full-out anger now, a chance to regroup.

"Don't think any of your friends are going to come here to take care of you," he snarls. "This is my house and I'll find ways to stop them. And I'll be there at the hospital, you can count on that. It's my health insurance you're on, so you can't stop me from coming. Just try it."

"Stay away," I warn, then phone the hospital and leave word he's not to be present when I'm a patient.

On the day of surgery, the boys skip school and drive me to the hospital in Troy. Will is nowhere to be found, and I'm relieved his promises to interfere were empty threats, as I suspected. The boys stay with me while I'm prepped for the OR.

"Look at that guy by the gurney over there," Eric leans down to whisper in my ear as I eye the IV tube taped to my arm and feel the sedatives kick in. Kyle snickers and I chuckle, too, at the improbable sight of a man in a full canary-yellow suit. I'm so grateful for a moment of levity with these two that I can't stop laughing, though the drugs surely help.

Eric and Kyle are the first ones I see when I wake up. The kids send flowers, which are delivered after the boys have left. I lie in bed and admire them as I drift off to sleep, a splash of joy that reminds me of the unbreakable bond I have with my children and lifts my spirits after the difficult months we've all survived.

The next morning, a friend drives me home. My first school year is over, prematurely. Old church friends and new work friends band together to bring meals and visit. I'm exiled in Cambridge with instructions to rest and walk, enjoy the early summer weather, recover. The worst is over, they tell me.

But I know better. This is only the beginning.

TWELVE

Waiting

One Sunday evening in July, Will slinks down the stairs from our bedroom holding a grocery bag stuffed with the few of his clothes that remained in our closet. He's heading back to the lake, where he's been living since he left the house in late June. I stand at the landing.

"Will, the mortgage is overdue. Can you deposit your paycheck or at least give me enough money to cover it?"

He comes toward me unfazed, as if he's heard nothing.

"And you need to stop telling Kate she can ignore me."

"Move." His left eye twitches as he slides against the wall to push past me.

"You can't just take her whenever you like, without telling me where she is. She's still my daughter." The smell of beer hangs in the air around him.

Eric emerges from his bedroom off the kitchen and blocks Will's way just as he reaches the landing.

"Dad, Jesus, grow up! What the hell's the matter with you?" Eric is red-faced, hyped, ready for action. He throws his body in front of his father and gives him a shove.

"Get out of my way," Will barks.

The two of them scuffle, limbs flailing and bodies thrown about, smashing a hole in the wall at the base of the stairs. I shout at them to stop and call to Kyle to take Kate into Eric's room. She doesn't need to see this.

But Kate wants her dad, of course. Will wrestles free and runs out the back door, Kate right behind him.

"You can't ride with him. He's had too much to drink!"

The Full Catastrophe

I run after her, but I'm too late. Kate hops into the truck, and they drive away.

Kyle returns to watching Road Rules, a safe escape. Eric storms back into his bedroom and cranks up his music, losing himself in the Stone Temple Pilots' throbbing beat. My cheeks are wet, and I absentmindedly wipe them with the back of my hand as I look at the wall of crumpled sheetrock facing the stairs, then turn away. Damage to the house is inconsequential when we're each crumbling ourselves.

All month long, Will ferries Kate back and forth from camp, rarely letting me in on their plans, ignoring her scheduled tutoring sessions and therapist appointments.

When Kate's home, she challenges me at every turn.

"You can go play with friends as soon as you've picked up your room," I say.

"I don't have to listen to you. Dad lets me do whatever I want." She plants her hands on her hips, glares at me, then dashes out the door.

Seeing me at the dining room table paying the bills, she says, "Sure, keep spending money. You know Dad doesn't have any. You're pathetic," an eleven-year-old girl parroting the scripted lines she's heard from her father for years.

I watch as she stalks off—leaving is how I picture her these days—and think instead of her joyous arrival. My daughter—*my daughter!*—the little girl I'd prayed for and felt so close to in her infancy and toddler years. How far we've come from that full-circle moment, when holding her close reminded me of the bond I'd had with my own mother. How far away from each other we are now.

Waiting

In Kate's bedroom a few weeks later, I fold shorts, tops, and underwear into outfits and place them in her suitcase, adding swimsuits and PJs, sneakers and flip-flops and water shoes. A shiver tickles my spine as I picture her last week, eyes wide and doing a little happy dance when she learned we'd agreed Will would take her to Annapolis to spend a week with his sister. I pray some time with caring adults away from this mess we've made will do her good.

Kate comes by on Saturday to get her things. I hand her a small cooler filled with homemade chocolate chip cookies, her favorite, and juice for the road, brush her unruly bangs away from her face, and wrap her in a hug. She allows me to hold her just long enough to breathe in her citrusy shampoo and catch a whiff of the peanut butter sandwich she's just polished off. Then she pulls away.

"Have a good time, and don't forget to call!" I shout after her as she runs out the door into Will's truck, idling in the driveway. He throws it in reverse, and I run through the house to the front door just in time to see them fly past, too late to wave goodbye one last time.

All week, between work and visits with Mary, I try to picture what Kate's doing. Is she taking a sailing lesson? Is she crabbing with her aunt and uncle, preparing a gourmet meal, walking around the harbor? Is she having fun? Does she miss me, even a little?

I doubt it.

On the afternoon of her return, I start dinner with one eye on the clock. Ring noodles and eggs boil on the stove, the steam rising from the pots adding to the August heat. In my largest bowl, I add chopped celery and onion, cans of tiny shrimp, thawed peas, and Miracle Whip to the al dente pasta and sliced egg, then mix it all together, sprinkle it with parsley and paprika, and pop it in the fridge. Marinated chicken breasts sit ready for the grill.

Messy from cooking, I climb the stairs to put on a clean top. Kate's door is ajar. *That's odd,* I think, remembering how I'd pushed it closed to keep the cats from messing up the bed I made with fresh sheets after she left. I step in to investigate.

Her dresser is missing. Her bookshelf, too. Frantically, I check her closet. Empty, save for a few things, discards scattered on the floor: old hair ties, a chapter book I bought her last month, a photo of the two of us a couple of years ago, our smiles genuine, our embrace sincere.

My head throbs as I labor to process what I'm seeing. When I sort it out, I'm sick to my stomach: Will has moved her out completely.

How did this happen? When? Will must have come yesterday, with help, while I was gone until evening, driving from preschools to homes for therapy, getting groceries.

I call the camp. No answer. I call his parents' house, looking out my kitchen window at their car parked in their driveway as the phone rings and rings. I finally hang up. I call camp every thirty minutes until, late at night, Will answers.

"Where is Kate? Is she okay? Why is everything gone from her room?"

Will sounds giddy, as if he's won a battle and is holding his trophy high. "She's going to live at camp with me now."

"She has doctor's appointments and tutoring. We've planned play dates and a shopping trip. You can't do this," I say. But he already has.

How could I have been so dense, believing we could work together for the good of the kids? How could I have been so blind, not seeing this trip was all part of a bigger plan?

But I wasn't dense. I wasn't blind. I was hopeful. Hopeful

our kids could have two loving parents who were separate but happy. Life would be so much better for all of us if this were true.

I'm beginning to see that a situation is only as sane as the least sane person in it. Because Will has refused to communicate and requested repeated delays, there's no separation agreement or custody order, so there's little I can do. He's her father, and he has the right to take her wherever he wants, whenever he wants. Though we've had one court appearance, without a legal document he can refrain from providing financial support of any kind. More intent on making things difficult than concerned about our defaulting on the mortgage and other bills, he views this as permission to do just that. I'm reduced to cashing in my life insurance policy and using the little savings I have left to pay the bills.

I petition for custody of the two younger kids, still minors. Will counters, requesting only sole custody of Kate. He knows it's futile to tell Kyle where he has to live. When it becomes obvious arriving at any sort of agreement will be near impossible, I sit in my lawyer's office and worry aloud.

"We can't go to trial. Eric's already upset, and Kate is more aggressive every time she's with me. Kyle stays quiet, but he's suffering, too."

"These things never go that far," he assures me. "They settle at zero hour. It'll all work out. Trust me."

Within weeks, it's obvious a trial is exactly where we're headed. It feels as if trusting him has not been my smartest move.

At night I lie awake, dreaming up ways I can continue financially and missing my daughter, now completely under her father's spell. I think of how not being the one to tuck any one of my children into bed at night seemed inconceivable a year ago and obsess about problems that have no answers.

But just before Labor Day, when I've all but given up hope, Kate calls from the lake. She begged her dad to bring her home for the start of school, she says, but he refused. After multiple phone calls to and by my lawyer, a temporary custody order is issued. Will and I will share physical custody, alternating weeks.

Will moves back in with his parents across the street. Every other Sunday, when it comes time for Kate to return home, she and her father stand on the corner between our houses, hugging, a long tearful goodbye. I find notes from Will to Kate, decorated with hearts and written in his awkward hand to what would seem like a child much younger than a sixth-grader: "Hang in there honey, your time with *her* will go by fast. You'll be back with me before you know it. Daddy loves you."

Soon, Kate refuses to come home and stays with Will for the week. By the end of the month, he petitions for full custody of Kate until the trial, citing our inability to "get along."

I'm devastated, grieving the loss of my little girl. Exhausted from fighting a no-win battle, I concede.

—

My friendship with Suzanne has been lifesaving. Since spring, Bruce Cockburn's lyrics have steered me toward a sense of peace, especially when things seem so relentlessly dismal and unfair. We refer to him now simply as "Bruce," like the personal friend he's become.

Some weekends, Suzanne drives to Cambridge and

spends the night. She floats through the door, arms over-flowing with flowers and Chianti and brie for melting, enveloping me in a hug and a cloud of patchouli. We talk endlessly about a new way to see the world and grapple with how some of these heady ideas apply to the messes in both of our lives.

I've felt a strong connection to God since I was a little girl. But now the rules of religion seem less important, and I see how we all belong to each other. This both comforts and challenges me in ways I could never have predicted.

I fight my way through each foreign concept.

We are all one is something I've heard since I was small, in church after church, and I believe it's true. But it's tough to feel "one" with Will and his lawyer, with his mother, with all the people who have turned on me when I need them most.

What I give I receive? I've been giving my whole life, and it sure doesn't feel like I've gotten back in equal measure. I mean, "If I'm nice to you, you'll be nice to me" has never really been true for me. Often, it's just the opposite.

The more I think about these ideas, though, the more they make sense. I've worried so long about whether I have enough love in my life—that mental Rolodex still haunts me. But gradually I see that when I scramble to get all the love I need, certain it's in scarce supply, I forget it's already mine. What good is my belief in God—in a higher power who lives within us and connects us all, whatever I name it—if I don't believe I'm inherently loved and lovable?'

One morning, I go to the playground to pick up a student for therapy.

"Seriously? You come at the worst times." The young special education teacher hired for summer program shakes her head.

I think of all the things I could say. *We made this schedule together. M's speech and language needs are severe. My work with her is a linchpin of her program.*

Instead, I return her hostility with generosity and patience.

"This must be so frustrating for you. You're tossed into this class with little support, given minimal information about each student's needs, and expected to conform to everyone else's plan. I'm sorry about that."

She softens. "Thank you. That means a lot, and it's not really you I'm mad at. Maybe you could work on helping M tell us what she did at home last night?"

But when the school year begins a few weeks later, a teacher accuses me of talking with a student's mother behind her back, though it's my job to communicate with parents about speech and language progress. Today, empathy has no effect. Later in the afternoon, she accosts me in an unusually empty faculty room.

"You're so calm about everything. You don't know what it's been like for me this year." She stands too close for comfort, scowling, and though I try to assure her I'd like to understand, she isn't done. "I know you think I'm awful." This couldn't be further from the truth.

This isn't about you. She's operating out of fear—don't meet it with your own, I remind myself, feeling more sympathetic than angry. How difficult it must be to walk through the world looking for a fight.

Weeks later, she stops me in the hall. "I owe you an apology," she says. "I was upset I was given such a challenging class. You got caught in the middle."

Sometimes resolution never comes. Sometimes there's no stopping someone's anger. Still, the idea that defending myself invites attack clicks into place for me. Forgiving someone—even if they're not sorry—releases me as much as it does them. Maybe more.

I get this in theory, but I know living this way won't be easy. Sometimes it feels safer to be angry than open, to put up walls instead of trying to connect. Vulnerability is hard. Especially as I fight to protect my children.

———

Eric's wildly successful junior season only a memory, senior-year soccer is disappointing for him. With many of his friends off to college, the team is rebuilding, and Eric's enthusiasm for the sport (and for school in general, his grades dropping along with his motivation) is not what it was. Still, I attend all the games I can, driving south to the Capital District or east, well into Vermont.

Then, mercifully, two bright spots appear in Eric's world only weeks apart. One night in October, he meets Ashley. She's a year or two younger than he is and lives a town away. He's smitten. He introduces us at one of his soccer games. She flashes me a sparkly smile, and her long blonde hair shines as it catches the sun. Ashley's clearly as taken with Eric as he is with her. I'm relieved to see the light return to his eyes.

The following week, I venture into the high school guidance office for advice about potential colleges for Eric. While personalized support for top-tier students appears plentiful, kids like my son, those who have caused more headaches than pride for faculty in recent semesters, are given little attention. *Screw ups*—I believe that's the technical term. I'm fairly certain the only way we'll get the answers we need is for me to show up in person and ask all the right questions. I'll stand in for Eric: patiently navigate the information, investigate his options, and apply just the right spin to help him see all the world could offer outside of Cambridge.

Predictably, the counselors are busy, but they steer me to a computer with a program that allows a filtered search. Carefully—as though his life depends on it—I enter the criteria, channeling Eric the best I can: industrial drafting and design, his current passion. Dorms. Intercollegiate soccer program. *Bingo*. South Portland Technical College in Maine it is, within driving distance, yet far enough to allow him some relief from the turmoil at home.

I gather materials and make my pitch. Eric is surprisingly enthusiastic, and in early November we drive to Maine. As we tour the campus, Eric realizes he's had good preparation, having already taken many drafting courses in high school not available to some of the other students on the tour. And the coach is bursting with enthusiasm for what Eric could add to the team.

We drive back a little lighter, a little more hopeful. After years of my guiding Eric through life closer to home, he seems ready to broaden his world to a life that just might include South Portland.

With Eric potentially on the right track—in the whac-a-mole fashion that has come to define my life—I lay awake worrying about what Kyle's up to out there on his skateboard with his new crew of edgy friends, not the soccer crowd he hung out with in elementary school. These kids wear metal band T-shirts, have multiple piercings, multi-colored hair, and a vague air of discontent. Now Kyle does, too.

Forbidding Kyle to spend time with them would be

fruitless. They'll hang out at school anyway, and it'd be easy enough for him to run to his father, as his sister does, where he, too, could do whatever he pleases. I'm not about to alienate him from the one parent he knows he can count on no matter what. So I invite his friends to stay and feed them; knowing where they are and what they're doing is better than the alternative. To my surprise, I often find myself laughing with them, and I see through their practiced tough exteriors to the sweet kids that live inside.

Kyle and I meet with the *guardian ad litem*—our lawyers call her the law guardian—whose job is to advocate for the kids. I speak with her first, then return to the small waiting room while Kyle goes into her office alone. Before long, he reappears and plops into the chair next to me, seething.

"She told me to shut up," he says, scowling.

"What?! Are you sure? She wouldn't say that to you." I don't doubt he's said something out of line, but surely a law guardian would use more professional language to deal with a teen stuck in the middle of a contentious divorce.

Weeks later, my lawyer tells me the law guardian's secretary overheard what I'd said to Kyle and reported back to her. The law guardian is incensed to think I'd doubt she'd told him to shut up. He clearly deserved it, and, by the way, maybe I would do well to be more authoritative, too.

What's worse, my lawyer adds that Birdie has been in frequent contact with the law guardian, reporting on the things she observes as she watches us from the bay window across the street. The almost-mother who helped plan my wedding, baked my birthday cake every year, and treated me like her own daughter in all the ways that matter has now cast herself in the role of enemy informant.

No use dwelling on things I can't change. *Push it away*, I tell myself. *Soldier on.*

THIRTEEN

On Trial

A week before Christmas, I sit clutching a manila folder in the family court waiting room beside a sad tree with worn-out ornaments. Just as I see Kate with Will and his parents around the corner sitting as far away from our group as possible, Kyle bursts in. As he tugs off his coat, he spots me and grins.

"Whoa, you can spot a room full of teachers a mile away!"

The educators here, me included, gasp in mock offense, then laugh. We're all grateful for a break in the tension. I'm relieved, too, to see Kyle has preserved his sense of humor. He and Kate are here to meet with the judge and law guardian prior to the proceedings—a Lincoln Hearing—something I know he isn't looking forward to.

I steal a glance at the nervous faces of good friends along with teachers and therapists I know less well. They've all risen early and driven the better part of an hour to support my case for full custody of Kate. No one enjoys this, taking the stand, promising to tell the truth, all the while staring out at people they've known for decades who stare back at them, watching them choose sides.

Though I try to stay in the present and find my peaceful center, the events of this terrible year play in my mind. It's laughable to think that a case could be made that living with Will would offer Kate what she needs most: stability, structure, and the steady love of a parent who puts her needs first. Yet here we all are.

The Full Catastrophe

The uniformed clerk appears beside my chair and tells me they're ready. I breathe deeply, stand, and follow her into the unknown.

—

Next to Will, his lawyer leans back in the swivel chair across the aisle from my lawyer and me like he knows he has this thing all wrapped up. The air is thick with the scent of furniture polish and men's cologne and fear. I riffle through the papers in the folder I've placed on the cherry table in front of me.

The two of us and our attorneys have stood together at soccer games and waved as we dropped our daughters off at birthday parties. My lawyer gave Eric rides to the mountain, and Will put tires on his car. Will chatted with his lawyer at Girl Scout meetings, and I waited on him at the bank. Yet it's doubtful any of the collective goodwill we've previously harbored has a chance of surviving what will happen today.

Will somehow looks smaller than usual. He fidgets in his seat. I can almost hear him thinking about the cigarettes in his pocket and how good it would feel to have one right now. A long drag might calm his nerves. I see our hands clasped, resting on the shifter of his souped-up car, the cigarette glowing between the fingers of his free hand more like a beacon than an emergency flare back then. The two of us so young, so full of hope.

This feels like an emotional ping-pong match, me volleying between urgent prayer and quiet trust. I've never been in a courtroom before, much less been the plaintiff. The barely detectable flutter in my chest tells me the old arrhythmia is back. Perfect.

On Trial

After nearly a year of feeling unheard, I'm relieved to finally have a chance to tell my side of the story. *Let the games begin* crosses my mind, which reassures me my sarcasm's survived.

I'm confident about our case. I've been a caring mother and a strong advocate for my kids. Then there's Will's history, his mercurial behavior and issues he's had at work and with friends over the years. Each time, I chose to believe the things he said: others were unfair to him, fabricating events that weren't true. He was the victim. The truth is much clearer to me now. I hope we can make it as clear to the court.

The counselor who saw our family last year when we were still together starts things off for our side. He describes Kate's relationship with me as "close and conflicted," and explains I provide more of the structure she needs given her ADHD diagnosis, structure she alternately accepts and rejects.

Kate's current therapist is next. My attorney asks why Kate would choose one parent over another, and she describes Kate's protective posture toward Will. How she checks in with her dad to be sure he's okay and writes his appointments into his datebook, confirming the time is good for him. How she makes sure the therapist knows Will doesn't have any money.

"This behavior from an eleven-year-old indicates 'parentification,'" she explains. "This occurs when a child starts to worry about the parent as if the parent were the child. Kaitlin worries her brothers are hurting Will. She appears to view them not as siblings—it's not a clear relationship for her," she adds. "But neither is the relationship with her father."

Next, Kate's music teacher describes running into Will

The Full Catastrophe

sledding with Kate one afternoon when school was closed. Will left, he reports, then returned later smelling of alcohol. Will's lawyer steps up, sneers at the previous comment, then asks about a dinner party the teacher and his wife attended with Will and me last winter.

"Was Mary there?"

This question stops me cold. Will has often had a problem with anyone he sees as my ally, but with Mary in particular. It's become apparent he considers her my new "love interest" in the stories he's spread around town, yet I haven't expected her to be mentioned today, if only as an insinuation. A friend of Eric's recently asked him at a party if I was a lesbian; she'd heard the rumor from her uncle—Will's lawyer. *As though, were it true,* I though then, *that damning indictment would seal the deal.*

One teacher after another is asked about Kate's learning style and challenges, about what type of support she needs to succeed. Each describes her need for praise, structure, few transitions. They discuss the many times they've met with me over the years, the phone calls and emails we've exchanged, especially during medication changes. They explain how frustrating homework is for Kate, how angry she is when I set boundaries and refuse to function solely as her friend.

"Given her learning issues, isn't it true Kaitlin should have been retained?" Will's attorney asks on cross. "Doesn't her anger have less to do with parenting style and everything to do with her being promoted inappropriately?"

"Not at all," her current special educator replies. "The decision to move her on with effective supports was agreed upon by the school psychologist, the principal, and her teachers. There was no question this was best for her."

We break for lunch. The court clerk's sympathetic smile

as I pass through the heavy doors unnerves me. In the hall near the metal detector, my lawyer tells me the evaluator concluded substance abuse is not an issue for either of us. Will reported drinking far less than I know is true. He was taken at his word.

——

Finally, I take the stand.

"Kate tells me, 'My job is to make Daddy happy,' and 'I can do whatever I want, because Dad will take me to the lake,'" I explain.

"Unfortunately, she's right. There are things all kids need—consistency, predictability. But when ADHD is a factor, it's so much more than that. For Kate, fun and spontaneity are important, but they have to be set into a backdrop of clear parameters, positive reinforcement, and loving consequences."

"Having said all of this, what would you like to see happen?" my attorney asks.

"I want Will to have reasonable visitation with Kate, but he either can't or won't provide the support she needs. If she's with me more regularly, I can help get her going in the right direction again. I want my daughter back."

"And what do you predict will happen if she stays with her father?"

"I worry about her now, and I worry about her future. I don't see Will following through on the counseling she needs or on the medications that were helping her before this all began. I'm concerned he won't set boundaries, and I picture him defending her no matter what outrageous things she does. He's never valued her doing well in school, and I worry she'll end up dropping out. I'm afraid their dysfunctional relationship will result in a future for Kate that's so much less than it could've been."

My attorney turns his attention to the boys. "Kyle's report cards indicate he's failing English, and comments have been made about the boys' inconsistent performance in school and their not completing homework. What makes you think you can do a better job with Kate?"

"I've always been involved with all of the kids. Kate struggles academically, but it's never been because her homework wasn't done. Until now. Kyle's passing all of his classes except English, though, believe me, I'm not happy about that English grade. But he's had a lifetime of mixed messages from his father, and so has Eric. Will would tell me to 'lay off' about homework, then he'd follow Kyle around the house and yell at him about getting it done. He's taken Kyle's bedroom door off the hinges for months at a time so Kyle can't shut it when Will chases him to his room."

"How are the boys doing in general?"

"Kyle is taking a full Regents course load. He's in the band, plays several instruments outside of school, and is also a ski instructor. Eric has succeeded despite having a learning disability, has been well-liked by his teachers, and is making plans for college next fall. He teaches snowboarding, plays soccer, and has coached a PeeWee soccer team for several years. I'm proud of both of them."

My lawyer asks about the car Will bought for Eric, then left him struggling to make payments on. Yet another example of inappropriate parental decision making, I say. All three of the kids are suffering, I say. The boys feel rejected by their father. Kate, on the other hand, has been given all the power. She's crumbling under the pressure.

On Trial

What I don't have a chance to add is this: when kids have power they aren't old enough to handle, power they haven't earned, it's not their fault when they misuse it. And it doesn't prepare them to function in the world as adults. To me, this goes without saying, but I hope the judge will connect the dots.

I step down and return to my seat at the table, satisfied I've had the opportunity to make my case. Unsure I've been heard. Worried so many things could still go wrong.

Lost inside my head, I'm startled when the judge bangs his gavel. Our side has rested. We're on to round two.

———

It's nearly 5:30, the defense is only now beginning its case, and I silently beg for this not to spill over into tomorrow.

Will's mother testifies on his behalf. With her best proper British demeanor, Birdie adjusts the bow on her blouse, smooths her skirt, and describes her relationship with the kids from an early age. For a moment, I'm right back there, Birdie babysitting on school-day afternoons and during vacations, the kids running back and forth between our houses, the close-knit extended family I'd dreamed of. I hear her even now, each time I came through the side door into the kitchen. "Hiiiiii," she'd say with a smile in her voice. "Can I get you a cup of tea?"

Sitting rod straight, she swears her son is a stellar parent and describes how I turned my back on my family. Will's lawyer grimaces, feigning sincere regret, then encourages her to elaborate on my recent neglect.

"I became aware Casey wanted Will out after she finished

college. After the marriage collapsed in January, Will stayed in the house until summer, when he and Kate moved to the lake. Casey treated him like dirt. Poor Will had to sleep in the living room."

Wait, what?

The boys don't come near her house, she says. They've treated Will badly, though things have recently improved with Kyle.

"But the first time I saw Kyle's change in appearance— dying his hair, wearing terrible clothes, an earring and everything—I told Will, and he was quite worried. Will has a problem with Kyle looking this way. I don't know if Casey does. I watch the house when she's not home"...*there it is*..."and there are boys with skateboards. Girls, too. Unsupervised. Their hair...it's long, and I'll bet it's dirty, too."

"Do they smoke?" probes Will's lawyer.

"Cigarettes? No, I didn't see cigarettes. I'm too far away, so I can't hear if they're cursing."

Listening to her testimony, I understand that for Birdie, who's been far more than a mother-in-law to me, I've been a means to an end—her grandchildren. Now that they're here, and I'm no longer the daughter-in-law she expected, I'm disposable. It destroys me to hear her paint me as the enemy. I pray she won't convince the judge I'm as worthless a parent as she describes. But she's done a fine job convincing me of one thing: The love I felt from her, the love I so desperately needed, is no longer mine. Maybe it never was.

The psychologist who met with each of us individually takes the stand. Still upset by his recommendation, I remember how I'd almost felt bad for the fresh-faced, impossibly young-looking doctor when we met as he

On Trial

stumbled through his questions. Now Will's lawyer draws out the information beneficial to their case. Over and over, the doctor confuses information and reports things I never said.

"Which parent would Kate be safer with, in your opinion?" Will's lawyer asks.

"My recommendation is that she live with her father."

I bite down on my lower lip so hard I check to see if I've drawn blood.

"The ongoing conflict with her brothers would affect her development. Mrs. Simonson has difficulty managing the children's behaviors. Kate has a fear of conflict, and her mother is overly harsh regarding homework. Based on Kate's reports, that is."

Hearing this conclusion from someone claiming to be an expert in human behavior, I want to crawl out of my skin. Will has broken every rule of parenting—encouraging Kate to act out toward me, pitting her against her brothers, removing any academic or behavioral expectations. Of course I have difficulty controlling her. Of course I'm upset when she refuses to do her homework. I insist she completes it, she shouts, pushes past me, and suddenly I'm shouting too, words I later wish I hadn't said. Then I feel defeated and ineffectual and ultimately deserted by the daughter I love so much.

And Will has chosen Kate, while rejecting his sons. Can no one see how harmful this is, to all of them?

As though he's read my mind, my attorney zeroes in. Yes, the doctor confirms, people with ADHD do need more structure. Yes, it is better for a parent to make her do her homework as opposed to no enforcement at all, though there must be a balance. The same applies to bedtime and attending school, he agrees. It's not good to let the child make the rules, and inconsistent rules between parents is damaging. Yes, yes, this is even more challenging with children with ADHD.

"And if you knew that Kate has said it's her job to keep her dad happy?"

"That doesn't mean much," he replies. "Kids feel that way anyway."

Will is sworn in. He looks more jittery than usual. I take a tiny bit of comfort in this.

"The boys treat me awful," he testifies, his face quivering slightly as he speaks. "They're greedy. They only get in touch when they want something."

Now I understand their case is predicated in large part on a Will-and-Kate versus me-and-the-boys scenario. How could I have missed this?

My lawyer steps up for cross examination. Will can't name even one of the kids' teachers. He has no idea what an IEP—an individualized education plan, which guides a special education student's program—is. When asked about what happens when Kate refuses to do her homework, he insists it's always done, shrugs when reminded the teachers report otherwise, then finally says he'll take away TV privileges if she doesn't do it. But that's never happened yet.

Questioning turns to the time when Will was removed from the house by the police and taken to the mental health facility. Will doesn't recall saying he had a gun or refusing to give us supplies for Kate, a baby then. The police came to get him, but the diagnosis was depression, not alcoholism. He's not sure he was told to stop drinking. He doesn't drink in the garage; well, only a few times a week, sometimes non-alcoholic beer. He stopped drinking heavily about ten years ago. When told Kate reported her father drank a lot to the

On Trial

DARE officer at school, he offers "that depends on how you define 'a lot.'"

Will's lawyer fires questions, one after another, drawing out details of my abusive behavior. I say terrible things about Will in front of the children. I hit Kate, sometimes scream at her. I tear up her homework, toss it in the trash, and make her do it again. I drink too much. Will had to stay in the garage, night after night, before he left the house for good. How could he be expected to come in for dinner and face my constant criticism?

I cringe, listening to these lies and half-truths. Yes, I'm frustrated when Kate refuses to do her homework. No, I don't hit her (*seriously?*) or throw out her work. Yes, Will and I did argue often, and I did complain—about his drinking, about his never joining us for dinner, about not setting boundaries for Kate. No, I don't drink to excess. But he certainly does.

Will provides his version of the July fight with Eric on the stairs, new details replacing the ones I provided. Eric started it, Will was only trying to get away and keep the peace. I asked Kyle to take Kate to Eric's room not to protect her but to punish her. I often asked the boys to discipline Kate. Then Will launches into his version of the day he moved her out. He had to protect her from me. What else could he do?

I try hard to suppress my reactions, but it's not easy. When my mouth drops open repeatedly I force myself to close it, and I groan as silently as I'm able, hoping to avoid being reprimanded by the judge. I've told my side of the story, now it's Will's turn to tell his. But logic does little to dull the sting of listening to his lies.

"Did you help take care of the kids when Casey was at college?"

The Full Catastrophe

"Oh, I did everything." Will brightens as he eases back into safer territory. "During those years, the kids were never fed, except by me."

It'll take me more than two decades to understand that each of us has our own story, our own version of events as they happened for us. *Were these lies Will was telling, or were they his truth, the things he honestly believed?* I'll wonder then.

It's after 7 p.m. when the judge finally declares the trial over. I've been expecting him to announce another break, after which we'd all be called back into the courtroom for a verdict.

"It's been a long day, and I think we're all ready to go home," he says instead. "You'll have the law guardian's written recommendations by December 23rd, and I'll issue my ruling by Christmas."

I didn't understand in the flurry of preparation for the trial that we'd walk away without a verdict. I drive home, exhaustion descending in one consuming wave. Sleep will come soon and without struggle, and that's a good thing. I have work in the morning.

FOURTEEN

Out of the Frying Pan

"We won!"

I never tire of saying these words as I make one call after another on this happiest of New Year's Eves. I can't imagine a truer cause for celebration or a better reason to put the nightmare that was 1997 behind us.

In disbelief, I scan the ten-page decision, which reads like a clinical diagnosis of Will. Judge Houser lists his concerns regarding Will's parenting: his lack of involvement in Kate's education and his lack of understanding of her needs as a child with ADHD for structure and super-vision. His lack of involvement in home life during our marriage.

And finally, this: "The court is concerned that the father has exhibited a long-time proclivity for withdrawal and avoidance in dealing with life in a solitary way and leaving responsibility and accountability to others." There, in a nutshell, is what my heart has been shouting for years. My eyes fill with tears as it sinks in: I have been heard.

"The mother is not without fault," writes Judge Houser, and of course he's right. "She may at times be oppressive in her pursuit of structure and responsibility. Yet testimony supported Kaitlin's need for these things, though she would of course wish to resist it."

Perhaps I've exercised poor judgment on occasion in exposing the children to our disputes, he adds. *Perhaps I have,* feeling a pang of guilt over all of the things I couldn't protect them from, all the times when, out of desperation, I used them as sounding boards for my fears. Yet, the Court

167

continues, I'm better able to meet Kate's needs, provide her with a role model, and guide her through life than her father is.

"The mother sets goals," the judge asserts, "works to achieve them, meets challenges directly, and is responsible to follow through." He understands Kate has asked to live with her father, "yet she is but eleven years old and is unable to deal with even the minimum amount of stress."

I have been awarded legal and physical custody. Kate will be with Will every other weekend and at other prescribed times. This is too good to be true. Kate can come home, and I can help her find her grounding again. Will will be angry, but we'll adjust. At last the law is on my side, on the side of what's right for Kate, where it should have been all along.

Judge Houser has restored my faith in the system, maybe even my faith in the Universe. It's possible things sometimes actually do work out the way they should.

———

Moving Kate home requires multiple trips, she and the boys carrying her things out of their grandparents' house into my car. Will meets Kyle at the door, shouting "You'd better get out!" Kyle ignores him, visits with Pop, then calmly walks past his dad and out the kitchen door.

"All of the terrible things that happened at your house in the past few years—your dad's drinking, him pushing you on the stairs that day?" Birdie says to Eric. "None of it was his fault, you know that, right? It was all your mother."

I begin to understand how hopelessly naïve I've been, thinking the worst was over. I hire a couple of high school girls to alternate helping Kate with homework after school until I get home. She's fine with them, but when I come through the door, she's itching for a fight.

Tonight, it goes this way: She's not eating dinner. She won't do her homework, either. She'll do it, but I can't be in the same room. I'm not allowed to see her agenda book or, God forbid, cast my eyes toward her book bag, two rooms away. She doesn't have any of her materials.

At 10 p.m., she suddenly does. "Ha ha! I had them all along. You're pathetic," she says, parroting her father's frequent term for me.

I try everything: reasoning with her, being loving but firm, finally making myself clear.

"You can't talk to me that way," I warn. "It would be so much easier for you to just do the work, Kate. I'll help you if you want me to, or you can do it on your own. Either way, it has to be done."

"What? Are you talking to me? You're not making any sense." She pushes past me. "I'm telling Dad you're starving me!" she shouts, then runs out the door and across the street to Will.

This continues on and off for weeks, mostly on the day or two following a weekend stay with her dad. At first when I call her grandparents, they insist they haven't seen her, though when I set out on foot to find her, there she is. After that, she runs, I call, they calm her down and send her back, no less hostile. Other days she goes rogue and no one can find her. "She's MIA again," I tell Mary when I call for moral support.

Kate's out of control. I fear she's failing in school. I know I'm failing at motherhood. Will and his lawyer will be the first to point this out.

I dreamed of having a daughter for so long, certain we'd have an unbreakable bond. Realizing we have no bond at all destroys me. The things Kate says are hurtful, but I try to see past them to the hurt little girl inside. Occasionally, she shouts something so transparent, so obviously straight from Will, I soften. I tell her I love her, that I only want to help.

She turns to me, pauses, then regains her steam. "I hate you. I want Dad. He doesn't care what I do."

In February, we appear in family court to finalize a temporary order of support. For the past year, I've struggled to meet expenses. Now that we have a custody order, I'm eager to get something official on paper.

After a year of hearing nothing but "no" in relation to finances, things go better than I expected. I'll receive child support, a little below standard but enough to make ends meet. We'll split the kids' medical expenses and contribute to maintaining the house until it's sold or one of us buys the other out, when profits will be split evenly. Kate has settled in over the past couple of weeks, doing better in school and seeming happier at home than she has in a year.

I walk to the car and turn my face toward the winter sunshine. I'll take these moments of hope wherever I can find them.

———

The calm doesn't last long. I spend every day of February break putting things in order for Eric to receive support at college through a program for individuals with disabilities. Will takes Kate to Lake Placid for five days, unbeknownst to me, though I have legal and physical custody and he is obligated to let me know where she is.

When they return, Will's mission to get custody shifts into overdrive. After they complete the long goodbye on the corner between the two houses, Kate bursts through the door ready for a fight. The next morning, I give her the medication she takes to help with ADHD. "I'm not taking that crap anymore. Dad never makes me," she shouts. "And I'm not going to school, either. You can't tell me what to do."

When I try to get her out the door, Kate gives me a shove, and I stumble.

"Dad says I need to decide whether I want to live with you or him. He says the judge could still change his mind." She runs out the door.

It breaks my heart, seeing her put in this position. Too late to get to work, I take another sick day. I'm running out of time, in more ways than one.

And if I thought my financial woes were over, Will has a plan for that, too. I send endless detailed accountings of the kids' medical expenses. He drops off a crumpled note with a scrawled, "Not paying this," or a scribbled message on loose leaf paper with sentences that trail off and make little sense. Child support is due on Thursdays; he leaves it on Saturday in another torn and crumpled envelope, the first payment $60 short, "HA!" written on the front.

Poking around in the garage for a wrench to repair a broken door, I find a voice recorder stashed away in Will's toolbox. Curious, I press play and lean against the rough-hewn wooden support, astounded as I hear Will's voice prompting Kate.

"We're having a great time here at camp, aren't we honey? Tell me about all the things your mom makes you do when you're at her house." Her long descriptions of how terrible I am, about how much she wants to live with him, provide Will the evidence he hopes to use to prove the judge was wrong, that he's the better parent.

The Full Catastrophe

On the day before Kyle's sixteenth birthday, he, Kate, and I are on our way to church. Last year, Will gave Kyle an amp from his own musical days. Because Will has refused to talk to him on the phone since the trial, much less in person, Kyle has written a letter asking permission to trade it in for newer equipment. When the three of us open the doors to hop in the car, Kyle finds a note addressed to him on the passenger's seat in his father's unmistakable handwriting. I assume it's a birthday card, but as Kyle reads, his face morphs from hope to shock to outright anger. He throws the note on the ground—"Thanks, Dad. Happy fucking birthday"—and storms into the house.

I pick up the crumpled paper and read: "My equipment is still mine. I want everything back." My heart breaks for my son.

Kate explodes. Angry at Kyle, angry at me, angry is all she knows. She storms through the house, up the stairs and into her room, where she slams the door, locks it, and loudly threatens to climb out the windows of the dormer onto the porch roof, jump to the sidewalk, and run to Will.

After twenty minutes of talking through the door, fearful of what she'll do to make her point, I call the police. An officer who lives next door responds. I put aside my worries about what he's heard through open windows, what he's heard around town, and what he thinks of me and attend to the crisis at hand. He immediately begins to formulate a plan. We discuss calling the county mental health clinic, then think better of it, hesitating to put wheels in motion we may not be able to stop.

Instead, the officer calls CPS—Child Protective Services—which makes sense to me, fills them in on the background and the current situation, then puts me on the

Out of the Frying Pan

phone while he goes upstairs to talk with Kate. The investigator assures me I've done the right thing by seeking support. I explain our contentious divorce; she says she's certain ours could be considered a domestic violence situation given Will's manipulation of our finances that leaves me scrambling to pay even basic bills, among other things.

When I hang up, Kate's calm, listening to the officer, and agrees to listen to me as well.

———

Eric's friend John comes by on Wednesday morning before I leave for work. He's on college break, and the two of them have plans to head to Stratton Mountain for a day of spring snowboarding. I wouldn't typically agree to Eric's cutting school, but today I rationalize it this way: tomorrow is his birthday, he's on the downhill slope of his senior year, and he rarely gets a chance to hang out with John. Besides, I suspect Eric might go with or without my approval.

"Hey, Casey, how's it going? We're headed out." I'm in the bathroom upstairs putting the finishing touches on my hair when John hollers up from the kitchen.

"Wait, don't leave yet. I never get to see you!" I shout, starting down the stairs a little too fast. Suddenly, I'm lying on the floor at the landing, covered in shattered glass, the framed horticultural prints that hung in stair-stepped fashion along the wall and broken glass scattered on the rug around me. My right ankle is twisted inward in an unnatural, nauseating fashion. I look up to see the boys staring down at me, their faces a cocktail of concern for my welfare and anxiety their plans may be dashed.

"I've been watching you two play soccer for fourteen

years now, rolling around on the field in agony with every hit. What do you suggest I do?" Though I'm probably in shock, I figure humor remains the best approach with teenage boys.

"Get up and walk it off," they say with a grin, nearly in unison. Each one takes an arm, and together they attempt to hoist me to my feet. Instantly it's evident this is not a "walk it off" injury.

John and Eric help me to the car and drive me up hospital hill. I have x-rays, then we wait. The boys are sympathetic, but I know what's on their minds, and I have to laugh. I find someone willing to take me home once I'm done at the ER and send the two of them on their way.

"It's okay, we can stay," they protest weakly as they head out the door before I rescind my offer. Who could blame them?

Finally, a diagnosis: I have a tibia/fibula fracture and a bad sprain. The attending physician applies a temporary cast, refers me to an orthopedist, and sends me home with crutches. I spend the next several weeks driving the forty miles to and from work with my left foot and navigating the building in a wheelchair.

So I don't have enough to manage? I ask the Universe in mock offense. I don't believe I'm being punished, and I've never been one to ask "Why me?" Sometimes, when I edge into self-pity, I force myself to remember how lucky I am to be fed and clothed and relatively safe, without the worries folks in South Sudan or Somalia or other war-torn regions struck by famine live with daily. But I'm no martyr either. I'd happily erase all of this if I could.

On Saturday, Eric's girlfriend Ashley throws him a party at our house. She drops off soda and chips then drives off, leaving me to come up with the rest of the food for a group of hungry teens. John's younger sister, who's been like a little sister to Eric, comes by to help. Still figuring out how to carry a dish to the refrigerator while hobbling around on crutches, I'm more grateful than she knows.

Yet how I wish it were Kate who was eager to be part of her brother's celebration, excited to decorate the house and his birthday cake, happily immersed in a mother-daughter project. Instead, she's peering around the curtain of her grandparents' window across the street or driving away with her dad, devoted to being anywhere other than where I am.

———

My sons have been two entirely different creatures since birth, and each has dealt with the conflict in our home in his own way. Eric's characteristic enthusiasm is often replaced by the same brand of energized anger that flared during the pushing match with his father on the stairs over a year ago.

If I see him at all when I arrive home from work, he's usually leaving.

"Headed out again?" I ask, hoping to have some time to chat.

"Meeting up with Luke (or Kevin, or Evan)," he shoots over his shoulder, halfway out the door, no time to answer questions. On the evenings he's in, we have dinner, then he retreats to his room with the door closed, on the phone with a friend, fighting with Ashley, or both.

Though Eric prefers not to hear anything about his father, his anger flares when Kate rebels or when there's a problem with the car Will bought him and refused to make payments on. "Jeez, Mom," he says. "Why the hell does he keep doing this shit? What a jerk."

In contrast, Kyle is an enigmatic combination of rational peacekeeper and disenfranchised rebel. With the notable exception of the day Will asked for his amp back, Kyle has mostly avoided attention. Though he's heartbroken by his father's total disregard for him and disgusted with Kate's behavior, he says little and continues to visit his grandparents regularly.

Still, he often dares me to try to enforce the kinds of rules any parent of a sixteen-year-old would impose. While Eric is in and out, Kyle is often nowhere to be found. When he finally appears, things don't go well.

"Kyle, you missed dinner. Where've you been?"

"Hangin' in town with my friends."

"Which friends? You need to at least tell me where you're going and be home for dinner. What about homework? Your five-week notices don't look good, and there's no reason for you to be failing. This is crazy."

"Yeah, whatever." He grabs a peach Snapple, heads upstairs to his room, and shuts the door.

But just when I fall into despair over the state of our relationship, he arrives home chatty, all joking and sarcasm. This is when we have good talks.

He fills me in on what's up with the kids I know, the ones who used to hang out at our house in elementary school. He chats about his classes and shares the things that have been tripping him up. Our connection is the one thing I've counted on as I watch my relationships with Eric and Kate become shakier by the day.

I know I shouldn't talk to the boys about the financial strain, the upcoming trial, my struggles with Kate. But sometimes I crack, mostly when Will or his mother has thrown yet another wrench into everything I try so hard to set right.

I slam the phone onto the receiver one evening.

"Can you believe Gram told me Kate wasn't there, when she obviously is? And now your father's refusing to pay his share of the bills. I can't believe he's not worried about providing a home for his kids," I fume, knowing even as I do how wrong it is to expect them to sympathize with me.

"Yeah, Mom, we know." Eric retreats to his room and closes the door.

Kyle settles onto the sofa, turns on the TV, and zones out, leaving me to wallow in how alone I feel, how hopeless.

It's such a tangled mess, the web we've woven—Will, his mother, the boys, Kate, and me—that I can't keep it straight. I am, without question, not my best self.

FIFTEEN

Into the Fire

The envelope I pull from the mailbox is white and thick. I note the return address—Washington County Family Court—and my stomach drops.

I open it slowly, knowing once I've seen this it can't be unseen. It's an official filing, judging by the standard heading and listing of plaintiff and defendant that rarely bring good news. Will's lawyer has filed a child custody modification based on a change of circumstance. I can't handle Kate on my own. I've had to involve the police. Obviously she would be safer with her father.

Staring at the document in my hands, my mind races. I've listened to the judge, the police, the CPS worker, and now they're using it against me? I implemented loving, consistent consequences with Kate. I followed through on the prescribed arrangements and stayed in touch with school and lawyers, therapists and doctors. None of this seems to have kept our situation from becoming darker, more hopeless. Will, on the other hand, does as he pleases when he pleases and refuses to respond to even the most civilized attempts to communicate. Instead, he floats every random idea he has to derail any of my efforts to help Kate feel safer and more stable, then waits to see what sticks.

It all seems to stick.

But more surprises lie buried here. Judge Houser has been replaced by the other family court judge in our county, who won't have heard the case we presented at the trial. Though a change of circumstance is meant to deal only with whatever has changed since the previous decision, I worry that someone with little idea of the history won't see through the allegations Will makes about my parenting fails.

We're back to square one.

———

Since elementary school, when Eric was one of a remarkably close bunch of boys and girls who had third-grade dance parties, he's seemed comfortable in the role of big brother and best friend to a cast of girls. Nightly, the phone rings repeatedly, and I answer to Heather-from-Cambridge, Becca-from-Greenwich, Lindsay-from-Schuylerville.

"Hi there, it's Sarah," chirps the voice on the other end of the phone this time. "Is Eric around?"

Sarah-from-Clifton Park calls nearly every night. I like her, though I've only met her once or twice.

"What've you been up to?" she asks. We chat for a while, until Eric shouts from his room on the other side of the kitchen wall.

"Mom! Get off the phone! She's calling for me!"

I laugh, say my goodbyes, then Eric picks up the extension next to his bed. Behind closed doors, he's on the phone with Sarah for at least an hour, usually longer.

Still, none of these girls has had anywhere close to the impact on him that his girlfriend Ashley has.

When Eric and Ashley first met in the fall, I was happy for him, but as he throws himself into their relationship, he seems to have lost himself. His single goal most afternoons is getting to her house, thirty minutes away, his usual Tribe Called Quest replaced with Christina Aguilera—Ashley's favorite—blasting on his stereo. Eric's mood and academic performance rise and fall in direct proportion to whether the two of them are getting along.

Eric's relationship with Will is practically nonexistent. Not only aren't they speaking, each avoids being in the other's presence. I've hoped Eric would stay close with me, that I could be the anchor he needs to get through the onslaught of challenges he's faced in recent years. The stress of the divorce and the pain of a strained relationship with his dad were difficult enough. Now, as he watches his friends, already away at college or planning their own hopeful futures, he seems less and less interested in life beyond Cambridge and has committed himself to a relationship that isn't strong enough to carry the weight.

There seems to be little I can do but watch, be available to listen, and beg God to take care of him.

———

In years to come, 1998 will be little more than a blur. It will appear in my mind like a pixelated film, out of focus just enough to prevent me from making out the thread that ties each scene together, the map that allows a concatenation of events to make any sort of sense.

Maybe Kate is out on her roof again, angry, taunting me to just try and make her come inside. Or, living mostly with me now, maybe she's doing better in school this week, a little happier, more stable. Maybe Eric's wrapping me in a bear hug and Kyle's playing his guitar, impressing me with his talent and entertaining me with his sarcasm. Or maybe Eric's hostile and Kyle's incommunicado.

Maybe this drags out over months, or maybe all of this happens on the same day. In the end, it doesn't really matter.

The Full Catastrophe

All I know is that this morning, though the daffodils have burst into bloom overnight, there's no splash of cheer in sight for me. I drag myself out of bed and stand in the shower, letting the warm water flow over my scalp, cascade off my face and the curves of my body, and slide silently down the drain. In my fantasy, I drain away along with it and hide down there where no one can find me, beneath the world of struggling children and a hostile spouse, beneath a legal system designed to protect only itself. I'd stand in here forever if I could. If I never leave, I'll never have to do what's ahead of me today. I'll never have to live this life.

Then I dress for confidence, square my shoulders, and drive to family court.

Well over a year since I filed for divorce and more than four months since I was awarded full custody of Kate, I'm ushered into a room with my lawyer and the law guardian. This woman supposedly represents my children's best interests, but she's been so clearly aligned with Will and his lawyer that I feel defeated before we begin. Still, I won't let her destroy me, and I won't stop trying to make her understand.

"I'm telling you now, Eric is not going to survive this," I say through tears, forcing the words past the tightening in my throat. "Will isn't speaking to the boys. They're both suffering, and Eric is angrier every day. No one is protecting them. I thought that's what this system was supposed to do. When Kate's back here in her teens, delinquent, I hope you remember your recommendations."

She looks at me with the slightest of shrugs, collects her things, and leaves the room.

I picture Kate standing in front of me a couple of weeks ago, arms folded, chin jutted forward. "Dad says if I fail the third marking period, I can live with him."

If this is the court's idea of providing for a child's emotional wellbeing, I'm seriously out of the running.

Inside the courtroom I watch, frozen, as things go according to plan—their plan. New psych evals are ordered for both of us, and the kids are ordered to meet with the psychologist as well. If we can't agree, we'll sit through it all again in September: a second trial with new witnesses, fresh testimony, more documents memorializing our virtues and our fatal flaws. Then the legal system will render its verdict, solving with a stroke of the gavel the issue of who is best to care for and guide our daughter. This is the most frightening thing I've ever heard.

As I head for the door, I catch a glimpse of Will, who wears a self-satisfied expression. How will I break this to his other two children, the ones he's apparently forgotten altogether?

———

At my request, depositions and the inevitable trial are put off until the school year is over. But just when I think there will be a little respite, Kyle comes home on Friday afternoon with big plans.

"Gotta run."

"Where are you going now?"

"Doesn't matter. You don't need to know."

"What about homework? Will you be around over the weekend? I need a little help with some things outside. I can't lift those heavy storm windows."

"This is fucking ridiculous," he barks, which sends us both into a tailspin.

The Full Catastrophe

"You can't talk to me that way!"

"Apparently I can!"

We talk over each other, shout. I cry. He gets angrier. Finally, he stomps up to his room, bangs around for a while, then pounds back down the stairs.

Kyle swings his Burton snowboarding pack, jammed full, onto his back and heads for the door. I flash on the day we bought it late last fall, the two of us at the mall for lunch and a hunt for the perfect bag. We enjoyed each other's company that day, anticipating winter fun and talking about anything but the mess our family was in.

But now: "I'm outta here. I'm not taking this shit anymore."

"Kyle!" I shout as he disappears down the front steps. "Come back and let's talk about this. Fine, then! You don't care who you hurt!"

Mary and I talk that evening. She's seen Kyle skateboarding with friends near the traffic light, so at least I know he's safe. Early Saturday morning, when he hasn't returned and I'm beside myself with worry, Mary calls to let me know he spent the night at her house. Thank God. If he needs space, I understand—who wouldn't want to escape all of this?—and I know Mary will take care of him.

But on Sunday, when Kyle still isn't home and I call to ask if she knows how he's doing, Mary gently divulges he's picked up his bag and has gone to his grandparents' house. With Will. As the "safe parent" (how I've come to despise that role), I've become Eric's target, and there's no question where Kate's allegiances lie. But now I've lost Kyle, too. Everything that's held me together is gone.

I hang up the phone, and my world goes dark.

I fall to the floor, head in my hands, and sob, releasing

the pain I've held inside for years, fearing that once it was out I could never shove it back in. Now I'm up and pacing, waving my arms and wailing, then calming in spurts, wild with frustration and grief, angry and stricken and entirely spent.

The voiceover continues, as it has since I was small. *You'll remember this forever*, I told myself as I stood poised for action at the top of the staircase in second grade, as I lay on the sofa one December day just before Mom died. As I opened the door for the first time to the young man who would someday be my husband, the father of my children.

Now the internal narrator intrudes again, with her unwelcome need to impose order. But she won't win, not today. I'm grateful I'm alone. I know I need to fall apart without considering who might be watching, what someone might think.

All I've ever wanted was these babies. I held myself together with my eyes on *someday* during my teens, channeling the pain of losing my family into dreams of the future, intent on creating a storybook life if it killed me. The world had sorted itself into the things I knew I wanted, consisting mostly of antitheses and split infinitives (to not raise children in an unstable home; to not have them live in chaos; to not feel unloved; to not stand alone) and those I couldn't imagine ever existing in my life.

The Not-Mine life included everything else—an education that took years to complete, too long to go without a family of my own. A high-level job of which I knew I was more than capable, but who would listen to me, the sweet girl who did what I was told? A life with enough money, not only to provide the home and future my kids would deserve but to allow their parents to have their own fulfilling lives. And oddly far down the list, a well-rounded intellectual and emotional life shared with a man who, beyond being a reliable dad, knew how to love me.

These dreams were too big for me. Instead, my main goals were to blend in, have a few deep and lasting friendships, a marriage that was reasonably drama-free if not exactly happy, and a decent job close to home so that I could be there for the incredibly joyful, well-loved, talented, free-spirited, socially adept, and—most of all—devoted children who were surely destined to come.

One recent Saturday night, I half-watched the 1964 version of Zorba the Greek, hoping to stifle my obsessing over the hopelessness of our situation and wishing I could explain, even to myself, how I'd gotten into this mess. Suddenly, Zorba said it for me: "Am I not a man?...I'm a man. So I married. Wife, children, house, everything. The full catastrophe."

That's what I wanted, too. Bring on the sleepless nights and the messy diapers, the overwhelming years of lessons and sports practice, the college expenses, the inevitable relationship challenges. I wanted all of it, everything I believed I'd been denied, and I was committed to making it happen.

Perhaps I should have been more careful what I asked for. I made the life I believed I could have, set grander goals aside, and filled in the gaps where reality failed with wishful thinking.

Of course, that couldn't last.

I did it, didn't I? I got the family I wanted, not two but three beautiful babies, the Craftsman bungalow on a tree-lined street, grandparents across the way, jobs and cars and a boat at the lake. I had those breakfast-in-bed Mother's Days,

Into the Fire

those out-for-brunch Sundays, the Christmases with three happy kids tearing into their gifts. Unadulterated joy.

Yet here I am, watching this life implode, losing it all, along with a sense of my place in the world.

Here I am, immersed in the full catastrophe.

Why go on? courses through my mind on repeat, like lyrics to a song I can't shake. *Who am I without the love of my children? What if they never come back to me?*

But as usual—even in this worst of times—I am fundamentally rational enough to know that, in this moment, I'm completely irrational. I cannot stay here alone.

Mary and Suzanne are both busy, so I call Grace, a coworker who's been a good friend throughout this ordeal. She tells me to meet her at school and she'll drive me to her place in a setting so remote that even with directions, I'd have a tough time finding my way in the dark. I toss a few things into an overnight bag and drive out of town, still sobbing.

How will I ever return to the house that was supposed to be our sanctuary? How will I ever save myself?

Grace's post-and-beam house is warm and inviting. After a long chat, she shows me to the guest room, straight out of the pages of an LL Bean catalog, with lace curtains and bed skirt and a log cabin quilt. I crawl into bed and sleep well for the first time in months. The next morning, my eyes are swollen nearly shut. This happens whenever I cry these days. Maybe I'm allergic to tears, or maybe I've used my lifetime supply, and the ducts have run dry.

I lay a cool compress over my eyes and ride with Grace to work.

Often in the midst of this nightmare, I've driven to work teary, then composed myself and behaved as if nothing were wrong. I pick up my mail and head to my office, take off my coat, and magically activate the part of my brain that identifies me as an effective, caring adult, the very thing I no longer seem to be at home.

Today I barely make it through my sessions, break down in the hallway, and stop in to talk with Suzanne. I'm forced to skip students and pull myself together behind my closed office door.

Alone in the quiet, I splash water on my face and remember I get to choose how I react. I can rail over how unfair this is. I can feel it all—the pain, the frustration. The grief. Not only can I do this, I *need* to do this. No amount of spiritual bypass—denying my emotions and pretending platitudes protect me—will get me where I need to go, any more than dulling the pain with drinking or drugs would. I might find a moment's relief that way, but it doesn't last. And it isn't real.

I also know this: when I feel bad enough, long enough—when I wallow till I can wallow no more—I can find a new perspective.

The kids are hurting. They're looking for any escape from this shitty situation. Who can blame them?

SIXTEEN

Keep Going

Parents like to think they understand their kids.

"Trust me, I know him," we often say, confident that having raised our child, maybe even having carried him for nine months, having lain awake nights worrying about his physical and social and emotional well-being, we have a bond that goes wider and deeper than any other. But there comes a time, for many of us, when we have to swallow a difficult truth: suddenly, we don't know that boy at all.

It happened so gradually it's been hard to see when typical teen behavior ended and something more ominous crept in. I can hear the conventional wisdom—"Teens test their boundaries, struggling to free themselves from parents who don't let them grow up"—but nothing can stop the other voices in my head, the ones that wake me up at night. Sometimes they torment me with the fear I've had since Eric was small, visions of him dropping from a sudden heart attack in his twenties like my brother did. More often, the nightmare is less clear, something about a boy with unrealized potential, a traveler who's lost his way and me helpless, powerless to guide him home.

It is, indeed, more than growing pains that has caused the transformation in my formerly gregarious boy. Eric is justifiably angry and hurt over, among other things, our rocky divorce and his father's hostility, which has affected us all. But I'm not blameless either. I think of all the times I've vented to him when I could've kept quiet. The little boy who was my sidekick, who made us a family, the one who started

189

it all, has become someone I hardly recognize.

Though we're only deciding custody of Kate, Will and I are each to bring all three kids along to our respective psychological evaluations in a small city an hour north. But with Kyle not speaking to me and Eric not speaking to his dad, this is impossible. Will and Kyle have already seen the evaluator together, and today Eric, Kate and I are meeting with him. Only a few weeks ago, I couldn't have imagined Kate would go anywhere with me or that Kyle would align himself with his father.

Dr. Fleming talks with Kate and Eric individually, then directs them to the waiting room of the center-hall colonial-turned-psychology office while I meet with him privately. I'm aware he's already heard Will's side of the story and figure he's already gotten the law guardian's opinion, too. Still, I smile, settle into the armchair, and wait for him to begin.

He turns from his imposing cherry desk to face me.

"Do you yell a lot at home? Kyle says most of the time you're fine, but once in a while you scream. That must be when you're yelling at Kate."

I'm stunned. Isn't he supposed to be impartial?

"No, that must be when Kyle is shouting at me, telling me he can do whatever he pleases, that he doesn't care about my fucking rules."

He presses on. "Kate says she wants to be with her dad. She says you don't use corporal punishment, but you pressure her too much when it comes to homework. She says you expect her to be an A student."

I suppress a laugh, though nothing is remotely funny. But Kate's anger when I so much as mention doing homework or studying for tests, her fleeing to Will's where she gets a free pass makes her insisting I expect top grades heartbreakingly absurd.

"It's obvious nothing I say will matter." All of my innocent optimism has drained away.

"You know, sometimes there are good parents who simply can't manage their children," he continues with a flip of his hand and a brief glance in my direction. I make one last attempt to explain our situation. Dr. Fleming isn't concerned about Kate's behaviors. Those will work themselves out.

"Kate says she's afraid of Eric," he continues. Of course she does. She sees Kyle as having defected to their side, but Eric remains the enemy.

"What about Will's drinking and driving?" I press, tears blurring my vision.

"I'm not sure there's really anything to that story."

I'm quickly dismissed. As beaten down as I've ever been since this entire ordeal began, I drag myself out of the chair and on through the waiting room. Eric and Kate follow me to the car while I rant. I can't help myself.

"This is so unfair! All I've ever done is try to be a loving mother. Your dad drinks day and night and takes no responsibility for anything, while I hold everything together by myself. And now he's the better parent? What more am I supposed to do?"

On and on I go, a wild river of fear wresting the control I've clung to like a life raft from my grasp. Horrified, I watch it float downstream and, with it, all hope.

We're still in the city, stopped at a traffic signal. I'm crying. Kate's yelling about what a horrible mother I am, about how much she wants her dad. Suddenly, Eric flings open the passenger's door and jumps out of the car.

"I'm not listening to this shit anymore. I'll find my own

way back to Cambridge," he shouts. "I'll walk if I have to."

"No!" I shout back. "Get back in the car, Eric, I'll stop, I promise! How will you get home?"

Kate is hysterical in the back seat. People in the cars around us stare. A woman in the car beside ours catches my eye and glares at me, her judgment cutting me like a knife.

The light is green. The cars in line behind me honk their horns, and Eric has headed off in the opposite direction. When he gets something into his head, there's no stopping him, no use in trying. I step on the gas, take the ramp onto the highway, and try to calm Kate, though it's all I can do to hold it together myself. I grip the wheel like I'm navigating a sinking ship.

———

Soon Ashley, her heart set on the night of her life at Eric's prom, learns he's landed on the academic ineligibility list. He can't attend, so neither can she.

Attending college in Maine—a plan that once held such promise—is off the table, since Eric won't leave Ashley; his failing grades have eliminated that option anyway. But college plans, which feel distant in Eric's do-what's-in-front-of-you approach to life, mean little to him in the face of this more pressing crisis.

Ashley is furious and their demise is rapid, though it's been a long time coming. I overhear heated phone calls. Within days, it becomes obvious their relationship is over. Instead, Eric is in and out with friends and back to regular phone chats with the typical rotation of girls. It's a little like old times, though he's more subdued.

Ashley fades from our lives, and I have to admit I'm a little relieved.

Keep Going

—

My relationship with Kyle has been reduced to written notes, which Kate delivers. I tell him I understand his wanting out of this mess, though I don't see how living with his dad makes that any better. I beg him to get in touch with me. *I need to know you're okay*, I write. *I'd like to understand if I've jumped to conclusions about your taking sides. I love you and miss you more than you'll know until many years from now. When the damage is already done.*

Ten days later, he calls.

"Kyle! Where are you? I'm so happy to hear your voice. Are you okay?"

"I'm at Dad's, but I'm not staying. I'm sixteen, and I don't want either of you to have custody."

"But why can't you move home?" I ask, edging a little too close to pleading. I'm far less concerned with who has custody than I am with knowing he's safe.

"Dad lets me do whatever I want. We don't really speak, which is fine by me." He sounds baffled that I don't already know this. "You have rules. Besides, I'm getting an apartment with friends in Saratoga."

I reason with him, using words that make sense to me, but even as I say them, I imagine he hears them as nonsense.

Finally, he's done.

"I'll call you back when you can stop laying a guilt trip on me," he says.

The line goes dead.

—

As I await Kyle's next call, it's become painfully obvious

The Full Catastrophe

I need a new lawyer. I suspect only someone outside of our county's "good old boys" network can make any headway on my behalf.

A friend recommends an attorney in Troy, a small city close to my school. Sitting in the firm's offices on the top floor of a stately old building downtown, soaking in the pervading sense of permanence and encouraged by Sam's take-charge, no-nonsense style, I already feel calmer. He rolls his eyes about the things that have been allowed to happen and makes strong, reassuring statements about next steps. When we're finished, I walk off the elevator and out into the summer sunshine with a to-do list and the sense that there is, indeed, something to be done. For the first time since January, I can breathe.

The next morning, I assume my spot in the janitor's closet, pick up the phone, and divorce my divorce lawyer.

Buoyed by this new spark of hope, I make it through to the weekend. It's the first Saturday in June, our annual Cambridge Day, with a 5K at the school, a silent auction at Hubbard Hall on Main Street, vendors and artists and music in various locations around the village. This year I have a houseful for an east-meets-west potluck party. Music plays on the stereo, tables and counters are filled with food, and Cambridge friends and work friends mingle. This couldn't have come at a better time.

The great room is full. So is the deck. The early summer warmth blows gently through the screen door, carrying with it the aroma of grilled salmon and vegetables and newly cut grass. Kate has postponed the hostilities and is enjoying the fun with Mary's daughter, Corinne. Eric, who's finally settled on HVCC—Hudson Valley Community College in Troy— for the fall, pops in with a friend and hangs out with us for a while. And there is Kyle, coming through the door like nothing ever happened. I don't know what this means or how long he'll stay, but for now, all is well. Ira, the special ed teacher who teams with Suzanne and with whom I work closely, is searching the fridge for another Old Speckled Hen, other school friends are chatting, and someone is tending the grill. Another guest is uncorking the wine. Suzanne and Grace have pulled up a chair next to Mary, and I catch their eyes and smile.

Seeing our home filled with laughter and genuine affection, I'm filled, too, with a sensation I need to sit with. There's the memory of something long ago, a time when I felt warm and calm and loved, when my thoughts were occupied with happy dreams of a bright future instead of fears of the darkness that may very well lie ahead. But I'm also glimpsing the life I intend to have, with a home that's a place where people want to gather, not one they fight to escape. I'll take this day for what it is, a cease fire. A little R and R for this battle-worn soldier.

Soon Eric's graduation is upon us and, glory of glories, he's brought his lowest grades up to passing. It won't be the celebration I've pictured. Instead, this feels like something to get through. Eric will pass his candle to Kyle at Awards Night on the eve of graduation, a Cambridge tradition, though it's unclear what exactly we're supposed to imagine Eric handing off to his little brother.

Birdie and I are on the phone firming up Kate's schedule when I ask her whether she and Stan will attend Friday's graduation.

"We haven't been invited. Neither has Will." Her clipped response conveys her annoyance.

"I haven't been invited, either," I point out. "Everything

that's been happening with the divorce has made us all edgy, and Eric's no exception. I often don't know exactly what's up with him. But we're the adults, he's the kid, and it's our job to support him and show we love him, whether he's hostile or not."

"Thank you for the lecture," she barks, and hangs up.

My sons are so handsome, dressed in their navy sport coats and khakis as we arrive at the school Thursday evening for awards night, Kate so pretty in her new buttery yellow dress, and I think of how easily we could pass for a normal family. *We may be struggling*, I think, *but we clean up well*. The boys walk the aisle, complete the ceremony, and the long list of award presentations begin. I applaud as the larger sums of money are bestowed upon students with top academic honors, athletic prowess, kids bursting with potential and promise, most of them Eric's lifelong friends. Smaller accolades are handed out, niche recognitions, of the "most improved" and "hardest worker" variety.

Nearly every student has received something. I swallow hard. Is Eric really going to leave empty-handed? How quickly the charming adolescent with the perennial smile, star soccer player, and everyone's favorite snowboard instructor has fallen from grace. No longer seen as the hard-working student, now he's the kid who scraped through, doing the minimum. Finally, they call his name and hand him a certificate that's basically presented for showing up. I think of it as the "Thank God We Got Him Out of Here" award.

Kate is scheduled to return to Will's tomorrow at 4 p.m. to begin her week with him. I send a note asking he allow her to stay through the evening so she can attend graduation. He answers succinctly: "No."

This is how it happens, then, that Eric is in his cap and

gown, walking down the aisle, taking his place on the stage, reaching out to shake the board president's hand and receive his diploma, while Kyle plays in the band and I sit holding back tears, Mary beside me. Will and his parents have bowed out of attending. I'm devastated for him, sad for the family I thought I'd built, hopeless that it will ever again resemble something good and true.

The commencement speaker talks of knowing who's got your back. "Find your families in the audience," he instructs the graduates. Eric looks around and his gaze lands on me, though he's clearly uncomfortable. "Send them love and appreciation for all they've done to get you where you are today."

I think my heart is about to break.

A penny ricochets off the windshield, grazing the knuckles of my right hand, white from clutching the steering wheel. Another coin, this one silver, careens from the passenger's seat to the windshield, then past me into the back seat and is followed by another, and another—a barrage of ammunition. The next, projected by the careful flip of thumb off finger, comes too close to my face and bounces off my glasses: a rim shot. I squeeze my eyes together, briefly, tightly, hoping to keep the tears from spilling over while I try to see clearly enough to make the little course corrections required to keep the car on the winding country road.

I can't let Eric know how afraid I am. I need to hold it together. I wish I knew where I could find the closest police station. I wish I could pick up my cell phone and call 911. I don't dare. There's no telling what he'll do then.

The Full Catastrophe

"Turn the car around. Take me home!" he shouts, out of coins.

"But HVCC is what you've wanted. I've spent all spring putting everything in place for you. College is your ticket out. You're going." The strong mother line.

"Fuck that."

"It's just orientation. Go, listen to what they have to offer you. You want independence? This is your chance."

Silence. Agitated silence.

Eric slumps in the seat beside me, seething. I can almost see the charged ions swirling around him, an electric field that at once repels me and draws me in. I want to get away. I want to fix it. If I could only make him remember how much I love him, how I'd do anything to make whatever's gone horribly wrong inside him into everything that's right. No, I won't walk away. I won't let him run, either. Not like he did a few months ago, when he flung the car door open at that stop light an hour from home.

I prefer to remember the boy I've known. It's been only a couple of years, though it seems like decades, since those evenings when I'd wander into his bedroom just off the kitchen. There he'd be, stretched out in shorts and a T-shirt, his tanned, muscular legs ending with feet pushed against the footboard of his bed. It was too much to resist, then, grabbing onto his calves and, giving them a little shake, saying, "Where did these tree trunk legs come from? What have you done with my son?!" He'd laugh, more of a smirk, really, pretending not to like this routine. I knew better.

Only a year ago, Eric was the charismatic kid who taught his teachers to snowboard, who settled the soccer ball and read the field with equal parts intensity and grace. Then, he answered my serious observations with that light-hearted,

Keep Going

"Thank you, Captain Obvious!" I can't see that boy anymore, though I have faith he's still in there somewhere. I'd give everything I have to see that smile again.

But here we are, the walking wounded. Me scared, yes, and committed to stopping this game of chase-me-till-I-catch-you, push-me-till-I-jump that can't end well. And Eric? I honestly have no idea. Eric made this plan, I tell myself, though to be honest, it went more like this: He said okay, and I threw myself into making it work. I'd thought it a fine balance, then. Now it appears ready to topple.

I'm still trembling when we arrive at the college, find parking, and get ourselves to the first meeting. Eric drags along behind me, a sulking ball of passive aggression, staking out his emotional territory: *You may think you got me here, but you're dead wrong. You can make me come; you can't make me listen. And you sure as hell can't make me care.*

He's right, of course, and I know it, but what good does that do me? I think back over the past year and half—Eric alternately his father's prize and totally fatherless, his own volatility and fall from extroverted teen to angry young adult—and I struggle to imagine how we can possibly make it to the other side of this intact. One thing I do know: this is not how it was supposed to be. Not for our family. Not for me. And certainly, most crushingly, not for my beautiful son.

Though I have little influence at this point, I'll be damned if I don't keep trying. Eric will get to college and he'll know I'm on his side. Yet as I watch him take a seat in the back of the room and half-listen to the program chair describe the courses, the requirements, the articulation agreement for transfer to Rochester Institute of Technology—RIT—after graduation, I detect a glimmer of interest. Eric sits a little straighter in his chair.

The speaker lays it on the line. "Fewer than half of the freshmen who begin this program will complete it. But for those of you who do, the future is bright."

I can picture him then, my beaming son at his college graduation, having moved beyond this rough patch, safe on the other side of whatever this is, a little course correction. It's clear to me—Captain Obvious—how it can all happen.

I see what I need to see.

———

Financial planning for Eric's college life is a complicated and precarious puzzle, especially without support from Will—student loans and the learning disability funds I put in place in February, TAP and Pell grants to cover tuition and textbooks. The job he's landed at Walmart will cover food and a little spending cash, and I've rented him a room in a house near the college, thirty-five miles from Cambridge. His living at home is not a viable option for either of us. With no sway over what he chooses to do, I cannot sit by and watch him cruise or crash.

Then there's the matter of a car. Eric's had one bucket of bolts after another in the past year, one engine seizing before he remembered it burned oil and needed constant attention. It'll take at least $3,000 to find a car reliable enough to get him where he needs to go. But when I buy him a used Audi sedan, I get back into my own car and burst into tears. How did I think I was going to pay for this? The savings bonds Will and I have purchased since Eric was small won't even cover the cost of this car, much less gas and maintenance. I'll make it work. I have to.

Suzanne and I meet for lunch and, distraught, I share my

Keep Going

dilemma. As we leave, she hands me a check for the portion of the car I can't fund. I well up with relief and gratitude.

Now I commit myself to proving that Kate is better off living with me. Gathering evidence—of expenses, of my parenting skills, of Kate's improvements in school and Will's negative impact on her well-being, about his rejection of the boys, of practically everything—has become a way of life. Sometimes I dream of living an undocumented existence. Such a luxury, to go about one's business unfettered by the need to record, to prove.

Though typically I can only be overcome with worry about one kid at a time, now I don't know what to do about any of them. About Kate, who has added Kyle to the list of people she's dedicated to protecting from my evil ways. About Kyle, who's back at home now but in and out, sometimes with Will, sometimes who knows where, doing who knows what. And about Eric, whose alternating anger and agitation have me awake at night, searching for a way— any way—to help him.

Kyle and Kate have both seen counselors; Eric needs someone to talk to as well. I make an appointment with a psychologist recommended by a friend, and Eric agrees to go.

At our first session, Dr. Reid meets with each of us individually. A week later, we sit side by side in his small office and listen as he provides his appraisal of our situation, based on a single visit.

"You shouldn't be talking about the problems you have with your husband in front of the kids. Eric shouldn't know about these things. He wouldn't be so upset if you'd protected him from all of this."

I've shared my fears with the boys when I shouldn't have,

and I feel guilty about this. But the suggestions that my keeping quiet would have solved everything—as if Eric weren't the target of Will's juvenile behavior himself—feels like a patronizing oversimplification of a deeply complex situation. It infuriates us both.

Eric, so angry he's shaking, leaps from the chair and storms out of the office. This time, I can't say I blame him. This guy is splashing droplets of water on an inferno that would take a brigade to extinguish. Beneath Eric's reluctant agreement to meet with a counselor surely lay a deep hope that he'd find some relief or he wouldn't have agreed to come. I hoped for that, too.

Eric's gone, but I still have things to say. I turn in my chair to face Dr. Reid, hot tears stinging my eyes.

"You have no idea what our family has been through. Eric's dad, who lives across the street with his parents, hasn't spoken to him for more than a year. He didn't attend Eric's high school graduation. Neither did his grandparents. Eric has lost more than a father. He's falling apart with anger and grief. And you think not talking about those things would have prevented his pain?"

He stares at me, expressionless. I continue. "Sometimes," I say, speaking more slowly now, with the vaguest note of anger creeping into my voice, "when an adult is emotionally abusive to a child, it's important that someone who loves that child let him know it's not his fault."

I rise and leave, knocking Eric's empty chair out of the way in my rush to escape. We do not return.

SEVENTEEN

Oh, the Places You'll Go!

When we are no longer able to change a situation, we are challenged to change ourselves.

I want to live by this wisdom from Victor Frankl, I really do. But I can't seem to figure out how to make it happen.

Should I push forward with what will inevitably become custody trial number two, put myself and the kids through more drama and trauma, stubbornly holding out faith that one day the legal system will see things my way? Or should I let it all go? And how can I do that? The little bit of child support I already get is essential to my shaky financial solvency. But these worries pale when I consider how frightened I am for all three of my kids. Closure feels elusive when the process that gets us there has wrecked us.

I try to untangle it all with Suzanne.

"I know I need to see things differently, but it's a maze. Kate's clearly better off with me, but Will won't stop his attacks until he wins or takes them all down with him. How can I stop fighting for what I know is right?"

"Which will bring the most peace?" she asks, a question that reminds me of the one thing I seek for all of us.

I know what I need to do.

Our lawyers agree to this new plan. Kate will switch houses on Friday evenings after school, spending a week at each place and avoiding the drama of the Sunday night return. Kyle can stay where he chooses, and Eric will be off to college soon. Though this isn't the best solution for Kate in the long run, it's all I can do for her now.

The Full Catastrophe

I've always believed if I offered love and compassion, everything I gave would be returned to me. I wasn't all wrong, but it's not a simple equation, not a way to control the outcome. What does it mean then? For me, it's a question of pushing deeper into becoming who I want to be. Do I want to be a person who carries all these grievances? Do I want to be miserable and mad? Do I want to be right, or do I want to connect?

Now I understand I can't control any of it: not how Kate sees me, not what Kyle decides he wants or doesn't want, not even whether Eric takes the path laid out before him. I pray life will settle down for all of us. I pray I'll find a way to meet expenses. Mostly, I pray for the peace that's eluded me for so long.

On a late August Sunday—the day I bring Eric to college—I sit him down in one of the two flowered Queen Anne chairs near the bay window in the center of the house, thinking of the family dinners and birthday parties that have happened here when it was still the dining room, before we added on to the house. The voices of my cousins and their young families, Esther, Will's parents and sisters ring in my ears. I remember Eric's friends, Kyle's too, circling the old pine table, each pretending to be Bob Kovachik, our local weatherman, tween boys trying on the cockiness of confident men before bursting into unbridled laughter.

Eric's curious when I steer him to the chair, until he spies the copy of Dr. Seuss's *Oh the Places You'll Go* I'm holding.

"This may seem silly but there's so much wisdom in this book," I tell him. I've written a note on the flyleaf, and I read it aloud:

Oh, the Places You'll Go!

Dear Eric,

Read this book twice—once for its humor and once for its heartfelt message. As you've already learned far too well, life is a roller coaster at times, with exhilarating highs and frightening dips.

The message in this book is clear, true, and echoes exactly my faith and confidence in you. You will figure it out, and with great courage and style.

Independent living, college life (!), and the world await—go for it! All my love to you...

With wings to fly and feet planted firmly on the ground...

Mom

Eric peers at me and looks half touched, half amused, but he seems to sense this is something I need to do for him. For myself. I ask him to listen as I read him the book.

"Your childhood starts and ends with Dr. Seuss," I say, laughing. And then I begin.

I read the text and turn the pages, the silly rhyming verse declaring the very excitement of the journey ahead. So much to look forward to! And you? You're in charge. You're smart. You'll fly past them all, writes Dr. Seuss.

Yet.

Though I've read this book a dozen times, my voice catches as the tone shifts. Now he warns of things that may go awry. You may fall, hard, get hurt, he tells us. Your friends may leave you. And it may be tough to recover. You may be confused. You may get stuck.

He's already been there. Tell us something we don't already know.

But wait! No, you'll find your way!

Thank God. So it'll all work out.

Yes, you'll be ready, and you'll have fun "because you're that kind of guy!"

Yes, he sure is. That's my Eric.

Oh, god, but now you'll be lonely. And scared.

What is Seuss doing to me? I'm crying now, but I'm going to finish this book, dammit.

"You'll face up to your problems, whatever they are." Like a knife in the heart.

So...shit will happen...be careful...it's all about balance...and yes! You will succeed!

I put the book down and Eric stands to hug me. "Are you okay, Mom?" he asks.

God, I love this boy.

Soon it's time to leave. I drive along behind Eric and Kate, who proudly rides shotgun. Today, there's no hint of animosity. When we arrive, Kate hands him Wrinkles, her most prized Beanie Baby from her extensive collection, and hugs him tight. With all the hostility of the past eighteen months, the arguing, the defending her father and striking out at Eric sometimes as vehemently as she did at me, one thing is clear: Eric has never stopped being her big brother. She's never stopped loving him.

And neither have I.

———

On a crisp October morning, I sit alone in a conference room at Supreme Court while our lawyers negotiate the financial terms of the divorce in an office next door.

As I wait, I remind myself that Will is not the enemy and I'm not his victim, that holding onto my anger will never

Oh, the Places You'll Go!

bring me peace. It's remarkable how calm I feel when my attorney comes through the door with the final offer. We've given some, he tells me, and we've gotten some things in return.

This was never about winning, I think as I gather myself and leave the courthouse, *only about finding a place where we all get what we need. Maybe we're finally on the right track.*

El's daughter Sandy visits for Thanksgiving, bringing warm memories of holidays spent at her house growing up, memories of belonging to a large and loving family, though it wasn't my own. Now we spend a long day Christmas shopping at the mall an hour from home. Finally, the strains of "I'll Be Home for Christmas" playing as we enjoy a late dinner, I remember. *Kyle!* He's moved back home now but isn't yet old enough to drive, so he's counting on me to pick him up from his restaurant job. Here I am, at closing time still forty miles away.

We gobble down our dinner and get ourselves home pronto. Dashing into the kitchen, I see the answering machine blinking frantically. Ten new messages. These days, it's a toss-up, which Kyle to expect—the often frustrated, annoyed teen or the witty, sarcastic kid who makes me laugh. I suck in my breath, say a little prayer, and gingerly press the button to hear the authoritative robotic voice of the man inside the machine.

Saturday, 9:34 p.m. Hey Mom, it's me, um…it's like 9:35 and we're pretty much done, so be here *at* ten. Okay? Bye.

Saturday, 9:49 p.m. Hi Mom, it's me again. I just wanted to call to remind you to, uh, drag it?

Saturday, 9:55 p.m. Hey Mom, it's me again. Uh, Mickey's big hand is on the ten…where are you? (*around him, the muffled laughter of teenage boys…*)

The Full Catastrophe

Saturday, 9:59 p.m I'm waaaiiiittttiinnnggg…

Sandy and I laugh out loud. This is Kyle at his best, funny and forgiving, and the pride I feel in him surprises me.

Saturday, 10:06 p.m. Hey Mom, it's me again. I was just wondering if you realized how irritating it is when you're done like, twenty minutes early, and your ride doesn't come for like, I dunno, ten, fifteen minutes after you get done. I just thought I should, you know, say that…

Saturday, 10:15 p.m. Mom, I'd like to go home sometime today, please…um, if it wouldn't be too much trouble, could ya please pick me up here? It's, like, 10:15, ya know, I got done at, like, twenty o' ten, I been just sitting here waitin' 'n waitin' 'n waitin'….Anh, I guess I can let it go…Bye.

Saturday, 10:24 p.m. Ten, Mom. Not ten-thirty. *Ten!* Thank. You.

Thankful he's still amused, I check my watch and see it's nearly eleven. I hope these messages don't go downhill fast.

Saturday, 10:27 p.m. Hey, Mom? Uh, I was just wondering if you remember where I worked, you know, Benson's Diner, you're, like, goin' to Hoosick Falls on Route 22, right next to the first blinking red light. You know, you take a right *(there's that snickering in the background again…)* and you go to Johnsonville, go straight and you go to North Hoosick. We're right there on the corner, we've got an ice cream shop right by the road *(stifling his own laughter now)*. I would really appreciate it if you'd come pick me up sometime. I've been done for about an hour now…I been gettin' kinda bored, so maybe I'll see ya sometime soon. Bye!

Sandy's doubled over now, and I'm in stitches, too. A huge sense of relief from the worry of today and of the past couple of years leaves me with a feeling that borders on hysteria. I take a deep breath and press play again.

Saturday, 10:29 p.m. Hey, Mom? I was just wondering if, uh, next time I could bring a tent, or a sleeping bag, or something like that, 'cause this just isn't working. I gotta like, get home at some point, ya know? I don't know... *sigh* ...I'll see ya later.

Saturday, 10:34 p.m. Hey Mom, it's me. Bo's gonna give me a ride home. And Mom? I know Rome wasn't built in a day, but you really gotta work on this.

End. Of. Messages.

Kyle bursts through the door smelling of cooking grease and sugar as the last message fades away.

"Oh my God, Kyle, I'm so sorry. We were at the mall and I completely forgot you needed a ride!"

"Nice, Mom. Hanging around here yucking it up with your friend while I sit abandoned after a long day at work. Really nice." He's nodding his head slowly and trying not to smile.

I roll my eyes with exaggerated drama. "What?! You could have walked! It's only five miles. Piece of cake."

"Oh, sure, why not? Just goes to show you no one ever remembers the middle kid..."

Sandy's boisterous laughter drowns us out as Kyle and I match each other, barb for barb.

I'm still smiling as my head hits the pillow when I finally crawl into bed. This is the most fun I've had in a very long time.

———

A few weeks later, a punch in the gut. When I get my credit card bill and see the charges, I panic. Eric has my gas card and has found a way to get extra cash, lots of it. He quit the Walmart job not long after school started. The finely tuned budget I've put in place for each of us has been blown to bits.

I sink into a chair, hurt, angry. Desperate, too. When I confront Eric, he's sorry but offers no solution. When I learn he's talking to his father again, it's obvious Eric understands my financial well has run dry. Regardless of what's made him open to a relationship with Will, I'm relieved it's happened, for both their sakes.

I won't shower Eric with Christmas gifts I can't afford when he's been helping himself to cash I need to pay the bills. I return much of the snowboarding equipment and keep a few things to put under the tree. There will be other holidays. Of course there will. This year, he'll have to learn a tough lesson.

Eric moves home for break in mid-December, and the house feels fuller than it has in months: dirty laundry awaits washing, Eric's shoes and coats are scattered around the house, and the phone rings constantly again. With all three of the kids in and out, at Will's or with friends or at Willard Mountain on their snowboards, I'm never sure whether to expect a houseful for dinner or complete silence. Either way, I'm thrilled to have Eric home.

Though I've seen no grades, I suspect the semester has not gone well, and I can't shake the vague sense of doom I feel hanging over this otherwise happy scene. I ask Eric for details.

"I really screwed up, Mom," he admits. "I worked hard at first, then I started cutting class."

"Oh, Eric, I'm so disappointed. You have so much ability. This is such a waste." I prop my elbow on the kitchen counter and rest my hand against my cheek. Holding my head up without added support suddenly seems to require more energy than I can muster.

He frowns and studies his shoes.

"Yeah, well, I started smoking pot with my friends, and after a while it didn't make much sense to go to class. I'd already missed so much."

I'm upset yet unsurprised. Oh, how I wanted this to save him. Still, I realize now how stunned I would've been if it had.

"So what do you think you'll do now?"

He looks up at me, lost.

"Listen, Eric, I did everything I could to help you make this plan, and it hasn't worked. But now I see this was my plan. I'll do everything I can to help you figure out what's next, but the decision has to be yours."

He nods slightly, his face expressionless.

"The way I see it, there are three options: You could go back to college and really work at it this time. You could find a job—a real job and an apartment, not working part-time at Willard and living at home. Or you could join the service."

"No way on the last one. That's not for me."

When Eric's grades arrive the following week, option one is out. He's failed every class and can't return for at least a year. A few days later, he's decided. The military isn't such a bad idea after all. There's a Navy recruiting office in Troy. He's made an appointment.

Things move quickly. Eric passes a drug test and spends a weekend in early January at a regional Military Entrance Processing Station undergoing a physical and taking the Armed Services Vocational Aptitude Battery, otherwise known as the ASVAB. He calls from the exam site, at his recruiter's urging, to tell me he's done well on the Armed Forces Qualification Test (AFQT). The recruiter comes on the line, full of enthusiasm, and talks about all the options this opens up for Eric.

"This is a wonderful score. We think the best fit for Eric would be to complete basic training, then attend aircraft technician school (*how perfect for him,* I think) at our Naval Air Station in Pensacola, Florida. With hard work, he has the potential to go far with the Navy. I'm so excited for the opportunities he'll have. You should be very proud."

Proud, anxious, skeptical, cautiously optimistic: none of these do justice to the massive amount of anticipation and overwhelming burden of fear I feel when I imagine Eric's future. For now, I'm going with unadulterated hope.

—

When Eric walks through the front door holding the note a week later, I think nothing of it.

Until I see his face.

As a child, Eric was easy to read. Whatever was happening inside him seeped through to the surface as though no barrier existed at all. Now I sometimes stare at him when he's not looking, wishing I could peel away a bit of the teenage mask to see, really see, what he's thinking. Who he is.

But recent events have shaken us up, and now some of our connection has been restored. My boy is back, and I've missed him. With his decision to enlist in the Navy behind us, I've thought there would be time to catch my breath, to look forward to a future filled with possibility.

But looking at him now, I see trouble.

I ask what he's holding, and he sinks into the recliner,

staring at the small white paper torn from a note pad. "I'm not sure, but it can't be good."

"Who's it from? Where did you find it?"

"I was getting in the car to head to Willard, and it was stuck under the wiper," he tells me, looking dazed. "It's from the village cops. They say I should stop by the station today."

At least he hasn't been ticketed or, God forbid, arrested for anything. The crew he's been spending time with since most of his friends left for college last year mostly hang around in one of their parents' basements and appear to have no future plans. I'm sure they smoke pot—though I don't know the details—and I suspect the police are hoping to press Eric for inside information.

"Well, whatever it is, Eric, just be honest. You can't go wrong if you tell the truth."

"Yep. I'm heading over there now so I can get up to the mountain. See ya later, Mom."

With that, he's off, leaving me with one more thing to add to the pile I push to the back of my mind so I can function on at least a basic level. The pile keeps getting bigger, and still I sweep. Something tells me I'm going to need a bigger broom.

This struggle between fighting to ensure life works out as planned, however fruitless, and finding peace is anything but linear. Sometimes I find that place of rest, then another crisis erupts, and I'm overwhelmed and hopeless again. Maybe this is simply the way life works, but it exhausts me.

Late in the evening, the stereo in Eric's car thumps a pounding bass as it turns into the driveway. I need to get to work early tomorrow, but I've waited up.

He sits at the kitchen table and fills me in. The cops knew he's bought pot in town and want him to wear a wire. This

The Full Catastrophe

doesn't sound like a good idea to me, and I tell him so.

But there's more.

Eric glances at me and waits a moment before he continues. "Remember Heather?" I do. Heather was one of the legion of girls who used to call Eric nearly every night, wanting to talk about boyfriends and music and anything, really.

"She moved over the border to Shaftsbury with her parents when they left here a few years ago. They got a divorce, and she was living with her mom. One day last fall, we were talking on the phone and Heather said she knew where I could buy weed in Vermont. I drove over there."

I watch him, and a wave of anxiety ripples through me.

"Well, apparently she's in the custody of the state now. She wouldn't listen to either of her parents, so she's in foster care or something."

"And?" I'm confused.

"So last week, her mother was cleaning out her room and found a journal. Heather had written about the time I was there." A pause. "She wrote that we had sex."

"Oh, Eric, seriously? But you hardly knew her."

He fiddles with the lanyard on his key chain, wrapping it around his fingers, and stares at the floor.

When Eric was younger, we stressed the wisdom of waiting until he was in a committed relationship. But as he got older, we had frank discussions about when it was okay to take that step. I'm not clueless. I'm pretty sure he was sexually active with Ashley when they were together.

"Was it consensual?" I ask, still having a hard time believing we're having this conversation.

"Yes! Jeez, Mom. Of course it was!"

"The cops asked if it was true and I said yeah, but we

Oh, the Places You'll Go!

both wanted it. I figured it was best to tell the truth, like you said. Then they asked if I knew she was only fifteen. I knew she was younger than me, but I never thought about figuring out her age. Now her mother wants me arrested for having sex with a minor."

I stiffen. "You've got to be kidding. That can't be right!" Eric thought he had nothing to hide—seriously, weren't most of his friends having sex?—so he cooperated. He's known these guys, the village cops, his whole life. He trusted them when they said he didn't need a lawyer, that he wasn't charged with anything. That they just wanted information.

"We're hoping you can help us out," they said. "If you wear a wire for us, maybe we can make this go away."

Everything out on the table now, there's nothing more to discuss. Eric goes to bed and I do, too, praying this was a poorly thought-out strong-arm tactic, praying we've heard the last of it. Praying the Navy will save my son.

———

I'm standing in the kitchen near the desk in my dream that night when Eric bursts through the door. The lights are bright, and he is too: bright and shining, smiling that brilliant smile. But something's wrong.

"I've been hanging out with my friends," he says, laughing. "We're having a great time. Everything's cool!" He's just come in, but he's already heading out again. Places to go, people to see. Classic Eric.

Then I see it. His perfect white teeth have been sawed in half, horizontally. Right across the middle. Every one of them is ruined.

"Eric, what's happened to your teeth?" I cry out, my eyes

blurring with tears.

"Aw, David and I were just fooling around!" He's beaming, happier than I've seen him in years. It's my boy. He's back. The pleasure and the pain, side by side, are overwhelming. Too much to take.

In the next instant, I'm somewhere else, as happens in dreams, driving through the village. I pull over on the side of the road, up at the top of North Union Street, and other cars are there, too, filled with friends from town and from work. I notice we're parked across from the cemetery and wonder why we're here. I line up behind the others, but my thoughts are interrupted as Karen, my take-charge supervisor, comes dashing over. I roll down my window.

"Why are you parking back here?" she challenges, motioning for me to pull to the head of the line.

"Lead!" she insists. "If you lead, others will follow!"

I'm confused, but I comply. As I move my car up to the front, I'm suddenly back in the kitchen again. Eric left but has returned now, smiling that broken smile. Still upset, I try to make him understand.

"Eric, honey, it's your teeth! You've done damage that can't be fixed!" I'm pleading, my voice rising to a fevered pitch.

"It's okay, Mom." He comforts me, flinging an arm across my shoulders. The grin never leaves his face. "Don't you get it? It's okay! I'm happy now."

And with that he's off, out the door. Leaving me, as usual.

When I awaken, I'm already sitting up straight, eyes open wide. I've been having recurring nightmares about my own teeth, loose or severed, sometimes falling out, these symbols of my fear of losing a part of myself. They've been happening throughout the divorce and the struggles with Kate and custody. Since Eric found the note a week ago, I've almost expected them.

But this was more like a vision, a visit, than a dream. And it was Eric's teeth this time, not mine. I jump out of bed and write down everything I remember in a race to record what I've seen before it leaves me.

One of these days, I think, *I'll figure out what all this means.*

EIGHTEEN

Pacing the Cage

I'm dozing on the sofa one evening a few weeks later when sixteen-year-old Kyle shuffles through the front door, shoulders slouched, and drops his skateboard to the floor. His hair is green this week, and he wears baggy jeans and an old '92 Metallica tour T-shirt under his Burton snowboarding jacket. He plops onto the cushion on the opposite end of the sofa with a groan.

"I don't know how to get my shit together, Mom."

Suddenly I'm wide awake. "What do you mean, exactly?"

"I want to do well in school, I really do. I want to have goals. I wake up every morning telling myself I'm going to pull it together. But I've been screwing around all year, and now it's too late. I can barely wake up until the day's half over. Sometimes I want to ask questions in class but I can hear what's in all of their minds: 'What, are you too stupid to think?' If I'd been paying attention all year, I'd already know this stuff. I'm a lost cause."

"Oh, Kyle, I'm so sorry you feel stuck, but it's never too late, you know? You're so smart, and I know there are teachers who would want to help you catch up if they knew."

He shakes his head. "I have an addictive personality, Mom, I know I do. I *have* to be up at Willard every day with my snowboard, even if it's just for ten minutes. And I'm already worried what I'll do to fill that void when winter's over. Nah, I know what I'll do, I'll be up at the corner on my skateboard, doing shit I shouldn't be doing."

These conversations, when we talk about his struggles

The Full Catastrophe

and work together to find a new way to approach them, leave me feeling proud of my intelligent, introspective son and his ability to understand his own behavior. He's been exceptionally self-aware since he was very young. But he's often unwilling—or unable—to turn his insights into action.

"Kyle, I really think Mrs. Borden would be a good person to talk to." Eileen is his English teacher, has a son Kyle's age, and has been a friend of mine for years. "And you should make an appointment with Dave." Kyle's typically open to talking with his therapist, something I admire.

He shrugs, and I hug him for as long as he'll tolerate it.

"I can help you structure your time if you like, and I'm great at coming up with study strategies. You know I'll do everything I can to help you catch up." All so much easier said than done. I'd go with him to talk with his teachers, help him get organized, hire a tutor. I'd set things up for success if I had any power at all, over the situation. Over Kyle.

Still, I know there's little I can do to set things right.

———

Eric is running the snowboarding program at Willard while the rest of his life is on hold. He's been arrested for sexual assault in Bennington County, Vermont, so entering the Navy has to wait.

With the magical thinking that comes when reality is too much to swallow, Eric insists he'll go into the Navy (as if that were even an option now) only if Ashley wants him back—he'll need to be someone, for her—but if she doesn't, who really cares.

This is yet another nightmare. I haven't seen any legal documents, no charges in writing, anyway. This will work

Pacing the Cage

itself out. We'll wake up, and it'll be over. It has to be.

When I arrive home one midweek afternoon, Eric meets me at the door.

"I met with Mr. Whitman in Bennington today. My friend's mother said he was a good criminal lawyer, so I made an appointment. He'll represent me if we give him a $5000 retainer."

"Oh, Eric, I don't know where we'd get that kind of money," I say, my voice thick with emotion.

I would do anything in my power for Eric. But the years of financial blows have left me with nothing, not a dime to spare and not an ounce of energy to fight another endless battle.

I feel stuck in a special circle of hell, one reserved for those who want to right every wrong and to know nothing about any of it. Beaten down by the divorce, the custody battle, hostility and betrayal from the kids, each suffering themselves, I still love them so much it hurts. It's becoming clear that I can't fix everything. Maybe, in truth, I can't fix anything.

When Eric hits a financial dead end with his dad, we attend the initial court appearance, and he applies for a public defender.

I'm relieved to learn he's been assigned a lawyer whom I met briefly at the coffee shop in town, a friend of a friend. I accompany Eric to meet with him, certain that Eric wasn't clear enough about the facts—that their relations were consensual, that Eric had no idea Heather was underage. And his confession was taken without a lawyer present. That can't be okay, can it?

The lawyer reads through the charging document, where the initials "HM" appear in place of the full name of the minor victim.

He looks up at Eric. "Who is HM?"

When Eric reveals Heather's name, the lawyer gently sets the papers on the table between us and looks up. "I'm so sorry, I can't help you, Eric. I was appointed her law guardian when she was taken from her parents and placed in care. This would be a conflict of interest."

My heart sinks.

"But make sure whoever takes your case knows this:" he continues. "That girl looks at least twenty-one. No one would have guessed she was only fifteen. The law is the law, but these circumstances should be considered."

Once the judge appoints a conflict defender then gathers information from each side, he decides the case will go forward. Eric is charged with sexual assault, based solely on his age and the age of the girl. It's time to steel ourselves for the long haul once again.

I'm on a need-to-know-basis with what's happening in Eric's life. He and Ashley are together again, but he doesn't appear to be any happier. Thinking of the talks we once had about his passions and dreams is too painful now. It takes all the strength I have to manage what's right in front of us much less how we'll get through the months ahead. How I'll get through today.

When I call home during my work day, the boy who once answered the phone with such gusto is gone. Eric's voice is thin, like air escaping from a deflated balloon. Other days, when I come through the door he's angry and unstable, someone I no longer recognize. He shouts me down and becomes so agitated if I attempt to ask him questions or offer advice that I sometimes worry he'll become physically aggressive. I begin to feel frightened to come home each night.

The advice of tough love advocates who preach providing no help to those who constantly violate rules courses through my mind.

"Set firm boundaries, then follow through with consistent consequences," they say. "If they keep breaking rules, provide no support."

"If you lock the door, they break a window," I counter as I think this through. They haven't walked in my shoes, and their solutions are useless. Caught in the vast chasm between wanting to protect my son while needing to protect myself, it's a dilemma I can't work out.

When Eric was small and needed me most, I promised to save him from danger, hold his hand when he was scared and make things right. What do I do now, when he's the one I fear?

Late one afternoon, I'm in my office catching up on a mountain of paperwork and worrying about Eric, as I do constantly these days.

What if he never makes it to the Navy? What if he only gets angrier and more hopeless? And the more immediate concern: *What if he's hostile when I get home?*

I imagine how confused and chaotic it is inside Eric's mind. His family has crumbled and college was a bust. Ashley might choose him, maybe not. The Navy is on hold, his entire future is unsure, and the possibilities are terrifying. How could he not be scared to death? I understand why almost anything he hears is too much for him, yet understanding this and knowing how to react to it are two entirely different things.

I drive home, reminding myself not to let my own fear launch me into a place where I can be of no help to Eric.

When I come through the door, he's upset, slamming things, headed out.

"Where are you going?" I ask.

He glares at me, practically daring me to question him.

"None of your fucking business."

It takes everything I have to hold my tongue. I breathe deeply before I speak, and when I do, my voice is low and calm.

"I love you so much, Eric. I know you're hurting. How can I help?"

I watch as the fight quietly drains away. Eric leans against the desk, drops into the chair, and talks about how afraid he is, how lost. We have a real conversation for the first time in a very long time.

For one moment, we're not slammed doors and angry notes and court cases we can't win; we're long days at the lake and trips to the mountain and a mother loving her son to the end of the earth. For one breath, everything feels right.

———

Eric's future is up in the air. Though he's obligated to the Navy, he can't go yet, with his pending legal issues. He works at the mountain until the snow melts away, then has a series of temporary jobs, including one at UPS and another at a motorcycle shop in Troy. He's in and out, sometimes living several towns away with a woman he worked with at Willard. She and her husband have young kids who call Eric their big brother, and she's found him a job near her house.

Also at Willard, he's become friends with a man with a young family who has just moved to the area from the Midwest and who, I'll later learn, paid for Eric to complete

Pacing the Cage

Professional Snowboard Instructor certification at Killington in exchange for Eric's help in building a deck on his home. Rick has contacts in the snowboarding world and has arranged for Eric to take a position at Mount Hood, Oregon, running a snowboarding program. When...or if...he's able.

And I'm relieved to hear Eric chatting with his friend Sarah again. She, her family, and her Clifton Park friends welcome him like one of their own. Maybe they'd agree to adopt me as well.

I miss Eric but realize his ability to seamlessly fold himself into these families and their eagerness to have him is probably for the best. I'm grateful for any time he's able to spend with adults who care about him and model healthy relationships. When he's home, surrounded by reminders of the plans that have failed and the current ones, indefinitely on hold, it feels as though I know him less every day.

Lines from a Bruce Cockburn song that's rung painfully true throughout the past year course through my mind on repeat: "Today these eyes scanned bleached-out land / for the coming of the outbound stage / Pacing the cage." Now they make me think of Eric, too, and the level of empathy they evoke is almost too much to bear.

At home, Eric's either agitated or, more often, sad, spending days on the sofa, frequently sleeping there. So frequently, in fact, that the chain from his wallet wears holes in the sofa cushions, which I repeatedly flip and switch with the others until they've all been damaged, and there's no way to hide it. This feels like a metaphor for our lives right now, all of the good sides worn away, only the frayed parts left to show the world.

That damn Dr. Seuss book haunts me. I hear it some-times, when I drive home in a quiet car, when I struggle to fall asleep, taunting me with silly rhymes about serious situations, making light of the furious careening toward nothingness. We're stuck there, in that waiting place. Neither of us is very good at it, yet fear of what we'll find at the end keeps me, and maybe Eric, too, from wishing it were over.

Lying in bed on a Saturday morning in early June, mesmerized by the patterns of light and dark the sun beaming through the lace curtains creates on the ceiling, I think about the patterns in my own life. Growing up with uncertainty and loss, I learned that putting one foot in front of the other no matter what came was the key to survival, that determination, when channeled in the right direction, could get me nearly anywhere I needed to go. Not that it was ever easy, but I'd learned not to expect easy.

When people asked how I'd survived my early years, I shrugged off their questions, minimizing the trauma I experienced by moving on to the one thing I couldn't weather. "I lost my whole family way too young, but if something ever happens to one of my children, just put me to bed and don't expect me to get up again."

Now nothing is sure. There are things vastly bigger than I am, so many forces beyond my control. What I can't imagine is how this all works out, and the more I worry over it, the more frightening it is.

But there's something else.

Daily now, I am of two minds—one person split in two, or maybe two distinct beings melded into one. While much of the time I obsess over how all of our struggles will ever be resolved, I'm gradually leaning into a new way to live.

There are only two paths for me now, I think: hold tightly to everything I'm convinced I know or find another way. This begins, of course, with believing there is another way.

Pacing the Cage

What if the things I hold most tightly were gone? The mother in me, who loves my children more than life itself, shakes her head and rages against the thought. But another voice reminds me we'll always be connected, even if we're separated by miles or prison bars or, God forbid, death. It assures me this letting go doesn't mean the thing I fear: that I don't love my kids enough.

I've been making the movie of my life since I was small. Freezing the frame, whether on film or in my mind. Holding onto the things I couldn't make last. Seeking a new perspective. The skills I honed as a little girl, as a tormented eighth grader—they've served me well. Now I'm sometimes able to rise above the landscape in a new way. I see us all here, scurrying about, protecting our territory at all costs, thinking this life we've created is all there is. It's easier, from up there, to see the whole picture.

I am not the whole picture. I never was.

We each have a journey, a life to live, choices to make. I can't make those choices for my kids any more than they can make them for me. And I certainly can't make things work out the way I'd like them to. Though it's been a long time getting to this place, I've begun to pray not for a specific outcome but for the courage to accept whatever comes.

I hear the kids, all three of them, rustling about downstairs, making breakfast, watching TV. It's a rare weekend with all of them home, and despite the dark cloud that hangs over each of us, this makes me happy. I push back the covers and sit on the edge of the bed, working up the energy to join them. My heart is heavy, grieving the life I've been so sure would save me and worrying over the future. But more and more, as I feel the pain I also recognize I'm choosing to feel separate, convinced love is in short supply when, in fact, I have enough to share.

Every day, it seems, our situation worsens. And every day, the peace I find when I push past the fear feels more lasting and real.

—

In the first days of June, Eric meets with his public defender and returns with news, none of it good. My former divorce attorney who has been a friend to Eric, the Navy recruiter, and several of Eric's former teachers have offered to write letters of support for him.

"None of it matters," Eric says.

"But are you sure they know everything?" I press. "This can't be right. Did you tell him it was consensual? Did you mention what the first public defender said about her? Did you tell him the police never said you'd been charged, that you were entitled to a lawyer? Did you mention they wanted you to wear a wire, and you figured they were using this to talk you into it?"

"Yes, Mom! Yes! All right?" He slinks into his room and slams the door.

I stare at the wall, the color of clotted cream. My son, my heart, has become a lost boy. Is it the proverbial sins of the mother, his epigenetic heritage, to struggle? Maybe he's always been a little lost. Like me.

The legal system has never protected me, not to mention my kids, so it's a tall order to believe it will protect Eric now. But I have to make one more stab at this, so a few days later I call the public defender from my office at the end of the day. I fire off questions, supplying the facts I've been sure Eric left out, but what his lawyer has to say leaves me speechless.

"I brought the case to the State's Attorney, but they won't entertain anything less than a full conviction. They have Eric confessing to having sexual relations with a girl who was fifteen, and that's all they need. In Vermont, it doesn't matter whether the abuser is nineteen or sixty-nine, whether the victim is a fifteen-year-old girlfriend or a five-year-old child. It doesn't matter that he didn't know she was that young, and because of her age, it doesn't matter if it was consensual, either. They want every person accused either in prison or in an eighteen-month sex offender program. My hands are tied. You can take it to trial, which probably won't happen until October. But he will lose."

I hang up the phone and sit, resting my head in my hands the way I do when all the life drains out of me. Then I pack my therapy bags, drive through the countryside, and sit on the floor with a four-year-old in her bedroom, enthusiastically eliciting sounds and expanding her utterances like it's my only job.

On Thursday, I steel myself and call my lawyer Sam during a break between meetings. I trust his opinion, and I have nowhere else to turn. I lay out the whole story and explain, weakly, that I haven't called him before now because I've felt shellshocked, as though I've been suffering from a sort of post-traumatic stress.

"Christ," he says, "you're the mother who should be on the steps of the courthouse with a rifle." I understand and appreciate that this is his way of sympathizing, letting me know he's on my side.

"Vermont's laws around sex offenders and statutory rape relating to consensual sex between young people are archaic. It's Jerry Springer prosecution. They're looking for another notch in the prosecutorial belt, regardless of circumstances, regardless of the lives it impacts. In New York, this would be a Class A misdemeanor."

So Eric's fifteen-mile drive over the border has likely altered the course of his entire life.

"I'm out of money, which is why Eric is using a public defender. But would it help at all if we found the right criminal attorney? I don't know how I'd pay for it, but I'd do anything to help him."

"It absolutely would. In situations like this, a case sealed in the back room can be a deal made in the back room. Don't let anyone tell you a conviction for Eric is set in stone. Listen, I went to law school in Vermont, and I'll be there this weekend. I'm out on Monday, but on Tuesday I'll call you with the name of an attorney. Hang in there."

I thank him, hang up, call Eric with this hopeful news, and head across the parking lot to another meeting. My friend and coworker Ira turns to me during a lull in the action.

"So how's Eric doing these days?"

When Ira and his family come to Cambridge from time to time, his little boys enjoy running into Eric's bedroom and jumping on his bed to wake him up. Eric likes Ira and called him once to mockingly harass him for leaving "bad beer" in our fridge. Ira gets Eric and likes him, too, so I tell him the whole story.

Then I blurt out the question that's plagued me for months: "How will he ever recover from this?"

Ira knits his brow. "We can't let this happen."

There hasn't been a "we" in my life in a very long time, certainly not in this situation, ever. Ira has no idea how loaded his words are, how much they mean to me.

But now that I've talked with Sam, there's hope. We just

need to get through the weekend and the annual Cambridge Day gathering. Starting Tuesday, we'll turn this thing around.

PART IV
DEATH OF THE DREAM

That helicopter was green and gray
Like the sky that hangs over the lake
And I knew that you would fly one day for sure
'Cause you were made for more

-Girlyman, "Superior"

NINETEEN

Fly One Day

I'm up at 5 a.m. Saturday, preparing for a late afternoon barbecue. It's going to get busy once everyone arrives, and I hate feeling behind before the day has even begun. Especially on Cambridge Day, though it'll be a much smaller group than last year, with schedule conflicts for many of the usual suspects. Kate's with me this weekend, and I'm expecting Suzanne and her son Evan, Mary and Corinne, and another Mary, a friend from work. Suzanne will run the 5K at school this morning, then we'll check out the auction at Hubbard Hall, do a little shopping, and relax on the deck. This is exactly the day I need.

Kyle's up early, too. He and Eric have been hired for the summer at a theme park an hour north in Lake George. Only Kyle is scheduled to work this first day, so a friend picks him up. Eric sleeps in.

I'm wearing a sleeveless summer dress, sage green with scattered cream leaves; a shift, my mother would have called it. I feel an odd sort of light—light and heavy all at once, really, like I might sink into a pile on the floor, immovable, or, just as likely, float away. Disappear.

This used to be my favorite day of the week, Saturday— next to Friday night, that is—all possibility, forty-eight hours of freedom stretching out before me like an empty highway, but these days I choose not to look. Most weekends, I feel less liberated than sentenced, two days and three nights of solitary confinement, no contact with the outside world. With the kids far afield, off with their father or friends, my

The Full Catastrophe

own friends busy with other things, I often pull into the driveway on Friday nights and wander the house, staving off depression through the salvation of email and instant messenger, till I drag myself back out to work on Monday morning.

But this weekend I'll enjoy my friends and the promise of fun today, relaxation tomorrow. What could be better than that?

Okay, so I can think of a few things. I love these friends of mine, but I wish there were a guy in this picture, one who was more than a friend. I long for the one person whose job it is to be sure I don't wind up alone.

It's been two and a half years since my marriage exploded, though I was on my own long before that. The road from then to now is littered with lots of pain and broken dreams, but there's beauty, too, in no longer being afraid to be myself. In the freedom to choose who to love. Still, I'm weary. It's taken a lot of strength to stay hopeful, to keep believing better things are coming.

Not only that, I wish I felt as though my kids loved me more. They're the kids and I'm the adult, and my heart breaks for their losses. But it would be nice not to feel disregarded, ignored most days, and at the worst of times, plainly the enemy. The hostility I feel from them—some more than others, some days more than others—is bad enough, but the double bind has become a constant companion: nothing they say or do to me hurts nearly as much as the grief I feel over the people they are (or aren't) becoming.

There's something else, of course, something huge. Sometimes I picture a weather disturbance, the meteorologist explaining its complexities. The swirling line of thunderstorms that form the hurricane sweep over considerable territory, leaving nothing as it was. The heart of the system has its own distinct rotation, a part of—yet separate from—the instability in which it was created. She points to the eyewall, the hurricane's most devastating region, the columns of brutal wind, intense rain. All of the energy of the broader disturbance is centered here, she says, sucked into its violent vortex.

That's how I see us now, the Simonsons, fiercely thrown about, projectiles, none of us untouched by this storm, not one free from damage. But it's Eric who's become hopelessly trapped in its most destructive center.

This scares me so much that it seeps into my dreams no matter how hard I fight to keep it out. I don't want to talk about it. I need to talk about it. It's all I can think about. I'd give anything to stop thinking about where this tornado of trouble, building momentum, gathering speed, will finally make landfall, and what will lie broken in its path.

Yet.

There is this peace. I know, none of this sounds remotely peaceful. But moments of clarity appear without warning, when I understand that life is fleeting, that it's all about how we extend love while we're here. Some days I grab onto this sense of oneness with all of it—with all that has come before and all that is now and all that will ever be—and I'm overcome with the knowledge that all will be well. All is well.

And then it's gone.

Who are we if not jumbled balls of incongruity? I, like most of us, am so accustomed to living within this paradox that I rarely notice it and, unaware that it exists, become confused by the unnamed conflict I feel but can't describe.

Until living unaware is no longer possible. Until fear, overtaking both wakefulness and sleep, threatens to

The Full Catastrophe

consume. Until the fear that nothing will change succumbs to the fear that everything will change.

———

Suzanne and Evan pull in, and we head around the corner to the school. Kate and Evan ride their bikes while Suzanne and I walk and talk. Soon she's off and running, and I bump into the mom of one of Eric's friends, who asks how Eric is doing.

"Do you really want to hear the details?"

"We love Eric, Casey. What's wrong?"

A half hour later, I've dumped the story, the whole of it, as best I can: his failing out of college, enrollment in the Navy, and finally, tragically, the story of the charges against him. She grew up in Bennington, has connections in Vermont, and promises to call me later this afternoon with the name of a lawyer. I'm grateful. We'll take all the help we can get.

We arrive back at the house just as Kyle calls to say he's forgotten his driver's license; he won't be allowed to start work and needs a ride home. I pop into Eric's bedroom off the kitchen, shake him awake, and ask him to fetch his brother. A couple of hours later, they're back. Eric leans against the railing of the deck, smart-alecky as I ask him to take the recycling and an old gas grill to the transfer station.

"Sure Mom, I'll do it later. I have places to be." Then he and Kyle are right back out again, off to the lake and who knows where.

Me, I'm in and out all day as well. The four of us— Suzanne, Mary-of-Cambridge (as we've come to call her, so many Marys among our friends), Mary-from-work, and I—

Fly One Day

gather at the house after the road race, hit the silent auction, then move back home to regroup. The others decide on a little more shopping and walk back to Main while I have an instant-messenger fallout with a friend. I get up from the computer and burst into tears just as the boys appear in the kitchen. Eric opens his arms for a hug, but embarrassed and upset, I wave him away—"be home for dinner!" I say between sobs—and run past him to cry in the bathroom. When I emerge, the two of them are gone.

I move outside to the deck, breathe deeply, trying to pull myself together, and study the sky. Against a canvas of the bluest blue, cotton-ball clouds trail along, little puffs of white, as though they've been pulled apart, tossed back into the atmosphere and suspended there, altered. Lovely still. The air is motionless. It's one of those afternoons when you feel nothing...not warm, not a chill, not the breeze on your skin, the good kind of nothing. Everything just is.

My friends return and join me on the deck. We fire up the grill and examine their purchases. Before long, Kyle appears at the screen door separating the deck from the great room. I thought I heard the boys drive in, but I wasn't sure. He looks at me through the wire mesh, and I sense something strangely out of sync, though I can't put my finger on it.

"The cops are at the door," he says, his voice flat.

"Tell them I'm not here." I'm only half kidding.

In the past few months, I've filed police reports detailing Will's threatening behavior, listed items mysteriously missing from the house, and fielded inquiries about the whereabouts of Pop's rowboat, which, as it turned out, had simply floated away. I've had enough of the law to last me for a long time.

Kyle isn't laughing. "Mom, you'd better come." He seems frozen in place.

The Full Catastrophe

I open the door and pass him, then turn to head through the house, wondering where Eric is. My eyes rest for a moment on the framed picture that sits on the desk in the kitchen, the one I took of the three kids on the front porch a couple of years ago, when we were still a family. I notice movement at the front door, a straight shot two rooms away, where all I can make out is a uniformed shape. I kick Eric's sneakers and several throw pillows out of the path. Later, I'll ask him—again—to put things back together after he drags himself off the sofa.

I arrive at the door where a single officer stands, a local boy, looking as nervous as I suddenly feel.

"Yes?"

"Eric's been in a serious accident on 22."

He shifts from foot to foot, kneading the hat he holds in his hands.

"You need to get up to the hospital."

I stare at him.

"Now."

I sense Kyle standing behind me before I hear him speak. His voice is urgent, unyielding.

"I'm going with you."

Then, barely audible, "This is all my fault."

"Why?" I'm confused. How did I end up in this movie? I never asked to play this part.

His eyes trained on the floor, Kyle's words are barely audible. "We've been driving around all day, up to the lake, out to try to get Eric's friend to come with us to the covered bridge on the Battenkill. Back to the lake again…Eric was drinking, and I was the DD."

He looks out the window, his breathing shallow, and shakes his head as if he could will this nightmare away.

Fly One Day

"Eric started getting on me, telling me I wasn't shifting right, basically being an ass. I pulled into the driveway, got out of the car, and told him I wasn't driving him everywhere while he yelled at me." He massages his forehead with the palm of his hand. "I said he'd better not be driving either. I tried to grab the keys, Mom, but he's too strong. I couldn't do it. That's when I came into the house."

I gently place a hand on Kyle's upper arm and meet his eyes with mine. I will the unexpected calm I feel—calm I could never have imagined in the face of such tragedy—to flow through me into him.

"Of course we'll both go, but you won't be able to hear anything I say once we're there, so you need to listen to me now. No matter what happens, none of this is your fault. Do you understand? Eric made his own choices. You couldn't have stopped him from driving away, no matter how hard you'd tried."

Even as I say them, I understand these words are as much for me as they are for Kyle.

As I move back to the deck where the others sit, unaware of what's happened, things slow down and speed up all at once. Thoughts flash past, unbeckoned.

Turning from Kyle:

You knew this nightmare was never going to end well. This is the day you knew was coming—the day you find out how the story ends.

Crossing the room:

You're just a character in this film. The script was written long ago. Your job now is to walk through it gracefully.

Stopping in the kitchen to gather myself:

Strange, this doesn't feel like chaos; it's more like the pieces are falling into place. I can see them now, dozens of jigsaw shapes, each a problem with no solution, whirling wildly in the air, suddenly assembling themselves into a finished whole, the one they were always meant to form.

Now it's my turn to stand at the door to the deck and deliver the news.

—

The Mary McClellan Hospital ER is tiny, unlike the hospitals of my childhood where I sat with a sick parent, a labyrinth of spaces that led to places where frightening things occurred. The waiting room is empty, as though they've cleared the place for us. I picture myself here in years past, with children ill or nursing minor injuries. Not three months ago, it was Eric and John waiting for me with my broken ankle, eager to be on their way to the mountain.

I take a chair beside Suzanne, who drove us to the hospital while the others hold down the fort at home. My body tense and hands clasped, I stare off, while Kyle paces outside. Though I'm mostly quiet, praying for a miracle, deep within I sense this is not how today will end.

The receptionist says they're stabilizing Eric and I can't go in to see him yet, which tells me there's something beyond broken bones going on in there. I run through the options, none of them good. I believe he could live on, paralyzed, and though there would be challenges, we would meet them together. He could still have a full and happy life. But other possibilities torment me.

If this is a tragedy we're having today, please let it be finite. As guilty as I feel even as this thought flashes past, there have been too many years of long-term tragedies for us. I don't know if we—if I—could endure another. The thought of our visiting Eric in a nursing home for decades into the future,

Fly One Day

seeing my effervescent son barely able to think or function, the core of who he is stripped away, is more than I can bear.

I stay outwardly calm, both for Kyle and, in no small part, because I am no stranger to sudden loss. Yet as well as I know the script, I've never been in this particular scene. It has never been my child.

When panic rises, I breathe deeply, quietly reciting the mantras that remind me of the things that have gotten me through the past couple of years.

Trust that you already have everything you need within you.
Eric will always be with you, no matter what happens today.
Stay open. Accept whatever comes.

Periodically, the what-ifs rise to the surface. I whack them down the best I can.

Finally, the vision of another person maimed or killed due to Eric's recklessness ties me in knots. I need answers. The emergency personnel—a pair of local men unlucky enough to be on duty that afternoon—are waiting solemnly with their equipment in the tiny vestibule between the ER and the door to the outside world. The looks on their faces as I approach tell me they would rather be anywhere in the world than here, talking to anyone other than me.

"Was anyone else in the car? Were other cars involved? Is Eric the only one hurt?" I know I'm badgering them. I don't care.

They shake their heads. An EMT wipes his eyes with the back of his hand and responds so softly I struggle to hear. "Nope. Just Eric."

A few minutes pass. Agitated again, I push the door open once more to reach the only people with the answers I need.

"How did this happen? I don't understand."

The Full Catastrophe

Silently, in a gesture that will stay with me for the rest of my life, one man cups his hand and drives his fingers downward, hitting an imaginary gulley, then makes a sharp turn upward and arcs through the air until, brought down by gravity, his fingers slam earthward, ending with a violent bounce.

Gradually, it becomes clear. He hit the ditch with great force. He flew. How like Eric.

Then he crashed.

Kyle is outside, pacing. Now he's inside with us, calling his dad's cell, a number I'm not permitted to know. I hear him telling his father the bare minimum, saving the hard truth for when Will arrives.

"Eric's had an accident, Dad. You need to get to the ER. No, it can't wait till you're done with work. Come now." Visibly frustrated, his voice gets louder, angrier. "Jesus, Dad, get the fuck up here!" He slams the receiver into the wall and storms back outside.

After what seems like hours but is in reality no more than twenty minutes, Dr. Bergen—who's treated me in the past and is on ER duty today—emerges. I picture her on my most recent visit, asking about the divorce and custody battle, then folding her arms as she met my eyes with hers. "Stress takes a toll," she said then. "The body can only take so much."

Here in the waiting room, she gently grasps my shoulders, her own shoulders stooped as if someone has given her a thousand-ton weight to pass on to me.

"I'm so sorry. We did everything we could."

I look at her for more. I need more.

"Eric didn't make it."

Everything is suddenly quiet in my head as I take in what seems like the only outcome that has ever made sense.

Fly One Day

Absorbing the inevitable.

What I hear Dr. Bergen say, as gentle as she is in delivering the news, is this: "Here. Hoist this onto your shoulders along with the load you already bear and carry that around for the rest of your life." I don't know how I can do this—I'm overwhelmed with fear just thinking about it—but if there's one thing life has taught me, it's that I have no choice.

Dr. Bergen steps back, assessing my reaction.

"I know what you've been through, Casey, how you lost your family, and I know the hell you've been living now. When they told me this was your son, I couldn't believe it. I am so, so sorry."

With nothing left to say, she disappears behind the door that separates me from what's left of Eric.

—

We like to think things happen sequentially, that if we could just gather the witnesses, a reasonably reliable recreation of the events of a day could be assembled. But time is a funny thing. It teases us with notions of its constancy, lulls us into believing in its immutable properties. Then comes a day when it takes a break, when no amount of recounting of events can bring order to what has happened.

I was in a rush that morning. I broke with routine. Get to the school, get back home. Get Kyle off to work. Get dinner ready; the guests will be waiting. Get on the computer. Get myself back together. I put aside the predictable steps that typically dictated my days. Maybe I dressed before doing my hair. Maybe the jewelry went on first instead of last. I don't remember, and why would I? Such inconsequential,

The Full Catastrophe

fleeting details.

But I do remember one thing: In my hurry, I forgot to wear my watch.

In later years, I would come to think of this as the day there was no time.

So for this reason, or perhaps for no reason at all, no matter how I try, I can't put a sequence to the events of that afternoon. Everything I said was the first thing I said. Everything I thought, I thought the moment I heard.

I turn to Suzanne, who stands beside me.

"I've been letting go of Eric for a very long time."

To everyone else, this seems like a tragic, sudden death. And it is, a clean break. What they don't understand is that Eric's been leaving me bit by bit since long before today.

"I have way too much practice at this."

I know too well when someone dies, they're not coming back.

In a few minutes, Will and his family will arrive. So will Eric's friends. I know they'll look to me for guidance. I may not receive exactly what I extend to them, but will I meet condolences with righteous anger? Be the victim? Or will I accept the comfort they offer?

No single person did this. Eric's death is a tragedy that will affect us all. I can choose conflict and blame in this horrific moment. Or I can choose peace.

Before long, a nurse appears and holds open the door from the waiting room to the inner sanctum of the ER. "You can come in now," she says.

I stand, smoothing my wispy summer dress and unsticking my bare legs from the vinyl chair where I've waited for a half hour that's seemed like days. Praying. Knowing yet not knowing. I look for Kyle but he's nowhere to be found.

Fly One Day

Suzanne follows me, and the nurse, somber and anxious, steers me to the first room on the right, the same room where I spent a long Sunday with one-year-old Katie who'd burned her hand on a space heater in a freak October snowstorm. She left bandaged and groggy, yet she'd be fine—*the worst is over*, I thought then.

But now Eric lies on a gurney in the center of the room. I study his face: the small scar near his widow's peak, where he had those stitches after sliding into the woodwork in his rush to get to the lake. The single dimple caused by jamming his knee into his face all those years ago, when jumping off a dirt pile was thrill enough for him. His eyes are closed but his mouth is open, and his teeth are as perfect as ever. It's obvious that the tubes and needles and various tools essential to a last-ditch lifesaving effort have been removed and hidden away out of respect for a mother's last goodbye.

The air is heavy and charged and smells of antiseptic. I stand on Eric's left, near his chest, and take his hand. A warm tear slides down my cheek. This whole thing is surreal. Hasn't it only been a few hours since he was dashing out the door, promising to be home for dinner?

Suzanne stands to my left, beside Eric's feet. A sacred witness.

I sense several nurses behind me, and one grasps my elbow. "Hold onto her, she'll faint," he warns. This high drama, however well-intended, is jarring. I shake him off and ask them to leave us alone. They don't understand—how can they?—that there is peace in this scene, peace with great sadness, but peace nonetheless.

They leave the room, and I talk to Eric, mostly in my mind. I tell him how much I love him, how devastated I am that he has to leave. That we both did the best we could, and

The Full Catastrophe

there's nothing to forgive. That I can't wait to see him again one day. I sense his soul knew better than to hang around while they made their fruitless attempts at bringing him back. I feel him in the room with me for an instant—a breeze on my face that sends shivers down my spine—then suddenly it's gone.

After a time, I turn to Suzanne.

"He's not here."

She hugs me, rubs my back. "I know."

Back in the waiting room, I ask for Kyle. Someone says he rode home with our neighbor, a member of the village police department. I sit.

I'm aware of a sound outside the window, a loud idling that's been there all along but only now registers. It hits me all at once: the helicopter is waiting to take Eric to a major medical center. If he needs it.

He won't need it.

I don't understand how we never heard it fly overhead as we sat on the deck. Or how we missed the fire siren and the ambulance screaming through the village on the way to the crash.

One by one, the emergency personnel, the doctors and nurses who have lived through their own personal horror this afternoon, offer their condolences. "This must have been so terrible for you," I say, taking their hands in mine as they stand in front of the chair where I sit. "Will you be okay?"

Mostly, they stare, nodding yes, they'll be fine. Some of them cry. I wonder if they think I haven't quite absorbed what's happened, if I don't yet comprehend my son is dead.

They may never grasp how fully I understand this loss.

News travels fast in the village, and friends arrive at the ER. My pastor and his wife. Another couple, whose five-

Fly One Day

year-old son was run over by a milk truck years ago; they know this pain firsthand. Each of them knows Will can be unpredictable, hostile, especially toward me. They're here as much for protection as for comfort. All eyes are on the door.

Soon Will arrives, desperate, and without a word, he knows. He collapses into me, limp and pleading, as I expected he would. "My boy, my boy," he cries, and I hold him and comfort him as best I can. He takes his turn with Eric and emerges much later, only after gentle prodding by hospital personnel. I say goodbye, dreading the funeral planning that awaits us this week. Grateful to be able to support him in this cataclysmic grief.

TWENTY

All Roads Lead Here

Finally, there's nothing to do but leave. Suzanne and I ride down to the village in silence and arrive at the house, where the Marys are waiting for us with food and coffee. Others trickle in. Calls are made.

Life blurs at the edges. At some point, Kate rides in on her bike, angry and oppositional. She doesn't stick around to hear the details; somehow, she already knows. Kyle's with friends, or maybe he's home and his friends are here. Momentarily I wonder where Eric is. Oh. I close my eyes and shake the tears away. The lump in my throat refuses to budge.

Nothing seems stable. Even the rooms look warped by this monumental shift in reality. I walk through the house from back to front, the same route I took a few hours ago. A lifetime ago. Everything swells with heightened, painful significance. The collection of pitchers and bells that march across the shaker peg rack shelf—"the empty vessel and the cry for help," as Mary likes to say. The flowered Queen Anne chairs, where I read Eric *Oh, The Places You'll Go.* The counted cross-stitch sampler, which I planned to give him when he had his first home—*In my father's house are many mansions. I have come to prepare a place for you.* More tears.

Reaching down, I pick up the throw pillows I kicked aside back when my beloved son was alive and place them gently on the sofa, mindlessly arranging them the way I do after he stretches out there. I set his sneakers neatly by the door and notice the frayed laces. *I'll pick some up tomorrow,* I hear myself think. *I'll add shoes to Eric's Christmas list. Maybe*

251

The Full Catastrophe

Adidas this time.

Walking back through the kitchen, I notice some of the food that's already arrived is piled on the desk next to the refrigerator, where the photo of the three kids—my whole world—has been knocked face down. I walk on and lower myself into a chair, suddenly too exhausted to do anything but sit.

Later, when all the guests are gone but Suzanne, we make up the pullout sofa so she can spend the night. I climb the stairs to my bedroom and strip my clothes off at a snail's pace, as though any alteration from the way I was this morning, when Eric was still here, requires nothing short of reverence. Moving forward feels like walking through mud. I imagine being sucked into the ever-present quicksand of the morning cartoons of my childhood with no hope of rescue.

In the morning I awaken, coming slowly to consciousness, gradually aware of the relentless cooing of a mourning dove outside my window. A soothing sound, it seems to me. A trick. My body knows before my mind does, in that odd way our cells have of knowing. My eyes fill with tears, and I shake without understanding why. My brain struggles to catch up. What has overcome me?

Oh. That's it. My son is dead. There's a rising panic and the first pang of "Why?"—the dangerous question I haven't allowed myself to ask in fully conscious moments. The otherworldly sound that bleeds through the windows is now inside the room. Gradually, I realize its source: it comes from me.

It takes Suzanne no time to move from the sofa downstairs, where she's kept vigil on this first night of inconceivable loss, to the bed beside me. She crawls in and holds me, and we rock together until the grief has let me go.

I think of other mornings when wakefulness also came

slowly, accompanied by the gradual integration of all the other deaths—my parents, Tommy, Esther and Mack and Louise. El, who came to stay after Eric's difficult birth—Eric, the child no longer with me. The grief of those mornings fades against the backdrop of this present loss.

—

All week long, I'm surrounded by precious people who turn up in droves, bringing food and bags brimming with paper goods and cleaning products, the things you neglect to think of when life comes to a screeching halt. Over and over, a friend lays food in front of me—a sandwich, a bit of a casserole someone has left—and pours me a glass of wine. Over and over, someone eventually removes the plate, food untouched, though somehow I'm able to get sips of the wine to slide through the constriction that has taken up residence in my throat.

Already I know I'll never forget these scenes: parents of Eric's friends sitting on the floor in the living room the night he died, having appeared at our door as soon as they heard, one by one, disbelieving. I see Kyle's buddy standing silent in the doorway, his presence more profound than any words he could patch together. My closest friends—the practical angels—bustling about in the kitchen, one of them spending each night with me until they feel sure I'll be okay on my own. And Corinne, Mary's younger daughter, taking Eric's place in the recliner and watching VH1 for hours one afternoon, sitting her own brand of shiva.

My cousins get in touch, all four of them, and friends from long ago come to reestablish our bonds, wondering how we lost them in the first place. People share their souls, their own grief, kept hidden for so long. Grief has shaken the illusion that we're separate from each other and dissolved the boundaries we think will keep us safe. This week those walls are thin.

Eric's friend Sarah calls and asks if she and another friend can come for a visit. "We need to be there," she says, weeping. Kyle, it turns out, called her house as soon as he returned from the hospital, then drove there to be with her as the devastating news of Eric's death spread quickly among their friends.

The girls come by more than once this week, spending hours each time, and they look to me and Suzanne to help them deal with this tragic loss when they're not yet out of their teens.

"Everything in this life is temporary," I say. "Eric is still with us, just not in the way we wish he was. His body is gone, but his spirit will be with us forever."

They nod their heads, cheeks awash with tears, and seem to find comfort in what we say. I'm comforted, too. In putting words to the beliefs that have carried me through all that's happened, I understand it better now than I ever have.

The girls reminisce about Eric, the things they've done together and the secrets they've shared. Sarah tells me that a combination of Hugo Boss and cigarette smoke will always be his scent to her, that she'll never forget him, that she'll love him forever. I'm sure I'll see more of Sarah in the weeks to come.

Alternating waves of deep sadness and moments of quiet clarity define my days. I fall into bed each night and try to untangle the emotions knotted inside me. I'd give my own life to undo what's happened, to keep Eric safe at home that day. His passing feels like the worst combination of the long decline of a terminal illness and the trauma of a sudden death. I began to process what it would be like to live without Eric—imagining that absence might be due to estrangement or, worse yet, imprisonment—long before the day he died, much as I imagine parents of a terminally ill child or one fighting addiction might.

I was certain I could never survive losing a child. Yet somehow, with love surrounding me and love deep within, I understand that I will.

Others, strangers until now, take me aside to whisper about their love for Eric and, most touching of all, his love for me. His teachers. His friends' parents. Childhood friends and new friends from college and work.

Rick from Willard Mountain comes by one afternoon. "Eric was such a great guy," he says. "One of a kind. We're more than fifteen years apart, but when my friends from Wisconsin, where I used to live, ask who my snowboarding buddies are here, I tell them, 'I met this awesome kid…'"

I smile through my tears. I'm getting used to this, the grief moving aside to make room for a pinpoint of joy when I least expect it.

"Eric was telling me only a couple of weeks ago about how he has a tough relationship with his dad, but he can talk to you about anything." I'm sad to learn Eric and Will still struggled. Eric's needed his father these past months more than ever, but knowing he felt he could confide in me is a gift. Rick's words feel like a message from Eric, so they mean more to me than any condolence possibly could.

Rick waits around as the crowd thins, then, when we're alone, quietly shares that his three-year-old son drowned several years ago. "We have a bond," he says.

Tragedy is everywhere, it seems. Yet life continues.

Between and during these visits, I alternately make and receive countless phone calls, breaking the news and accepting, again and again, the condolences others offer through tears. I'm grateful for all of it.

I've been so afraid of being alone, of having no place to belong. But now I question everything I thought was true. Maybe I'm not alone after all. Maybe I never was.

Suzanne and I have spoken often in the years since we met of accepting our roles as simply observers of what appears around the next bend. So this week, I'm blown away with the realization that so much of what I've learned during this time has prepared me for what's happening now.

One afternoon, a Bruce Cockburn CD playing in the background as usual, I shiver as I listen closely to the verse I haven't realized so perfectly fits the events of Eric's death. It's as if I were hearing it for the first time:

Black snake highway, sheet metal ballet
It's just so much snow on a summer's day
We all must leave, but it's not the end
We'll meet again at the Festival of Friends

Again I'm struck by how all roads have seemed to led to this day. Talking with Suzanne, I struggle to express the sheer wonder of this phenomenon, and we lock eyes.

"I know," she mouths again, silently. "I know."

———

On Sunday, another jarringly beautiful afternoon, Will and I, maintaining a tenuous truce, sit on the deck with the couple who run the funeral home to plan Eric's farewell. We agree to wait until next weekend to hold the service. My motives are mixed. I worry aloud that finals and Regents exams will keep his friends from attending during the week. The deeper truth is that I need them there, maybe more than they need me.

Will suggests establishing a memorial fund where donations will be used to send kids to soccer camp. I'll handle the money; he'll contact the school to set things up. Will wants to bury Eric at Woodland Cemetery—the one in my dream—in his parents' plot, where they have an extra space. We visit the funeral home, where Will selects the casket. I agree with all of it. Eric is with me everywhere now. That body is no longer my son.

While our house is filled with more friends than I knew I had, others have seen Will walking around town alone. Repeatedly over the next days, he appears at the door with offerings, things he found in the car—now at the body shop awaiting demolition—or at the accident site, far from where the Audi came crashing down, having been thrown from the vehicle with violent force. Like Eric. He has Eric's wallet. A piece of clothing. A bag that was in the car. A piece of the car itself.

It's clear he wants to be at our house, where Eric lived. I know he needs me, and I want to be there for him. I'm grateful for a reprieve from the hostilities, even a temporary one. But it's all I can do to hold myself together and support the kids. I'm not angry with Will. I'm sad for him. But I can't be his strength.

He comes in to look at the oversized felt boards where we've tacked up photos of Eric to display at the calling hours: Eric as a baby, with family, with friends. Eric in soccer and baseball, on his snowboard, on skis at the lake. I select scenes that include all the people important to him, who will, I'm sure, look to see if they've been included. *We were close, I loved him*, I imagine them thinking, as they slowly walk past the display, hearts heavy with grief.

I understand Will's need to visit the place where Eric died, but I don't share his compulsion. I have no need to see the car (unrecognizable, Will tells me) or the field of grain with the imprint of a mass of mangled steel marring its beauty. I don't need to go there to believe it's real; I don't need to avoid it either. When it's time, I'll know. I find greater meaning in Eric's life, in who he was…no, who he *is*, living on with me in spirit. Closer to me now, in many ways, than he has been in years.

———

A teacher from the high school stops by one afternoon with condolences and an unopened carton of yearbooks from Eric's senior year and sets the box on the floor. "I thought you might want these now. Maybe there are relatives or friends who would appreciate having them." I push them into the corner after she leaves and wait for them to call to me.

These days feel scriptless, stripped of schedules. Instead, I'm carried by the hours, doing what seems necessary in each moment, letting something—or someone—greater than myself order my steps. One afternoon, the box beckons me and, surrounded by friends from town and from work, I take a new yearbook and stare at its cover. I never got a good look at Eric's copy, its pages covered with handwritten comments about parties and other escapades, and that was fine. I'd figured there'd be plenty of time later to talk about his many adventures, long after his high school days were over.

All Roads Lead Here

"C'mon, Mom," he'd say, laughing. "Did you really think I was a goodie two-shoes back then?"

"Wanna bet he was elected Most Daring?" I say now, only half joking. I flip through the pages, hearing that brand-new-book crack of the binding, breathing in the scent of fresh ink on crisp paper. I've expected to feel the little stab of heartbreak that comes when I see his hopeful face in the senior picture, though I also detect a tinge of sadness in his eyes even then. My breath catches when I see the quotes he selected: "Live while you live," so reminiscent of my dad's approach to life, and, eerier still, "What is done cannot be undone."

Next I turn to the "class celebrities" section—most likely to succeed, class clown, most popular—and there they are, Eric and his friend Megan, side by side, proud to have been elected Most Daring. I never heard this news. Yet, somehow, I knew.

Being fearless and reckless are two different things, I think. How I wish he'd known the difference.

From the time he was mobile, there was always something about air with Eric. Air, and flying; joy mixed with danger. It was transcendence, really, that drew him in. His devotion to soccer was rivaled early on by his passion for the lake and, more specifically, the boat. Before he could ski, he begged to be towed on a tube, then held onto the rope and bounced from wave to wave with a smile so huge it took over his face, while I prayed he'd make it around the lake safely. Later, Eric missed no opportunity to get out on the water skis and jump the wake, the faster, the higher, the better. As soon as he cruised into shore, he'd clamor to go again. Again! When snow skiing, his winter thrill, proved too tame for his tastes, snowboarding became his obsession. Straight airs or spins, flips or inverted rotations, he told us how riding gave him the feeling of soaring and the freedom to fly. So foreign to me, never a risk taker, I took him at his word. Now it will be a line in his obituary.

I see the big picture now with the sort of clarity that often only comes when something is over. Eric loved soccer, water skiing, the mountain and the snowboard that seemed like an extension of his own body. But it wasn't the ball, it was the altitude and the flight, his ability to launch it into the atmosphere with grand precision, direct its path. It wasn't the water, it was the feeling of weightlessness, the out-of-body experience that allowed him to give up his grounding, break free from the gravity that held him down. And it wasn't the snow, either. It was the air—big air, he called it. The freedom to fly.

In death as in life, Eric went big. Failing to negotiate a curve, the police told me, his old silver Audi pitched wildly into a ditch, then went airborne. It nosedived into a field of alfalfa and Eric—Eric's body, by then, his aorta severed on impact, we'd later learn—came to rest amid the golden grain a distance from the crumpled car. He'd left us just as he'd arrived, just as he'd lived: with a bang.

Someone has turned to a section of the yearbook I missed, pages of photos of wide-eyed babies, kids now nearly grown. I smile when I spot it, the shot of him at three, standing on the top rung of the slide's ladder, his little face staring expectantly into the far distance, pointing at something beyond and above him, out of the camera's range. Pointing to the sky.

I took this picture back then, and I selected and submitted it in his junior year, along with this caption: "You always saw it out there Eric. It's time! Have courage, faith, and know we love you. The sky's the limit."

And apparently it was.

———

Since the crash, I've spent the greater part of my days inside my head, working out the spiritual and philosophical conundrums that consume me, trying to make sense of Eric's life and death.

I've thought a lot about this: all those years I worried Eric would die in his twenties, as my brother had, all of those medications and dietary modifications and visits to the specialist, only to have it come to this. I pushed him to live cautiously in relation to his FH, yet his cavalier behavior caught up with him in a different way. The fact that his autopsy revealed relatively little arterial occlusion only adds to the tragic irony.

Sitting at the kitchen table late one morning, I picture Eric before everything came crashing down around him. His inherent daredevil nature, amplified by the invincibility of youth, collided with the shitshow that was his life over the past couple of years and culminated in this tragic outcome. Yet the devastation of this loss won't destroy my ability to remember Eric as he truly was: a free spirit, so full of light and joy.

Soon a news crew appears on the front porch in search of an interview. The grieving-mother-sobbing-at-the-door scenario is not for me, but Kyle wants to talk to them. Though I'm wary, I move aside.

"Tell us about the last time you saw your brother," the reporter begins.

"Cut!" I step in front of the camera and hold up my hand.

The Full Catastrophe

"Stop right there. This will not be a melodramatic interview about the traumatic day his brother died. You can talk about Eric, who he was, what he was like. That is it." I speak with the authority of a woman with little left to lose, daring them to cross me now.

"Of course," says the reporter and begins again. She asks Kyle about Eric and gets her soundbite.

"The piece will air on the late news," she says as they pack up. "Again, we're so sorry for your loss."

When it's time for the newscast, my friends and I gather in the living room. Kyle's out, and Kate's MIA for the evening. A few calls later, I discover she's hiding out at a neighbor's, her way to avoid being around for the news. The VCR is set to record, and we wait for the segment to air. Suddenly, the full-color image I'm not at all prepared to see fills the screen: that silver Audi, Eric's ticket to college and a life away from the mess at home, mangled beyond recognition. I suck in an involuntary breath, then blow it out slowly.

Okay, so now I've seen it. Guess that's how it was supposed to happen. They go to commercial.

When the news returns, they display the photos I showed them of Eric walking off the soccer field, another of him in action. "He was a high school soccer star, a bright light on the field," the anchor declares. "Now, the light has gone out." Scenes of the village, of our house, a quick interview with Will. Then Kyle appears, the microphone tipped in his direction.

"Tell me about your brother," says the reporter. Kyle, looking so young and so old all at once, both authoritative and thoroughly lost, describes how they liked so many of the same things, the music, the sports. "I guess you could say we rubbed off on each other," he concludes with a small, sad smile.

I've been holding back tears all day. Now they finally come.

———

Midweek, I answer the front door again, this time to two county sheriffs—unfamiliar faces—who ask to come in. I offer them a seat, and Mary and Suzanne, who sense the need to monitor the situation, join us in the living room. The officers introduce themselves and offer their condolences.

I'm confused, unsure why they're here.

"Do you know where Eric got the alcohol?" asks the officer who does all the talking.

"I have no idea. But I don't understand. I know he was underage, but what does it matter now? He's dead." I'm not being sarcastic or argumentative. I honestly don't get what they're after.

He explains it's their job to investigate incidents involving minors and drinking, then moves on to a new topic.

"We know he was facing charges in Vermont. He must've been very upset."

"He was, of course."

"Upset enough to do something drastic?"

I see where he's going with this. They're deciding whether to deem Eric's death a suicide.

"Things weren't going well, that's true, but the trial wasn't going to happen until October. I really don't believe he was desperate enough to have done this intentionally."

I've imagined, in quiet moments, what Eric might've been thinking as he rode around, drinking, with Kyle at the

263

wheel, then drove away on his own. If he was thinking at all, with a blood alcohol level nearly three times the legal limit.

Fuck it. Who cares about risk? What have I got to lose?

But I can only do this in small doses. I'm not yet ready to go all the way with this scenario—put myself in Eric's place, feel the car hit the ditch and fly. Did he realize, too late, that he'd gone too far? Did he cry out, regretting the one mistake he could never take back?

What is done cannot be undone.

The hardest part is that I'll never know the truth.

Nodding slowly, the officer takes in what I've told him. He stands, draws himself up to his full six-foot-plus height, and extends a hand. "Thank you so much for your time, Mrs. Simonson. Again, we can't tell you how sorry we are for your loss. Such a tragedy. We'll be closing the investigation."

I see them out and fall into the recliner, praying for the day a knock on the door will bring good news.

TWENTY-ONE

Brighter in the Dark

When I wake up on Thursday, I know it's time. It feels as though I've lived a lifetime in the five days since the accident, sleeping and waking and going through the motions, alternately delivering the unthinkable news and accepting condolence after condolence, words wholly inadequate now. Yet as consumed as I am by grief, some vestige of the person I was before life changed forever remains: I need a dress for the memorial service.

I've left the house just once this week, making the short drive around the corner on Tuesday afternoon to the local printer, and I felt oddly neon. In our small village, there are few secrets. Two women I knew from the bank and the sidelines of soccer games walked past, glanced my way, then looked again, long, lingering stares. I imagined the thoughts that ran through their heads: *There goes the mother of the boy who died in Saturday's crash.* These were the things I was sure they'd tell their friends and family as soon as they got home.

I pushed open the door of the print shop, intending to ask the price for a memorial program with a color reproduction of my favorite photo of Eric, the one of him holding his snowboard. When the owner looked up from his work in the back room and caught sight of me through the glass, there was no question he'd heard the news. His eyes brimmed with tears as he said over and over how sorry he was. He'd print twice the number of bulletins I'd requested. No charge. Please don't argue. It's the least I can do.

Now I drive over winding country roads to the mall,

forty-five minutes away. There, no one will know who I am. I alternate between terrible waves of sadness and intervals of peace and sense Eric in the seat beside me. I talk to him, reach out and hold his hand, remembering those long-ago trips to the mall with my little boy, my sidekick, in those days still safe in the passenger's seat.

Eyes fixed on the road, I see myself in the kitchen last Saturday. The last time I saw Eric alive. When I ran past him to cry in the bathroom, how could I have known he'd never be back? I'd give everything I have for one more chance to take that hug and make it last forever.

As I drive, I give myself over to the embrace of farmland. I'm shaken by how intense the colors are, how the greens and blues of the earth and sky seem oversaturated, how the bright sunshine is almost too much to bear. How, incredibly, the world seems to have gone on without me. Without Eric.

I don't quite feel neon in the mall among strangers, but there's something else.

I may look like you, I think as I join several other women browsing through the racks, *but you have no idea who I am.* Maybe they're preparing for a daughter's rehearsal dinner, a son's award ceremony. Maybe they assume I'm doing the same.

A chatty saleswoman is helping another customer make her selection, and I prepare myself for the question I'm certain will come: "Is this for a special occasion?"

Silently, I rehearse my answer, sad yet serene. "Yes, it's for my son's memorial. He's the boy who died in Cambridge last weekend."

She doesn't ask. I'm a little disappointed.

Who am I now, if not the mother of the boy who died? If I can't help others know Eric, will anyone ever know me?

Brighter in the Dark

It feels as if I'm floating as I search for a dress I can't describe. This will be a day to honor Eric, to celebrate him and his vibrant life. I won't be the stereotypical black-veiled anguished mother of the boy who died.

I hang several pieces on the hook in the fitting room and slide the curtain closed. The first dress isn't right. Too morose. Too matronly. Not me. Next, I slip on a stretchy, slightly form-fitting below-the-knee dress in cream and black. It feels chameleon to me, as if it can be whatever I need it to be. As soon as it clears my shoulders and falls around me, I know: this is the one.

I hear Eric's four-year-old voice commenting in wonder, just as he did when I modeled a dress I'd tried on back then: "Wow, Mommy, you look just like a teenager!" Before I could feel too flattered, though, he followed up with the timing of a seasoned pro: "All except for the face." Even now, just days after the crash, this makes me laugh, a bittersweet chuckle somewhere deep within, equal parts reverie and heartache.

Other memories flood in. From leaping off that mountain of dirt at eight years old, to a lifetime of soccer, water skiing, and snowboarding, to an adolescent dreaming of the next big thing, each time a look of sheer determination alternated with Eric's freckle-faced grin. Pure joy.

The saleswoman produces a cropped black cardigan. I put it on and stare at myself in the mirror.

Yes, I am buying a dress to wear to bury Eric.

And yes, though I can't see it now, I will go on to have happy moments in this dress.

The unthinkable has happened. My son has died. Yet I'm awed at how those difficult years prepared me for his passing. Just in time, I understood our connection to those we love doesn't end with death, that nothing can separate us unless we choose to walk away. That it will all be over so soon for all of us, and what's important is what we do while we're here.

Though I know I can't skip over the pain of loss, I see now the best way to honor Eric is to choose a life of joy. The life he won't get to have.

———

Eric's casket, closed at my request, is surrounded by endless sunflowers and roses and hydrangeas, in vases on stands and on the floor, an enormous spray on the casket itself, beside the framed photos of the boy—the young man—we knew in happier times. I watch Kyle and Kate at this first public event with one-third of their trio absent. They mingle with friends and family they spot in the line as it snakes through the adjoining rooms, past the photo displays, along the rows of chairs and through the archway before reaching us.

Someone starts the "mourning mixed tape" put together by a couple of girls who've been Eric's friends since childhood. At some point standard organ-heavy "wake music" begins to play; I bristle, they switch it back, and I realize how songs like "Let it Be," and "Wildflowers" have calmed me. Even "I'll Be Missing You"—the rap tribute to a fallen friend that was Eric's obsession, uncanny now in its significance—has found its way onto the playlist. My usual concern over what others might think has flown right out the window.

Hundreds of people stand solemnly in that line, some of them crying, still in shock. I suspect they wonder how they would do it if were they the grieving parents and dig deep for what they will say to us. By and large, they come up short, but that's okay; they come. Many of them carry the guilt of not having been there for Eric like a weighty offering, blurting out their regret even when they have told themselves they wouldn't, that his family has its own struggles. Others wrap us in a desperate embrace, out of words.

I tell each one, sometimes through tears, mostly the things I need to hear myself: that whatever they wish they'd said to Eric, done for him, he knows this now. That they can, like him, rest in peace. That I believe God knew the day Eric was born that this was the day he would leave us, though we're just learning it now. That this is the life Eric was meant to live.

Since I was small, I've struggled to make sense of one senseless loss after another—a relentless march of deaths, the collapse of our family, the years of feeling so alone in the world. I've found meaning not in the losses but in the way I choose to see them. And I'm struck this week by the simplicity of the things I've come to believe.

Our time here is short.

Everyone dies at the end.

All that matters is love.

The funeral directors offered to move the casket to a private room so that those who wish to view the body could visit before the evening calling hours begin. Eric is everywhere now, yet I know this is where I need to be. Kate and Kyle want to see their brother one last time, and I won't let them do that without me. And though I'm certain Eric's spirit will remain with us, this is the last time I'll be able to see my son in the physical form I have loved since the moment I first held him, to study his face and memorize the features I will never see again in this life.

The Full Catastrophe

As I kneel next to Eric with Kate beside me, he looks as if he's sleeping, like he had a tough day and needs to rest a while. His mouth is slightly swollen, but it's my boy lying there. *No sign of a struggle*, I think, which strikes me as ironic, given how deeply he struggled in life. I speak to him softly, reminding him of how much he is loved, how he will never be forgotten, and wipe the tears that trail down my cheeks, knowing I don't need his body here to tell him this.

Covering the hands they crossed over his chest with my own, my gaze falls on his fingernails, bitten short as usual, and comes to rest on the oversized shirt I chose with care, wanting him to look like the boy—the young man—we've all known and loved. *Oh, Eric, you'd never have posed that way, so stiff and formal*, I tell him without words.

Though it's Eric's lifeless body in the casket, that's not what I see. Instead, he's a newborn, looking up at me as he nurses, eyes wide, pausing to flash a sated smile. He might've been signaling hunger, or need. But I loved him with a love bigger than any I'd ever known, and I was certain it was love I saw gazing back at me. I'm still just as sure of that now.

Now he's on his bike on the driveway, jumping over ramps he hammered together from scrap wood in the garage. Sitting on the floor, leaning against the wall near the front door on Christmas morning, eyes wide again as he opens his first set of snow skis and boots. Coaching PeeWee soccer. Doing tricks on his snowboard. Carting the water skis up to camp after a day on the water.

Mercifully passing over the recent difficult years, I see him walking the stage at college graduation. Standing at the head of the aisle watching his bride walk toward him. Holding his first newborn. In middle age, slightly balding, still playing soccer with his adventure-loving kids, telling me the stories I'll never get to hear, the ones about his misadventures as a foolish teen. And the hardest one of all: holding my hand as I lay dying, the way I've imagined it since the day he was born.

A wave of fondness and empathy overcomes me then, and with a sad smile that holds the story of all that's happened, I tell him how I understand. How I know he's been through the war and that he's earned this respite from the weight of it all.

I sense movement next to me; Kate is nestling Wrinkles——the Beanie Baby she gave her big brother when he went off to college and retrieved from his room sometime this week—between Eric and the casket's satin lining. I pull her close. She lets me hold her for a moment, then together we turn away to join the others in the outer room. The evening calling hours are about to begin.

Close to eight hundred people come through to pay their respects, and when we arrive at home, late in the evening, I've never felt as physically and emotionally depleted. But there's no time to rest. Several friends join me in folding and assembling the programs for the memorial service in the morning. When we're done, we collapse in the living room, and I work my way through the cards people left at the funeral home.

I look them over: lovely, flowery cards, signed in sincere sympathy; trendy, new-agey ones that send positive vibes; simple messages with handwritten notes, some telling their own stories of loss and assuring me there are happier times ahead.

But one card, so raw in its honesty, I will never forget. A young mother I know in passing has written only this: "I am so sorry this has happened to your family." It's the most real thing anyone could say. Your family has suffered a terrible loss. It sucks.

Barely able to keep my eyes open, I dig to the bottom of the basket, pull out the thickest envelopes, and begin to wade through the perpetual mass cards sent by Roman Catholic friends.

"Eric Simonson will be remembered for one full year in the masses, prayers, and good works of the Society," I read, and we wonder aloud, between collective fits of inappropriate laughter, what will happen to his soul when the one-year period is up. "Oh, this one gives him five years," I exclaim, setting us all off on another round of hysteria.

I don't intend to be sacrilegious. I believe in prayer, I really do. But I also know that when I finally stop laughing, when the crowds are gone and I'm alone with the exhaustion and grief, I may never stop crying.

———

On Saturday morning, I stand behind Will and his parents, who are seated in the folding chairs set up at the graveside. Sitting feels too claustrophobic, too boxed in, when Eric's spirit is in the air, blowing free. Yesterday, Kyle announced watching Eric's body being lowered into the ground is not for him, and he's gotten no argument from me. Until this morning, I wasn't sure I wanted to be there either, finding greater comfort in the spiritual send-off at the memorial service to follow. But Kate is with Will for the weekend, and it doesn't feel right to not be here with her.

Surveying the small group gathered under the huge maple tree, alone in our grief yet united in our love for Eric, I know I've made the right decision. A plane flies low overhead. Will has arranged this with a pilot friend, a tribute to our son. How fitting.

Mid-afternoon, the memorial service takes place at the church Eric attended since the week he was born. Sitting beside Kyle, Mary, and Suzanne in the pew, I look to my left and see Kate with Will and his family. I think of the bride's and groom's families at a wedding, each having an experience parallel to but separate from the other. The flowers have been moved to the altar. So have the photos. Eric looks out at us, happy, healthy.

The music that has saved me this past year plays over the sound system. The congregation is silent, save for the muffled sounds of weeping that come from behind me and from the balcony above. It's a shock to most who are here—the lively boy they once knew, gone without warning. They haven't watched him struggle. They've had no way of knowing it might all lead to this.

Eric's friend Leigh—his middle school girlfriend back when such relationships were innocent and sweet—sings "Amazing Grace" with a voice so clear and strong my eyes overflow again, then people share their memories of Eric. Ashley's father describes how close he felt to Eric during his visits to Brooklyn, laughing about driving along FDR Drive while beatboxing and jiving out to Sugar Ray's "Fly" as if he were a teen himself. That's what Eric did to you, he says, made you forget your worries and just let loose.

One woman tells the story of how one late-summer day at the lake, a chill in the air, seven-year-old Eric swore he'd ridden horses plenty of times. She helped him onto her horse and he took a spin. Dismounting, he 'fessed up—"Oh, I've never been on a horse before"—with a sheepish grin. Others speak of his driving through town, whipping into a parking spot and jumping out of the car to fill them in on his latest exploits, then shooting out to the next one. They describe a boy who never hit that teenage phase of being too cool for an enthusiastic wave and a shout. "Hey! What's up?"

I hear serious stories too, about how we need to remember to check in with each other, how we can't know when someone might be secretly tormented unless we take the time to reach out. I wonder what they knew about Eric's pain, the things they might assume, right or wrong. Some remind us they're here to help, whatever we need.

A boy who's struggled in recent years stands to speak. "Eric was a great guy. It's so sad that he had to die, and I don't understand why, but there's one thing I know for sure." We hold our collective breaths, wondering where he's headed with this. "If Jesus doesn't know how to snowboard, Eric is definitely up there teaching him!" A ripple of relieved laughter passes through the congregation.

Two of Eric's soccer coaches take the mic. The first reads a poem he's written, mostly an homage to Eric's love of the game and the day his team finally got "over the Hill." The second, also the father of one of Eric's friends, speaks from the heart about the boy he knew and loved. Finally, Eric's Sunday School teacher gives the eulogy. Few eyes are dry when he returns to his seat.

When the pastor asks if everyone who wants to has spoken, I hold my breath. *Please let there be someone else,* I beg God. *This is all I have of him now. I need more.*

No one volunteers.

Between the stories that have been shared and the inspiring poem Suzanne has written and read, words of love and peace, I sense a lightness in the room that wasn't here when we arrived. When "Festival of Friends" begins to play, surrounding us with comfort and hope, I'm more sure than ever that this is the way we were meant to close.

Outside in the sunshine, a table holds photos and memorabilia and a book for people to record their memories of Eric. The scene I imagined at the start of the service returns to me. I've pictured this gorgeous Saturday afternoon many times over the years, standing outside the church surrounded by friends and family of Eric and his bride, sharing refreshments and amusing stories of their childhoods, their antics and foibles. Everyone was smiling in my vision, celebrating a joyous beginning, never an ending. And never did it cross my mind we'd be saying goodbye.

TWENTY-TWO

Indigo Tears

What do you do the morning after you have buried your child? I've asked myself a similar question each surreal, formless day since the crash eight days ago.

"How are you doing?" is the question others have posed a thousand times, maybe more. I'm not numb, as many think—so clichéd—though in this new role as mother of the boy who died, there's an acceptance, a peace in the way that I move through the world, that even I can't fully comprehend, much less explain.

I vaguely understand it's time to resume "normal" life. I wonder if anyone can tell me how to do that. The kids, the two of them—another little stab somewhere deep as this hits home—are often off with friends, and the summer promises long days in the house alone.

I'm stung, too, by the way the days just keep ticking past, knowing Eric's death will not be in the present for long. Whenever I close my eyes, I see the calendar used in old movies to show the passing of time, pages flying off one by one, days turning into months turning into years. Each time I think of Eric's face and body, his very essence, receding into the past, fading from my memory, from everyone's mind, I feel hopeless. Helpless. It's another little heartbreak.

So this morning when John shows up at the door, he's a welcome sight. Eric's oldest friend, he's one of my favorites. With John away at college, there's been a distance between them of late, forged by miles and by his disapproval of Eric's recent choices. This troubles him now, he tells me. He needs

The Full Catastrophe

to get back to his summer internship in the city and asks if I'll ride with him to the cemetery. The burial was private, family only, and he wants to see where Eric is. I want this for him, too. I put on the green dress I was wearing when I last saw my son and slide into the passenger's seat. We agree to drive first to the place where Eric died.

This is it, I think—the moment I've known would happen when it was supposed to.

The road that leads north out of the village takes us through the most treacherous of passes, though the treachery lies not in the geography but in the emotional terrain. On my left the cemetery where, just yesterday, we laid my boy to rest under a sweeping oak beside a great grandfather he never knew. A little farther on, just where the road curves gently left, it's the golden splendor of a once-serene alfalfa field that, until last Saturday, drew the eye right and on to the horizon. Now, instead, I'm assaulted by the scar of deep tire tracks leading into the ravine and on through the field, left by the rescue vehicles I'm told. In the distance, I see the vast flattened area where the airborne Audi came to a violent halt on its roof in a mangled heap. The imprint of Eric's car will linger there until the crop is harvested late in the summer. The place where Eric lay, a good distance from the car they say, is not visible. I pause to thank God for this little mercy.

Repeatedly, I've imagined him thrown from the car and prayed a thousand things: that it was instant, that he felt no pain. That the many injuries reported in the autopsy were, as I've decided is surely the case, insults that happened to an already lifeless form. These things are, on the distorted scale of difficulty that has taken over since Saturday's horror, relatively easy to believe.

But I pray other things, too. I pray that shock took over

when the car took flight, that he didn't have time to be afraid. That he didn't know this mistake would be his last, the one that finally called his bluff. And in my darkest hours, I pray this horrible outcome was in no real way his goal, though I cannot believe this could be true. That he was simply seeking comfort, a respite from the chaos inside his mind. That though, in his pain, Eric may have thought he wanted any way out, he didn't mean that, not really. That this was simply an accident in every sense of the word, the last stupid risk in a line of increasingly stupid risks taken by a tortured young man, desperate to dull the pain.

We walk to the edge of the road, where Eric's friends have left flowers and mementos—a mixtape, a friendship bracelet, photos of them together, brimming with joy. And letters, so many letters, some sealed in plastic and others soaked from rain, the ink dripping down the page like indigo tears. I need to see this—where his car went off the road, exactly where it landed, where they found him—and I don't want to see it at all. The two of us speak softly about everything and nothing. How tragic this is. How senseless. We get back in the car and drive to the cemetery in silence.

Heavy black iron gates stand open, and we drive through them then turn right, passing ancient, moss-covered headstones, newer markers flush with the ground, monuments from centuries past. One boulder of pink granite stands out from the rest and catches my eye—a childhood friend of my father's is buried here—and I vow to find something equally unique to mark the spot where Eric lies. John sits by the grave, fresh and unmarked, and talks to him in whispers. As if on cue, a warm breeze blows, carrying the scent of late-blooming lilacs and freshly turned dirt as I drift through the cemetery. Eric is all around me here. Silently, I

The Full Catastrophe

tell him everything I cannot say aloud.

This is not where I expected to be visiting you, Eric. How did we end up here? You frustrated me so. I didn't know how to save you, but it wasn't for lack of trying. I'd have done anything, you know that. You were lost, my sweet boy, and you didn't want to be found. Or maybe you just didn't know how.

I don't understand why I'm here and you're not, but I do know this: I'm so grateful I got to be your mother. You've given us so many reasons to miss you. You'll be with me always now, perfect and whole. And I'm going to keep on saying your name.

My mind quiets, and "One Day I Walk," another of Bruce Cockburn's songs, blankets me with the knowledge that today is not forever. That one day, like Eric, I, too, will be home.

My eyes are drawn to the horizon, where a small hill rises to another section of the cemetery. There, a line of old oaks and maples stand tall against the sky. I picture Eric, maybe twelve years old, perched on top of the tallest tree, grinning, waving, shouting for me to look up. That's where I'll see him forever now, catching big air. Flying free.

———

I was already planning the funeral while Eric was still in the womb.

This thought descends in a thunderbolt one day in early July as I drive to see my summer students, though once it settles in it feels more like an old friend, something I've known for years but am only now beginning to understand.

After Mom died, my life was threaded through with a vein of "almost." I became practically a sister, nearly a daughter, a litany of close-but-not-quite that could add up to an almost life, if I wasn't careful. But then there was this baby, *my* son, no almost about it. If asked to explain this morbid rehearsal, I might reference my melodramatic nature, though deep down I know the truth: it was simply a need to rehearse grief, an antidote to the very real specter of another life ended too soon.

Oddly, it was only Eric, not his siblings, whose funeral loomed. Looking back, I see the young mother, teary as she tucks the baby in for the night, praying to see him through to adulthood, clinging to the dream of family. I wonder what, if anything, I have to offer her. She would say that life requires nothing short of bravery. She would tell you that love and determination and faith will carry her through. And, though she can't possibly know the measure of courage these things will require, I see now, she would be right.

Nearing my destination, I think of how sometimes we rehearse for rehearsal's sake, to help ourselves grasp the irrational nature of our obsessions, a desensitization of sorts. At other times, rehearsals simply fold without warning, giving way to a command performance. For me, it was the latter, the knock on the door on that gorgeous June day cueing the curtain's rise.

———

All summer long, everything feels swollen with meaning and utterly meaningless. Between the calls from collection agencies that punctuate these weeks, I make mixtapes of the music we played at the memorial service for friends who requested one. Home alone so much of the time—Kate with Will, Kyle working or who knows where—this gives me purpose. Yet I'm also overcome with the need to do what feels right at any given moment.

The Full Catastrophe

A friend introduces me to singer-songwriters who are new to me: Dar Williams, The Nields, Catie Curtis and others. I listen to Bruce and these artists constantly, and their lyrics bring a depth of comfort I can't explain.

Two of Eric's friends are performing in *Into the Woods* at the local theatre company and invite me to attend. I'm vaguely aware Sondheim's musical intertwines the paths of Grimm's fairy tale characters as they journey deep into the darkness—and light—found only in the woods. Kate and I sit in the front row on folding chairs arranged along the floor in the middle of the room. Actors move from the stage at one end to another makeshift stage at the other, often performing in front of us. We are, essentially, in the middle of the action.

The lyrics, ripe with significance in the best of times, are almost more than I can bear only weeks after Eric's death. On the other side of a frightening journey through a dark wood, where she disregarded her mother's cautions and strayed from the path, Little Red Riding Hood reflects on what she learned. Scary may be exciting, but nice and good are not the same. There are things it's better not to know. She should have heeded her mother's advice, but the wolf was so tempting. Oh, how I wish Eric had listened.

When the witch laments, grieving our children's refusal to take our advice and the inevitability of losing them to bad decisions, the pain is exquisitely perfect, written only for my ears. I fight to hold back tears, aware others are watching. They see me here, Eric's mom, and wonder how I'll manage.

I count by threes, this is how I do it. It's oddly calming and splits my focus, the full weight of the words too much to take on their own. I love this play. I hate it. The lyrics tease me with the glorious comfort of language that says exactly the things I feel: How do you guide your children when you haven't figured it out yourself? When they won't listen to you anyway? What good is being a good mother if they're just going leave you in the end?"

Is this what life is then, a series of people to love and lose? Hopes that rise and fall and ultimately cause only pain? A never-ending march toward a home I will never find? And how do I continue, knowing it's an exercise in futility? These are the things that have crossed my mind in the depths of my grief. Somehow Sondheim knows this. Somehow I've ended up at this play.

But there's redemption here, too. The witch sings on, this time about loss, about people leaving. But the leaving's not forever. And no one is alone.

I play the soundtrack over and over and add it to my "Have a Good Cry" playlist. Sometimes that's exactly what I need these days, song after song that cuts me in two, gets straight to the broken part, and puts me back together, transformed. Closer to whole. I'm getting there.

It hits me one day not long after Eric's crash: my father, my brother, my son, the sad symmetry of having lost these three men an odd comfort. They're together now, Mom, too. I think of how I never got to know any of them adult to adult. Not even Eric.

For nearly twenty-five years, I've lived in a world where your whole family can die and leave you. Now, so can your children.

———

In July, my cousin's son, who lives in Esther's renovated house, invites me to a family party there. Kate goes with me, and as I take the work he's done in the fifteen years since I was last here, since that day I left with Will and our boys, certain I'd never return, it strikes me. This place is nothing like it was when I lived here. And neither am I.

Losing Eric and the family I so carefully designed has opened the door for something else. I would never have wanted this outcome, but it feels as if the stars have aligned to send me a clear message. I hear a voice, compassionate and wise, calling to me from deep within, fighting to be heard. It tells me I've kept myself small, nearly invisible at times, single-mindedly seeking the love I needed. But even that was not enough.

I mistook control for peace.

Sometimes, that voice insists, *the things we create have to crumble before we can rebuild them on a stronger foundation. Sometimes everything has to shift before we can find solid ground.* I need to make a life without Eric in the world, though our bond will never break. It's time to embrace who I am outside the roles I fill.

All of these years—from navigating friendships in childhood, through my teens spent with Esther, and on through most of adulthood—I've been on a quest for belonging. Now I've moved closer to understanding what that really means. It's not slipping seamlessly into a family as though I've always been there. It isn't being so much like everyone around me that I don't stand out in any way.

True belonging requires me to be myself, embrace my gifts and struggles, and share them without fear. Only in this space do I find the connection I crave and the strength to stand alone.

For years I've had the same haunting dream. I return to El's, and they're all there—my parents and Tommy, El and Henry and Sandy—the people who populated the happiest times in my childhood. Expecting they'll greet me with open arms, instead they're annoyed. "Go back to your own life," they say. "There's no room for you here." I awaken in tears.

These days, when I return there in my dreams, I'm welcomed home.

———

It's Saturday, the house is quiet, and suddenly I know what I have to do. Eric's room has remained as it was since the day he died nearly two months ago, untouched except for my crawling into his bed each night, comforted by sleeping where he once slept.

Recently I've begun climbing the stairs at night to crawl into a sliver of my own bed, the rest of it taken up with piles of folded clothes. It hasn't escaped me, the fact that I'm occupying as little space in the world as possible, but I'm giving myself permission to re-enter at my own pace. Most nights, I retrieve a piece of Eric's clothing from under my nightstand—a T-shirt, a jacket, his soccer jersey—one of the few garments from his hamper I had the good sense not to wash in the days after the accident. I hold it close and breathe him in as I fall asleep.

Now it seems right to take a small step forward. I begin by taking down papers and pictures and mementos Eric taped to his mirror, folding and sorting his clothes. I unearth a stack of photos from Christmases and birthdays and sleepovers with friends. We look so happy in these pictures from Eric's younger years, the scenes so idyllic. Three healthy, freckle-faced kids with a small-town life, grandparents close by, their school just around the corner, right down the path through the woods, not even a street to cross. Ball fields and the best bakery in the county, all a walk or bike ride away. Our house on the tree-lined street.

Summers at the lake. Winters on the mountain. Church on Sunday. And the Memorial Day parade, a prime photo-op, with assorted kids in assorted uniforms: Girl Scouts and Boys Scouts, band and baseball, little hands waving to the crowd.

But no shots capture the whole truth or show how it really was. Who photographs those? Look deep into our eyes and still you'll detect no hint of what stirred inside, no clue to who of us would find our way and who would get lost.

In the coming years, when I picture Eric's room just off the kitchen in this house where he grew up, I'll remember the unmade bed, the soccer posters, and the drafting table that hinted at a hopeful future. What I won't allow myself to fully reinhabit until years have passed is the dead weight of learning Eric was gone.

Nearly in a trance, I've gone to a place in my mind where I can bear to pack up his things without feeling the fullness of what it all means, when two clear thoughts appear, nearly at once.

When I meet new people and they ask me how many children I have, what will I say?

Anyone who comes into my life from now on won't have known Eric. How can they possibly know me?

Yet even now, even in the depths of grief, I understand it. What we all need when our time here is finished is the love and forgiveness of those who remain to keep the best of us alive. This will be my gift to my son. This one thing I can do.

Into the storage bin they go, Eric's favorite T-shirts, those sneakers with the frayed laces, strawberry candy wrappers, crumpled bits of notebook paper with "Awesome Eric!!" scrawled across them, treasures from his younger years. Photos and posters. His yearbook. I stash away the detritus of his life until the far-off day when deciding what to keep, what to let go, will somehow be easier. For now, it's one small step, one breath, at a time.

Overcome with fatigue, I close my eyes and picture Eric, little cheeks plump like apples, taking his first steps. Jumping in the truck to head to the lake. Boarding the plane for a visit with the Presleys. Heading out with John for a day of snowboarding. Leaving Kyle at home that June Saturday. Driving off. Alone.

These scenes string together like so many Christmas lights, guiding my eye from one to the next. They are, each of them, stories of connection—and stories of leaving. Now that the glow of Eric here with me is gone from view, what had dwelled in the spaces between the light is suddenly clear:

From the moment our babies arrive, we're learning to let them go.

There have been days, these last couple of months, when, amid the grief, I've been able to find my way back to a place of calm. I've resisted the temptation to fall into guilt or descend back into sadness—such an effortless drop. Instead, I'm resolved to take every peaceful moment as the gift it clearly is.

But as August comes to a close, my anxiety rises. As long as it's summer, Eric's death feels as though it's in the present, but the thought of taking the smallest step into another season has me feeling empty and sad. Needing to do something, I'm compelled to write the letter I've been mentally composing for weeks.

When I called my lawyer a few days after Eric died, he'd already heard the news. With deep regret in his voice, he spoke about the injustice of the Vermont law and its rigid interpretation. I asked him whether, when I was able to muster the strength to write to legislators about Eric's

The Full Catastrophe

situation, he would be willing to join me in signing the letter. He agreed.

As I write, it all pours out. I tell them—the State's Attorney, the state and US senators and representatives, Governor Dean—who I am, who Eric was. I explain how he didn't realize the girl was underage, how he told the truth as he'd been taught to do at home. I describe the inflexibility of the system, how not long before he died, his public defender told him the State's Attorney's office "wants every man charged with this in prison." That they refused to consider any of the facts regarding Eric's background and lack of prior legal involvement, their minimal age difference. That it was consensual.

Coming to my point, I continue:

My attorney has joined me in making this appeal for a new look at this archaic law and its inflexible enforcement. [He is dismayed by] *legislation that in no way reflects the message our culture sends its young people: that sex among teens and young adults is widely accepted. A like charge in New York State would be dealt with as a Class A misdemeanor, much more in keeping with the severity of the crime.*

We must ask ourselves whether...incarcerating a young man as a felon based on one consensual encounter with a girl four years younger reflects the intent of a law designed to protect society from truly deviant individuals. Does rendering promising young lives forever empty simply to put another notch in the prosecutorial belt appeal to our sensibilities?

When I finish, I sit back in the chair, drained, and reread what I've written. There. I'll never have to struggle to tell Eric's story again. I urge them to ensure that a hard look is taken at this law and its rigid application, then I sign the letter and send it along to Sam. He returns it to me with his own

Indigo Tears

signature, impressive credentials, and a single added line. I shiver as I read it: "I am truly disturbed by a criminal justice system that can fail as miserably as it has here." In this moment, I don't feel quite so alone.

Months later, I receive a lone reply from Governor Dean. He's very sorry for my loss. He tells me that, a year ago, the legislature revisited the law but declined to make any modifications. Maybe I should contact the head of the appropriate committee, he advises, though I've sent this letter to every member of the legislature already.

I'm not surprised, but I won't take this any further. I believe I'm capable of articulating my perspective on this complex and controversial issue, but I've done what I needed to do. It's time to move forward. Losing my son is something that happened to me, an overwhelming grief. But it's not my identity.

I refuse to let *mother of the boy who died* become all that I am.

———

As I suspected, the break in hostilities between Will and me is brief, and it's another year and a half before our divorce is final. Eventually, Kate decides to live with her father full time, staying with me on the weekends at first, though these visits soon become less frequent as she's swept up in the (even more) rebellious teen years. Kyle finishes high school, spends a half-hearted semester at community college, then moves to Saratoga for a restaurant job, alternately in touch and completely incommunicado. Though I want nothing more than to have him close, I understand his need to figure things out on his own and see that pressuring him to stay in

The Full Catastrophe

touch only yields the opposite result.

Sometimes I wonder who I'm supposed to be now. It feels as if I'm no one's mother, as if all three of the children I've loved so deeply are unreachable now. Yet when I take Kyle and Kate to visit friends in California, I'm grateful to have fun together again. As I reflect afterward on the warm nights at Disneyland, fireworks lighting the sky over the castle, drives along the Pacific, I see that we are, in fact, still a family. Not the family I pictured all those years ago, not the one I set out to create. We're in flux, the three of us, figuring things out. For this moment, that is enough.

PART V
Home at Last

I am not what happens to me,
I am what I choose to become.

-Carl Gustav Jung

TWENTY-THREE

The Full Catastrophe

Kyle in a tux—now there's something I never thought I'd see. But here he is, meeting me—in a simple off-white floor-length dress, a crown of fresh flowers in my hair—at the door of the Vermont inn, locking his arm into mine and leading me out across the yard toward my future. We pass the peace pole and walk on into the early September garden. My soon-to-be husband waits expectantly beside the officiant, along with the llamas, Guinevere and Llancelot, who stand watch behind the fence. Rows of friends and family turn to us, smiling. My eyes drop to the ground, and I smile, too, as I catch sight of the old-school black Adidas Kyle wears, a nod to Eric, who insisted that would be his shoe of choice if he ever went to prom.

It's been less than a year since I met Kevin, when we were counting the time since the planes hit the World Trade Center towers in weeks. I'd prepared carefully for our first date. Black tights, platform shoes, black wrap skirt. White shirt, boiled wool vest. My favorite scarf, with a pop of red, completing my favorite look: comfortable, yet put together. Dressed up, but not too. I'd straightened up the house and reminded myself to relax, be authentic but not give everything away. Holding a little back would keep me from making the same mistakes I'd made before.

As I lit cinnamon candles in the living room, I kept one eye on the heavy Craftsman front door with the panes of exquisite beveled glass, the one the previous owner had made us promise never to slam, a vow we'd broken many times long ago. Now, I imagined carrying each of my newborns through that door, kissing their little foreheads and welcoming them home. I pictured the kids running in and out a thousand times over the years, dashing to their grandparents', heading off to school, coming home sweaty and spent after a game. I saw the policeman standing there, only two years earlier, telling me there'd been a crash.

Finally, a knock.

"Come on in," I called and looked up to see Kevin stepping in from the porch. I recognized him; call me shallow, but I asked him to send a photo when I replied to his Match-dot-com message, which I'd read to a friend over the phone. He wrote about being a cyclist, loving travel and photography. How much he'd enjoyed being a father to his two kids. His long career as a social worker in the child welfare system.

Here's a guy who likely understands that even when someone does all they can to be a good parent, their kids can still struggle.

"Invite me to the wedding," said my friend, and we laughed. How likely was that?

Kevin strode into my living room in his khaki slacks and navy blazer, flashed his quintessentially Irish smile, stepped on my foot—the perfect icebreaker—then chuckled as he gave me a warm hug. *He can laugh at himself,* I noted. *So far so good.*

"Do you want to walk to the restaurant? It's only a few blocks from here," I suggested.

His eyes lit up. "Yes, let's," he said, and we strolled together under a full October moon, a carpet of fallen leaves crunching underfoot, past my former in-laws' home where Kate still lived with Will. I half-hoped someone was peering around the drawn curtains, wondering who that handsome man was beside me.

We talked through dinner about our jobs and our kids. Kevin had a son and a daughter, both in college, he explained, clearly proud of each of them.

"My daughter just turned fifteen, and my son is nineteen," I said, starting from the youngest child and working up. I weighed whether to tell the whole story, as I often did when meeting someone new, then forged ahead. No sense dipping my toes into the water if I wasn't ready to jump straight in.

"And my oldest son would be twenty-two, but he died in a car crash two years ago."

"Oh, Casey, that must have been awful. I'm so sorry." Seeing shock and genuine empathy in Kevin's eyes, I let out the breath I hadn't known I'd been holding.

Everything I'd have asked for in a partner, Kevin was funny and intelligent, handsome and engaging, and, as I learned when I visited his office one afternoon, clearly respected by those who worked for and with him. He was also the exact opposite of the low-key, articulate significant other I'd envisioned, almost laughably so. The irony of a speech-language pathologist in a relationship with a guy who talked a mile a minute, didn't finish his sentences, and was the king of malapropisms ("Let's order 'frajitas,'" he'd suggested at the Mexican restaurant, then commented on what a "ferocious" reader I was) did not escape me.

A couple of weeks and several dates later, we chatted across a table for two at a nearby English pub. Kevin ran his fingers through his wavy brown hair and looked intently at me, his blue-gray eyes dancing as he told one amusing anecdote after another.

"If you could travel anywhere in the world, where would

The Full Catastrophe

you go?" he asked, finally.

I didn't hesitate. "I've always wanted to visit Ireland."

That set him off on another story, this one about the time he'd brought his mother home to Sligo for her eightieth birthday. Riding along with a fisherman uncle and his cache of gasoline illegally procured in the North, they ran into trouble at the border.

"My mother's response? 'Aw, Kevin, it's too bad you weren't arrested. We would've had to go to the North of Ireland to spring you. Think of the stories you'd have to tell!'" He laughed, loudly enough to draw a few sideways glances, which I was pleased to find amused rather than embarrassed me.

We touched on our marriages, though it wasn't time for full disclosure quite yet. This tingling feeling of both comfort and possibility was a winning pair, like an old friend with so many secrets left to uncover.

As Kevin launched into another tale, the words he was saying blurred into the trombone-like *mwa-mwa-mwa* of the teacher's voice in Charlie Brown cartoons. I pulled up and out of the scene and saw us from the outside, as I'd done since childhood, in small moments that happened every day or ones that were pivotal and life-changing. I had the feeling this was the latter.

It struck me then: *I'll be sitting across the table from this man for the rest of my life.*

When Kevin dropped me off that night with a warm, lingering good night kiss, I allowed myself a glimmer of hope and excitement, but I wasn't going to get ahead of myself this time. I'd paid dearly for bad decisions, and going all in with the wrong person was out of the question. Still, as I lay awake that night, hour after hour, I could feel it: The winds had shifted. I pictured the weathervane spinning around in *Mary Poppins,* Dick VanDyke's character singing about new beginnings. The tiniest spark of the idea that life might someday be easier, that I might find the happy relationship I feared I'd never have teased me. Though essentially nothing was different, it felt as though not one thing was the same.

Six weeks later, as I left on a Thanksgiving trip to visit Sarah, who was studying in England, Kevin gave me a striking emerald and black scarf I'd admired on one of our first days together in Stockbridge. I wondered then if I'd be wearing it for years, whether he'd be walking along beside me when I did, back in the Berkshires or in New York City.

"I'll bring you to Carnegie Hall and Radio City…we'll have someone take our photo in Grand Central Station," he'd promised in intimate whispers. He was already planning ahead, decades full of optimism and fun.

I couldn't wait to see what that kind of life was like.

Now, that life is mine. A soft breeze rustles the leaves in the trees that surround us in the garden and dances across my face. I look up from Kyle's footwear, and there is Kevin, waiting for me in the late afternoon sunshine beside the officiant.

"Who gives this woman to be married to this man?" she asks in her soothing Irish lilt. It's a traditional setup for Kyle's not-so-traditional response—"Eric and I do"—and there's a barely audible murmur from our witnesses, the ones who know. They sense him here with us, and so do I. Kyle moves to the front, joining Kevin's son, Corey, his daughter, Ali, and Sarah, who's become something akin to a daughter to me and stepped in as my maid of honor when Kate decided not to attend.

I'm disappointed she's not here. We've come a long way,

The Full Catastrophe

yet Kate continues to struggle with the pull of her father, who can't figure out how to let her love us both. How perfect it would've been to have her here beside me, all five of our children together—Eric, too—witnesses to our commitment to each other and to all of them. Though I'd like to have fixed it all for her, I understand now that my daughter has her own journey. And it's far from over.

In the barn on the hill behind the inn, friends mingle in the glow of the white lights that hang from the ceiling. Kevin and I dance to a song I heard in an historic Saratoga café the year before we met. Even then, when Nerissa and Katryna Nields sang "Easy People" in that intimate space, I knew they were describing the relationship I craved.

> Haven't I paid my dues by now
> And don't I get the right to choose?
> I choose you to take up all of my time
> I choose you because you're funny and kind
> I want easy from now on.

Tonight, I can't think of a more perfect way to begin our lives together. As we sway to the music on the small dance floor, I'm overcome by the love I feel surrounding us, and I know I am exactly where I'm supposed to be.

———

Kevin and I build a house—*our* home—then Kyle and his girlfriend have our first grandchild. They give him Eric's name—first, middle, and last—and my Eric's presence is palpable as we welcome this precious baby into the family. I gradually become accustomed to hearing that name in the world again. "Eric and Kyle" are replaced with "Kyle and Eric," the altered order eliminating the need to explain which Eric we mean: the treasured young man we'll always miss or the treasured wee one we're just now falling in love with.

Will calls now and then, mostly in the first years after I marry and move away from Cambridge, to orchestrate Kate's dropoffs and pickups. We choose to leave the past behind and focus on what remains. When he dies unexpectedly, six years after my wedding, the victim of a freak snowstorm-related accident, I'm grateful the hostilities are behind us. Grateful, too, that I'm able to support the kids as they grieve another tragic loss.

I think of all our relationship gave me, those many years ago. Love, when I thought I had none. Three beautiful children. A family and a home that were truly mine. It fell apart, but that doesn't completely erase what was there. I was more at home in the rolling green hills of the Cambridge Valley than I'd ever been anywhere else. Cambridge will always be my hometown.

But this is my life now. And Kevin is my home.

———

Some people hold tightly to their story. When my story was all I had, I did that, too. *I've had a life filled with tragedy. I'll probably die young.* But I decided long ago that this is not what I want for myself. I decided to believe that my past is not my future, even when the present held no promise of better things to come. Even when relationships I had were not the sort I feared losing. Even when they were the sort I feared would last. I learned to hold things lightly, and better things came. In spades.

The Full Catastrophe

With the safety of the years that have passed and the embrace of a loving partner, I realize that of all the things I've come to believe, these six words have changed me most:

Everything that isn't love is fear.

It's been so easy to see myself as loving, eager to please. I knew my own fear well enough—fear of not having enough love, fear of being unlovable. Most frightening of all, fear of being alone in the world. I let those fears dictate how I lived my life, the decisions I made, and the things I valued, even when those things were the wrong things. Sometimes those fears led me to behave in ways that weren't loving at all.

What I couldn't see was how fear could explain the things others did that hurt me and those I loved, that most of the things other people do are not about me. Will's parents were unabashedly devoted to our kids, and isn't that a wonder, to have people who think the sun rises and sets on the children who mean everything to you? Birdie must have worried so deeply about her own son and about our kids that blaming me was the only way she could tame her fear. She didn't know she didn't have to choose at all. How much better it might've been for all of us if she had. This makes me sad for her now, and I remember the love we shared.

Will's lawyer. The law guardian. The mother of the girl who'd written about Eric in her journal, who pressed charges. None of them were doing those things to me, or to Eric. Not even Will. I believe each of them was scrambling to be sure they had all the love they feared they lacked, to push away the things they couldn't define, though that didn't look like fear to me. Or even, I suspect, to them.

Understanding this doesn't change what happened, but it changes me.

I married a man who was wrong for me, then held on for

far too long. I tried to mold him into someone he wasn't, and we both wound up miserable. I finally see that love sometimes means giving up the fight for something that was never meant to be. Loving those who did their best to love me back, even if it didn't look that way, and loving those who didn't. I turn this over in my mind, apologize to Will for the part I played in the demise of our marriage, and put it to rest.

It's taken me decades to understand that, like Eric, I've had a lifelong love affair with air and freedom. I've searched for it since I was small, seeking it out in religion and spirituality and in the ways I struggled to see the world as something greater than what was right in front of me. Yet it wasn't the knowing when to work harder, cling tighter, care more deeply that was the real challenge. Though these things have their place and time, I had another lesson this time around: learning when to let go.

My religion these days is kindness and compassion, the deep knowledge that we all belong to each other, and gratitude for all that was. For all that is. Maybe life isn't about getting it right after all. Maybe what it's really about is trying and feeling every bit of it, about allowing your heart to be broken and getting up again, bruised but wiser.

Sometimes I wonder if our souls all agreed to come here together long ago. I picture us negotiating the terms:

I'll be the mother; you be the son. You be the husband who teaches me to be strong, to forgive. You be the man who shows me what real love looks like.

We'll teach each other what we came to learn, and when that's done, we'll leave.

The Full Catastrophe

Kyle circumvents the traditional culinary school path and eventually becomes a talented chef via the school of hard knocks. Kate struggles, then finds her way, gradually realizing I'm not as bad as she once thought, and settles in nearby Albany. My relationship with each of them deepens as we work to make sense of where we've been and move forward together.

And Eric? He's with me always, the oldest treasure on the shelf, those we love nestled in around him. There he is, with that smile so bright it lights the room, teasing us, urging us to take the adventure. Reminding us to love each other. He sees the big picture far better than we do. He's the wise one now.

Our grief lives on that shelf, too. It doesn't disappear or diminish but is joined by all the other stories that are part of us, stories happy and sad, joyful and wise, and even the ones that tell of the mistakes we continue to make, because life doesn't stop, even when we think it should. The pain and pleasure live side by side.

When people ask how many children we have, Kevin takes the lead.

"Five," he answers, without hesitation. "Three boys and two girls between us."

This only makes me love him more.

One after the other, more babies arrive. We become Mimi and Papa to all ten of them. There are grandkids on the Canadian border and in Pennsylvania, in nearby Saratoga and ten minutes away. When we get together, all of us, the house is full and chaotic.

"How was your holiday?" my friends ask when we gather to debrief.

"A catastrophe!" I answer, laughing.

304

The Full Catastrophe

I've finally found it, I think as we move on to their stories of family dramas and joys. *The full catastrophe.*

Epilogue

One day when I was ten, I came home from school to discover my mother had set up an easel in our kitchen and suspended an oversized pad of art paper from the metal clips at the top. Using a compass, she'd drawn a series of intersecting arcs; some of the resulting shapes were already shaded in. For weeks, each time we passed through the kitchen, one of us altered the palette, bisected a line, offered something unexpected. In the end, we stood back, taking it all in. It was a thing of beauty.

Perhaps that stuck with me.

It would only be a few years before I'd put this skill to work for myself in a more serious way. Afraid of having no place to belong, I created a family that was mine, damn it, then realized what I'd done just in time to watch it fall apart. Just in time to say goodbye to my beloved Eric. After all my persistence, the palette had changed. Lines were bisected. Unexpected things weren't so beautiful now. Loved one here. Loved one gone. Repeat.

A fruitless fight for control taught me to accept whatever comes, though I still sometimes struggle mightily before I get there. Over and over, it seems, I've been fresh out of raw materials, yet I've ended up with a finished product of the finest quality.

It's turned out to be a knife that cuts both ways.

Though so much of what I dreamed of is here in front of me—or maybe because it is—nothing raises my doomsday antenna more than the "this could be the last time" refrain.

These days, I lie in bed next to Kevin and think about how much I love him, how thankful I am for the life I have now, how grateful to have him in it. I hang up the phone with Kyle or Kate, having agreed to get together or given a piece of motherly advice. "See you in a bit," I tell her. To him, "Hang in there, things will work out fine, I'm sure of it."

Alone with my thoughts, though, it begins: something I've come to think of as pre-emptive grieving, as though rehearsing the unimaginable will hold it at bay. It runs through my head like the still shots and movie script I've been compiling all my life. I hear the score, the music leading the audience to its inevitable, grim conclusion. "And that was the last time they spoke," says the narrator. Or, "They couldn't have known that by tomorrow he'd be gone." Another day, "She was feeling fine, then suddenly they found the cancer." It's a different sort of pivot point, the moment that leads from the light that is real into the darkness that doesn't exist.

There I go again, creating something from nothing.

I shake it off, that voice, put it aside and go on, determined to live the life I have and not the one I fear.

ACKNOWLEDGEMENTS

It's been said that birthing a book is not unlike birthing a baby, and I've found this to be true, though I'm grateful not to have carried my own children for the twelve years it took to bring this book into the world. And to continue the metaphor, the village it takes to raise a child is equaled only by the city that's required to raise a writer. Here are some of its inhabitants:

Diane Windsor of Motina Books Publishing: I couldn't have hoped for a better partner on this path to publication. You "got" my story, and isn't that every writer's dream? Thanks so much for being a kind, constant support. Thank you, too, to fellow Motina authors Ronit Plank, L.L. Kirchner, and Rosalie Mastaler. I'm proud to be in your company.

Marion Roach Smith: In three-hour segments, you introduced me to a world of memoir and creative nonfiction that would take hold of me and refuse to let go. It all began with you.

Ken Appleman, Donna Behen, Diane Kavanaugh-Black, Tina Lincer, and Mike Welch: Our biweekly "Salon" meetings in those early years were a crash course in writing and critiquing and gave me the deadlines I needed to produce essays on the regular. This book wouldn't exist without you.

Marea Gordett, Judith Fetterley, and Karen DeBonis: For me, our group will forever be affectionately known as "Third Act Writers." You've taught me so much and have become some of my closest friends.

Janice Toomajian and Sarah Schellinger Butterick: You, my dear friends, were my first readers (well, listeners), and with the patience of saints, you gave me the courage to write on.

Rae McAuliffe, our long phone chats and your wise comments gave me both perspective and validation. Thank you so much for your steady presence.

Bliss Broyard, Allison K Williams, Jill Rothenberg, Lisa Cooper Ellison, and Ann Hood: Your editorial wisdom and guidance taught me so much about craft and structure and drawing readers into a story rather than telling them about it. You helped me grow as a writer and feel part of a broader community, and for that I'm deeply grateful. Thank you, too, to the generous women and men who took the time to read this book and provide an endorsement. I'm forever in your debt.

Nancy DiMarino, Marea Gordett, Kate Jackson, Marjorie Larner, Tina Lincer, Donna Miller, Becky Moran, Jenny Currier Shand, and Alison Taylor-Brown: Beta readers extraordinaire, your comments both lifted me up and set me straight. Thank you for your generosity and your honest opinions. Margie, our rekindled relationship has been such a gift over these past few years. How lucky we were to reconnect after decades had passed.

Eileen Vorbach Collins, Karen DeBonis, Mimi Zieman: Where would I be without you three? When we met at the start of the pandemic in 2020, how could we ever have known we'd end up here, the four of us with books in the world we weren't certain would ever see the light of day? We haven't missed a meeting of "Writers' Tears" in what for most of us has been nearly five years. Now our bond goes far beyond writerly pursuits. Such gratitude.

Lindsey DeLoach Jones, Kirsten Ott-Palladino, Barbie Beaton, and Jennifer O'Brien: Our writing paths have

Acknowledgements

alternately merged and diverged over the years, but each of you has had an impact on my work. Lindsey, how I've valued our discussions about faith and spirituality and the importance of dwelling in curiosity.

Kate Jackson: I'm in awe of your talent, thankful for your guidance, and profoundly grateful for your friendship. Let's meet halfway, always.

Katherine Wilemon and The Family Heart Foundation: As an ambassador beside my husband, Kevin, I've learned so much about familial hypercholesterolemia and elevated $Lp(a)$ as well as the lifelong impact of undiagnosed genetic disorders on those who've lost family members at an early age. Thank you for the opportunity to blend passion with purpose, a combination we all seek but often struggle to find.

Sandy DeVille, Mary Laedlein, and Suzanne DeMuth: You, my oldest and dearest friends, not only walked beside me as I wrote this book but as I lived the events contained within it. Each of you saved me in your own way. Each of you has my undying love.

Sarah Schellinger Butterick: You are so much more than an early reader, dearest Sarah. You came into my life as Eric left it, or as I often say, you were the gift he left to me. Lo these twenty-five years later, here you still are, a part of our family. So much love to you.

Elizabeth, Bob, and Tom Mulligan: You, my beloved parents, my big brother, left me far too soon. But in the short time we had together, you showed me what it means to be loved unconditionally. I don't know how I'd ever have survived the long, lonely years that followed without your example. I will always miss you.

Eric, Kyle, and Kaitlin: Where do I begin? I dreamed of you all my life, my children who became the family I so desperately wanted. I cannot imagine my life without you. Here in body, here in spirit—you're mine, now and always. I'll love you forever.

To all ten of our grandkids (Eric, Brendan, Emily, Kate, Alexis, Robert, Porter, Lux, Ethan, and Caleb) and their parents (Kyle, Kaitlin, Ali and Jason, Corey and Erin, Tammy and John): Together, you have brought me the full catastrophe of life in all its best incarnations, everything I wished for when I felt so alone. Thank you for being our family, in all its beautiful chaos.

And, finally, to Kevin: I spent decades searching for someone who approaches life (and me) with intelligence and insight and humor, who loves a good adventure—a true partner in every way. How incredible it is that we found each other, how grateful I am for the life we've made. You have my whole heart.

Suggested Resources

BOOKS

Death and its Terrible, Horrible, No Good, Very Beautiful Lessons: Field Notes from the Death Dialogues Project, by Becky Aud-Jennison

Daring to Breathe: Stories of Living with the Foreverness of Grief, an anthology by Armen Bacon and Nancy Miller

The Art of Misdiagnosis: Surviving My Mother's Suicide, by Gayle Brandeis

When Things Fall Apart: Heart Advice for Difficult Times, by Pema Chodron

Love in the Archives: A Patchwork of True Stories About Suicide Loss, by Eileen Vorbach Collins

It's OK That You're Not OK: *Meeting Grief and Loss in a Culture That Doesn't Understand,* and *How to Carry What Can't Be Fixed: A Journal for Grief,* by Megan Devine

Motherless Daughters, and *The Aftergrief: Finding Your Way Along the Long Arc of Loss,* by Hope Edelman

Breath Taking: A Memoir of Family, Dreams, and Broken Genes, by Jessica Fein

Leading Through Loss: How to Navigate Grief at Work, by Margo Fowkes
Lost and Found: A Kid's Book for Living Through Loss,

by Rabbi Marc Gellman and Monsignor Thomas Hartman

Widowish, by Melissa Gould

Once More We Saw Stars: A Memoir, by Jayson Greene

The Fifth Chamber, by Anne Gudger

The Next Place, by Warren Hanson

End of the Hour: A Therapist's Memoir, by Meghan Riordan Jarvis

Finding Meaning: The Sixth Stage of Grief, by David Kessler

A Grief Observed, by C. S. Lewis

No Happy Endings: A Memoir, by Nora McInerny

Find Me There, by Sara Rian

Anxiety: The Missing Stage of Grief and *Conscious Grieving: A Transformative Approach to Healing From Loss,* by Claire Bidwell Smith

Modern Loss: Candid Conversations About Grief. Beginners Welcome, by Rebecca Soffer and Gabrielle Birkner

The Modern Loss Handbook: An Interactive Guide to Moving Through Grief and Building Your Resilience, by Rebecca Soffer

WEBSITES

GRIEF

21 Ways to Help Someone You Love Through Grief
http://www.time.com/5118994/advice-for-helping-grieving-friend/

GriefShare
https://www.griefshare.org/

Harvard Resources on Grief
https://www.health.harvard.edu/search?content%5Bquery%5D=grief

HealGrief
https://healgrief.org/

Modern Loss
https://modernloss.com/

Refuge in Grief
https://refugeingrief.com/

Salt Water: Find Your Safe Harbor
https://findyourharbor.com/

CHILD/SIBLING/GRANDCHILD LOSS

Compassionate Friends
https://www.compassionatefriends.org/

CHILD/TEEN/YOUNG ADULT GRIEF

Experience Camps
https://experiencecamps.org/grief-resources

Children's Grief Foundation
https://childrensgrieffoundation.org/resources/

Jessica's House
https://www.jessicashouse.org/

PODCASTS

All There Is / Anderson Cooper

It's OK That You're Not OK / Megan Devine

Good Mourning Grief / Sally Douglas and Imogen Carn

Grief Out Loud / The Dougy Center

I Don't Know How You Do It / Jessica Fein

Coffee, Grief, and Gratitude / Anne Gudger

What's Your Grief / Eleanor Haley & Litsa Williams

Got Grief / Craig Henry and Holly Sumpton

The Power of Love / The Dee Dee Jackson Foundation

Grief is My Side Hustle / Meghan Riordan Jarvis

Grief is a Sneaky Bitch / Lisa Keefauver

Healing / David Kessler

ABOUT THE AUTHOR

Casey Mulligan Walsh is a former speech-language pathologist who writes about life at the intersection of grief and joy, embracing uncertainty, and the nature of true belonging. Her essays have appeared in the *New York Times*, *HuffPost*, *Next Avenue*, *Modern Loss*, *WebMD*, *Circulation: Genomic and Precision Medicine*, as well as in *Split Lip*, *Hippocampus*, *Beyond*, *The Manifest-Station*, *Barren Magazine*, *Emerge Journal*, *Five Minute Lit*, and other literary journals. She is a founding editor of *In a Flash* literary magazine.

Casey's work is included in *Daring to Breathe*, an anthology about living with the foreverness of grief. She is passionate about supporting those who grieve all manner of losses, including those that are spoken of and those too often shrouded in silence.

She also serves on the Board of Directors of the Family Heart Foundation, an organization dedicated to raising awareness of the genetic lipid disorder that has affected her family across generations.

Casey lives in upstate New York with her husband, Kevin, a chatty orange tabby, and too many books to count. When not traveling, they enjoy visits from their four children and ten grandchildren—the very definition of "the full catastrophe."

Learn more at www.caseymulliganwalsh.com.

www.ingramcontent.com/pod-product-compliance
Ingram Content Group UK Ltd.
Pitfield, Milton Keynes, MK11 3LW, UK
UKHW012357080825
461699UK00001B/3